"WONDERFULLY WRITTEN AND SUPERBLY RESEARCHED."
—*Library Journal*

"The best assessment available on the state of knowledge on the Final Solution, on motives, resistance, and collaboration, as well as the reaction of the outside world."
—Walter Laqueur, Center for Strategic and International Studies, Georgetown University

"Written with sophistication and understanding . . . provides a perspective to a subject that has often been misshaped and contorted to fit preconceived ideas or notions."
—Raul Hilberg, Department of Political Science, University of Vermont

"Provides a clear overview of events and introduces the reader to a critical analysis of the scholarship of the last decades, even while emphasizing the problems which face historians when dealing with the victims, persecutors, and bystanders alike. It is indispensable for laymen and scholars who want to penetrate to a deeper level of meaning."
—George L. Mosse, The Institute for Advanced Studies, The Hebrew University of Jerusalem

"THE HOLOCAUST IN HISTORY is an example of what a historian should do: show that we are dealing with a historical phenomenon that is accessible to historical analysis, without denying the tremendous emotional involvement of all of us in the tragedy of European Jewry."
—Yehuda Bauer, Institute of Contemporary Jewry, The Hebrew University of Jerusalem

---

MICHAEL R. MARRUS, Professor of History at the University of Toronto, is the author of *The Unwanted: European Refugees in the Twentieth Century,* which won the Present Tense Literary Award. His *Vichy France and the Jews,* co-authored with Robert O. Paxton, received the National Jewish Book Award.

THE HOLOCAUST
IN HISTORY

MICHAEL R. MARRUS

A MERIDIAN BOOK

MERIDIAN
Published by the Penguin Group
Penguin Books USA Inc., 375 Hudson Street, New York, New York 10014, U.S.A.
Penguin Books Ltd, 27 Wrights Lane, London W8 5TZ, England
Penguin Books Australia Ltd, Ringwood, Victoria, Australia
Penguin Books Canada Ltd, 2801 John Street, Markham, Ontario, Canada L3R 1B4
Penguin Books (N.Z.) Ltd, 182-190 Wairau Road, Auckland 10, New Zealand

Penguin Books Ltd, Registered Offices: Harmondsworth, Middlesex, England

BOOKS ARE AVAILABLE AT QUANTITY DISCOUNTS WHEN USED TO
PROMOTE PRODUCTS OR SERVICES. FOR INFORMATION PLEASE WRITE
TO PREMIUM MARKETING DIVISION, PENGUIN BOOKS USA INC.,
375 HUDSON STREET, NEW YORK, NEW YORK 10014.

Copyright © 1987 by Michael R. Marrus

 REG. TRADEMARK—MARCA REGISTRADA

Library of Congress Cataloging-in-Publication Data

Marrus, Michael Robert.
    The Holocaust in history / Michael R. Marrus.
      p.   cm.
    Bibliography: p-.
    Includes index.
    ISBN 0-452-00953-7 (pbk.)
    1. Holocaust, Jewish (1939-1945)—Historiography. I. Title.
[D804.3.M37 1989]   88-21790
940.53'15' 039240—dc19   CIP

First Meridian Printing, January, 1989

2 3 4 5 6 7 8 9

PRINTED IN THE UNITED STATES OF AMERICA

For Jeremy, Naomi, Adam and Randi

CONTENTS

MAPS

PREFACE

In December 1941, during the evacuation of the ghetto of Riga, the Nazis shot and killed the famous Jewish historian Simon Dubnow. He was eighty-one. The story is told that Dubnow's last words were an admonition to his fellow Jews: "Write and record!" (in Yiddish: *shreibt un farshreibt*). Dubnow's anguished appeal, and that of countless Jews who expressed a similar yearning that their sufferings be made known, have echoed through the years. Many have taken up this task as a sacred duty, reflecting the deeply felt obligation of so many who lived and died in this period—to tell the story, either as witness, or in commemoration, or as a somber warning to future generations.

But along with this task, there is another that has inevitably grown stronger in recent years—to integrate the history of the Holocaust into the general stream of historical consciousness and to apply to it the modes of discourse, the scholarly techniques, and the kinds of analyses used for all other historical issues. In part this impulse derives from a concern that the history of the Holocaust receive universal recognition, that it be acknowledged as an important part of the modern historical experience and not just an episode in the history of the Jewish people. Another reason is the sense that historical methods can help us answer questions that have troubled observers over the years: How did Nazi policy evolve to mass murder? How should one evaluate the roles of collaborationist governments and societies, the allies of the Reich, bystanders, and the Jews themselves?

There has been no lack of writing of both sorts, particularly in the past twenty years, treating the Holocaust from many viewpoints and with a wide range of methods. Inevitably, the two approaches defined here overlap. There is no essential reason why one approach should preclude the other, yet in practice there is usually a difference.

This book is an assessment of the second kind of historical writing. Much, though not all, is the work of professional historians; much, though not all, has been written by Jews. Beyond this, there are few generalizations that one can make. As we shall see, the historians differ on many of the issues, and their writings reflect a variety of points of view. But this should not be surprising, for so it is with virtually any historical topic one could choose. There is, at the same time, broad agreement on certain matters, and I have tried to point this out as well. To make this assessment I have had to select from a vast historical literature, and I am acutely aware of how much my choices have been conditioned by my own experience, interests, acquaintances, and linguistic limitations. Necessarily, this is a personal view, but I hope that it is wide ranging enough for others to find in it something of use.

The chapters that follow address what I think are the most important themes discussed by historians of the Holocaust—and themes about which there has been serious historical investigation. I have had no difficulty excluding from this book any discussion of the so-called revisionists—malevolent cranks who contend that the Holocaust never happened. Regrettably this is no longer an insignificant current, and there are signs that those who concoct such fantasies are engaged in a much wider anti-Jewish enterprise. But while it is important that their activity be understood, I see no reason why such people should set the agenda for historians of the subject, any more than "flat-earth" theorists should set the agenda for astronomers. By the same token, I have tried to avoid polemical discussions about the meaning of the Holocaust—a much more serious body of literature, some of it by the same historians whose work will be considered in the pages that follow. Unfortunately, the Holocaust is frequently the object of angry controversy among those who use it to stake out political positions. As I write, one such debate is under way in West Germany, partly focusing on how contemporary Germans should view the murder of European Jews. Similar confrontations have occurred in Israel and within Jewish communities elsewhere. The issues raised in these contests are of course important: Is there too much preoccupation with the Holocaust, or too little? Have Germans or other Europeans come to terms with the past or have they not? What are the lessons of the Holocaust? Have Jews or others understood these lessons, or have they not? And so forth. To the outsider, however, it is usually evident that the participants in these polemics are really addressing present-day concerns rather than historical events. I have therefore avoided such writing, unless it has prompted new historical research and analysis. In most cases, it has not.

I want to record my thanks to my good friend Jehuda Reinharz, director of the Tauber Institute of Brandeis University, who first suggested that I contribute a volume to the institute's excellent series. Without his gentle prodding I would not have thought of undertaking this work and would not have had the opportunity of joining an illustrious list of fellow contributors. For the clarification of my views on the widely disparate subjects surveyed in this book I owe a great deal to the stimulating year-long seminar organized by Yehuda Bauer at the Institute for Advanced Studies of the Hebrew University of Jerusalem during 1984–85. I am grateful to the institute's director at the time, Aryeh Dvoretzky, and his excellent staff for providing the most congenial environment imaginable for our labors. Advice and encouragement have come from many quarters, but I take special note of the following, with whom I have discussed many of the ideas in these pages: Shmuel Almog, Yehuda Bauer, Christopher Browning, Richard Cohen, Saul Friedländer, Louis Greenspan, Yisrael Gutman, Jacques Kornberg, Dov Kulka, Dina Porat, and Bernard Wasserstein. For financial assistance I would like to thank the John Simon Guggenheim Foundation, the Social Sciences and Humanities Research Council of Canada, and the Office of Research Administration of the University of Toronto. For her excellent work in preparing the manuscript for publication my thanks go to Kathryn Gohl. And for everything else, I am deeply grateful to my wife, Carol Randi Marrus.

Toronto, December 1986   M.R.M.

THE HOLOCAUST
IN HISTORY

1. INTRODUCTION

THE HOLOCAUST, the systematic mass murder of European Jewry by the Nazis, sits uneasily in the history of our times. How is this ghastly event to be recorded? There is no dispute about personal memoirs—valued by all serious students of the subject as a message from a world that most of us scarcely imagine. But what about surveys of the modern era or the Hitler era? General histories do not seem to agree upon the place of the Holocaust as they do, for example, about the French Revolution or the First World War. In one traditional view, the Holocaust falls somehow outside history by virtue of its supreme importance—and hence it is held not subject to the wide-ranging investigation, discussion, and debate carried on with other aspects of the recent past. Close scholarly attention, it is feared, might diminish the horror evoked by the event, or lessen the respect accorded the most traumatic experience of the Jewish people in living memory. A related apprehension is that the dispassionate rethinking of some traditional notions of Nazism and the Holocaust might end up by trivializing the fundamentally evil nature of the regime. To others, the Holocaust remains an embarrassment, either because of a lingering antipathy toward the victims or because of an assumption that extensive historical investigation might suggest awkward particularist commitments. For both groups, academic discussion of the Holocaust has been uncomfortable. In the past, as a result, writers who examined the 1930s and 1940s often ignored the subject, gave it only a fleeting glance, or adopted a sacral tone—"consecrating the experience," as one writer has said, suggesting that the issue was unapproachable for ordinary analysts of the human record.[1]

My own sense is that things are changing, and the purpose of this book is to indicate how. Since the beginning of the 1960s, we have seen extensive historical investigation of the Holocaust and an increasing volume of serious publications treating it from every possible angle. The concerns and the disposition of writers in the postwar decade and a half remain intact, but are challenged now by a growing curiosity about the most venerable of historical questions: How could such a thing have happened? The following chapters review the very considerable historical literature on the Holocaust written in Western countries in the past two decades or so. Implicitly, they also chart a changed consciousness about the Holocaust, in which inhibitions to dispassionate historical discussion are gradually losing force.

Before beginning, a word about the spirit of this inquiry. As suggested, an important body of opinion opposes what might be called the "normalization" of the study of the Holocaust—its integration into the mode of discourse and explanation commonly used by practitioners of the historian's craft. "The Holocaust refuses to go the way of most history," writes Nora Levin, the author of a survey of the subject, "not only because of the magnitude of the destruction—the murder of six million Jews—but because the events surrounding it are in a very real sense incomprehensible. No one altogether understands how mass murder on such a scale could have happened or could have been allowed to happen. The accumulation of facts does not yield this understanding; indeed, comprehensibility may never be possible." In Levin's view, an impenetrable barrier will always separate the historian from the subject. "Ordinary human beings simply cannot rethink themselves into such a world and ordinary ways to achieve empathy fail, for all of the recognizable attributes of human reaction are balked at the Nazi divide. The world of Auschwitz was, in truth, another planet."[2]

Nobel Prize–winning novelist and poet Elie Wiesel returns again and again to these obstacles to understanding: "Auschwitz defies imagination and perception; it submits only to memory. . . . Between the dead and the rest of us there exists an abyss that no talent can comprehend." Holocaust writing, he feels, should dwell upon these limitations. "I write to denounce writing. I tell of the impossibility one stumbles upon in trying to tell the tale." Wiesel's self-proclaimed task has been a literary homage to those who were murdered. And from this point of view, much depends upon how worthy is the author in question. "Any writer may, if he so chooses, deal with the subject of the Holocaust," he complains in a recent article. His apparent conclusion: only the survivors, or perhaps those who are totally honest with themselves about the limitations of their powers, had better try.[3]

Wiesel is primarily concerned with artistic modes. Similar criticism has, however, been applied to scholarly discussion. Indeed, the careful qualification and guarded language that one associates with academic writing is sometimes held to be singularly inappropriate to describe the Holocaust.[4] Three kinds of concerns, I think, have prompted this apprehension. First, there is the feeling that the work of historians is necessarily *incomplete*, omitting vital aspects of suffering and criminality, and hence ringing false as a portrayal of what actually happened. Second, there is the fear that *inaccuracies*, however minor, will inevitably poison such accounts and that the parade of scholarly apparatus will validate a historical assessment that is flawed as a representation of the past. Third, there is anxiety that any *revision* of traditional interpretations of Nazism or the assault on European Jewry will open the door to apologists for the Third Reich, trivializing the evil nature of the regime. Survivors especially, I think, can feel violated by many historians' efforts and are far more comfortable with acts of commemoration and the compilation of eye-witness testimony.

The term *Holocaust,* widely used only since the 1960s, may originally have reflected such preoccupations and serves now to separate this particular massacre from other historical instances of genocide.[5] *Holokaustos,* we are reminded, comes from the third century B.C. Greek translation of the Old Testament, signifying "the burnt sacrificial offering dedicated *exclusively* to God."[6] As such, the designation of the massacre of European Jewry connoted an event of theological significance, and perhaps as well an event whose mysteries were not meant to be understood. In addition, *Holocaust* may have indicated a preference to focus upon recounting the experience of the martyred victims, rather than the victimizers. *Holo-*

caust, it has been suggested, is a nonspecific term that implies to most people a bolt from the blue—like an earthquake or a flood—rather than a deliberate, criminal act. It does not suggest perpetrators, and like the Nazis' own designation, *Final Solution,* may easily lend itself to abuse by misappropriation.

In this respect, it is well to remember how recent is the beginning of professional study of the Holocaust and how short a period of time the enterprise has had to establish itself. Up to the time of the Eichmann trial in Jerusalem, in 1961, there was relatively little discussion of the massacre of European Jewry. At Nuremberg, immediately after the war, crimes against the Jews were part of the proceedings conducted by the International Military Tribunal, but such crimes never assumed a prominent place. The most important Nazis who directed the Final Solution were either dead—Hitler, Heydrich, Himmler—or missing, or were not deemed important enough to be judged as major criminals. Several of the most sinister Nazi murderers were tried and executed subsequently—including Otto Ohlendorf, head of a murderous team of Einsatzgruppen that shot masses of people in the Soviet Union; Rudolf Höss, commandant of the Auschwitz death camp (and who appeared at Nuremberg as a *defense* witness); and Dieter Wisliceny, Eichmann's deputy, responsible for the deportations from Slovakia and Greece. But these trials did not draw wide attention and were not the occasion for recounting the full history of mass murder. Two surveys did appear in the early 1950s—by Gerald Reitlinger in England and Léon Poliakov in France.[7] Important collection of materials was also undertaken in those years, as was the establishment of institutes to house and study them. Little of this information reached the wider public, however, and historians outside a small circle of survivors tended to ignore the issue. Broadly speaking, general works scarcely mentioned the murder of European Jews, or did so in passing as one more atrocity in a particularly cruel war. This neglect prompted real fears among prominent Israelis that the Holocaust was being forgotten.

The trial of Adolf Eichmann, who was brought to Israel from Argentina after being abducted by Israeli agents, was meant to place the Holocaust in proper historical perspective. The proceedings were intended to be a grand summation of the persecution and murder of European Jews, along with the indictment of a principal perpetrator.[8] "We want the nations of the world to know," said David Ben Gurion, then Israeli prime minister. Also, he added, Israeli youngsters had to face the terrible events of the recent past. "It is necessary that our youth remember what happened to the Jewish people. We want them to know the most tragic facts in our history." The trial was not concerned with revenge, he insisted, but it was certainly preoccupied with establishing a place for the Holocaust in history.[9]

Since then, scholarship has proceeded apace, in this sense fully justifying the intentions of the Eichmann trial organizers. Based on a masterful reading of German documents, Raul Hilberg's *The Destruction of the European Jews* appeared in 1961—a landmark synthesis that remains unsurpassed as a survey of the destruction process. Hannah Arendt's *Eichmann in Jerusalem,* originally an assessment of the trial for the *New Yorker,* prompted a debate in the historical literature that echoes to our own time. Dozens of scholars in Western countries set to work. Arthur Morse's *While Six Million Died,* published in 1967, was the first important study of American bystanders, beginning a major genre of historical analysis. Yad Vashem, the Israeli institute devoted to Holocaust research and commemoration, has organized a series of important conferences since 1968, the published volumes of which show a clear evolution in the direction of detached, professional analysis. The institute's annual, *Yad Vashem Studies,* has become a major repository of research that is drawn upon extensively in this book. In Germany, meanwhile, several important trials of concentration-camp war criminals brought the Jewish question once again to the German public, including a group of historians too young to have been actively involved during the period of the Third Reich. Rolf Hochhuth's controversial play about Pius XII, *Der Stellvertreter* (*The Deputy*), presented the issue to German audiences in the early 1960s. Through the Munich-based Institut für Zeitgeschichte and its respected quarterly periodical, their work became known to a wide professional audience. An international symposium on the origins of the Final Solution was held in Stuttgart in 1984, bringing to the surface disputes that have their counterpart in other issues concerning Nazi Germany. We now have a vast literature on the Holocaust as a result of this scholarship. Indeed, the field is by now far too vast for any one scholar to master. A recent, select bibliography lists close to two thousand book entries in many languages and notes over ten thousand publications on Auschwitz alone.[10]

Some words of the English historian Sir Herbert Butterfield help define the focus of the chapters that follow. Writing about the history of international conflict, Butterfield observed that historical understanding moved through two phases. The first, which he called "heroic," is formulated in the heat of battle; it has a primitive and simple shape, largely dwelling on moral issues associated with the cause of one or another of the belligerents. The second, which Butterfield referred to as "academic history," represents "a higher and riper stage of historiography," in which the structural features of the conflict are disengaged and the overall view is less one of melodrama than of tragedy.[11] To be sure, there are limits to the application of this model. The Holocaust was not an international conflict in any normal sense: it took place within the context of an international conflict, and to a real degree there was what Lucy Dawidowicz has called a "war against the Jews." But there was no war of the Jews against Nazism, save for the resistance of those targeted for murder. In most cases, this was a war of the doomed. The Holocaust is about murder, and no amount of imaginative reconstruction will ever change that fundamental reality. Nevertheless, there is a sense in which our view of the matter has altered, has become more shaded, and our vision has acquired greater complexity. Academic history in the past two decades or so has helped contribute to a deeper understanding.

This book looks back across this period of scholarly activity and attempts to summarize its findings for the general reader. But it also accepts and approves of what I see as the historical agenda of recent years—to apply the tools of historical, sociological, and political analysis to the events of the war years and to understand what happened to European Jewry as one would understand any other historical problem.

In rejecting many of the protests that have been made about the normalization of Holocaust scholarship, I want to insist upon the respect that has to be accorded many of the concerns I have noted. No amount of historical investigation should be permitted to detract from the awesome horror of these events, and no license for theorizing should inhibit the sense of limitation that all should have when discussing conditions that are so utterly outside our experience. Those separated from these events—either by chronology or historical circumstance—can never penetrate their horrors or grasp their ultimate significance. In one sense, the Holocaust will forever be, as one literary analyst puts it, "unimaginable." [12] Yet as a thoughtful critic pointed out a few years ago, much the same could be said, mutatis mutandis, about many other things as well. [13] From the standpoint of theology, or even more humble ruminations on human nature, the systematic massacre of so many innocents is bound to escape understanding in some profound sense. So also do countless episodes of cruelty and destruction, however small or great their scale. Historians are used to tramping over their fields while suspending judgments on the fundamental human issues that are ultimately at stake. Once pointed in a scholarly direction most of us forge ahead, hoping to navigate safely using the customary tools of the trade. We simply do the best we can, knowing that our efforts are necessarily imperfect, incomplete, and inadequate.

With the passage of time and the fading of first-hand accounts, the inhibitions I have described will have less force. As Hilberg has suggested recently: "the era of researchers with personal experience of the period who could work with a sense of 'feel' for the documents, is coming to an end." [14] In time, as a result, the mystification will be dispelled and is bound to be replaced by the historical perspective. [15] Doubtless some of the exercises that result will be misguided. But the alternative, silence, is surely a counsel of despair—yielding the field to falsification or to oblivion. Rather than denouncing this trend, it is perhaps better to look upon it as a challenge, following the Israeli novelist A. B. Yehoshua: "As the number of surviving eyewitnesses to the period diminishes, the more freely will human imagination range in its attempts to achieve understanding. All of this will have to be met in a spirit of patience and openness. The horror of the events and the sufferings of the victims will not rob the new attempts—including new emotional and moral judgments—of legitimacy. The freedom of man's spirit suffers no restriction. Hence we must be aware that further study is liable to inflict new pain and will sometimes require that generally accepted views, which, it seemed, were firmly and solidly established, be abandoned." [16]

2. THE HOLOCAUST IN PERSPECTIVE

HISTORIANS STEEPED IN the literature of Nazi antisemitism or Nazi policies during the Holocaust invariably feel in the grip of the most powerful of obsessions—different in kind from the hatreds and campaigns of persecution that punctuate the history of practically every era and civilization. Validating this perception, Holocaust specialists have presented a strong case for the "centrality" of antisemitism in Nazi ideology, or the "uniqueness" of the Holocaust, even by the grim standards of twentieth-century massacres. At first encounter, these contentions do not sit well with the wider community of historians. Scholars often strain to justify their particular research commitments with claims that one or another patch of history deserves special attention and recognition. Indeed, students are frequently taught to begin their theses or research papers with some declaration of singularity. Most of us like to believe our subject is important, if not the most important, and the more deeply we examine a particular theme, the more we can be persuaded that it is truly "unique."

Yet there is substance to these arguments, which often began with the effort to make sense of preliminary findings. Isaac Deutscher, the biographer and admirer of Trotsky, a historian who certainly could not be accused of Jewish particularism, was among those who felt an "absolute uniqueness" to the Jewish catastrophe. Other massacres, he felt, had still some "human logic." This one, Deutscher said, might forever "baffle and terrify mankind" with "a huge and ominous mystery of the degeneration of the human spirit."[1] A closer look at assessments such as this will assist us in seeing the event in a broad historical perspective.

THE CENTRALITY OF ANTISEMITISM

Informed theories about the centrality of antisemitism in Nazism do not rest upon claims that anti-Jewish ideology was a predominantly German doctrine or a constant preoccupation of the leaders of the Third Reich. Research on the background to the Holocaust, indeed, has suggested the opposite. George Mosse pointed out long ago that if one were situated in Europe in the 1890s and asked to name the country most dangerous for the Jews, one might easily settle upon France. (Czarist Russia would also be a strong candidate.) Repeating the exercise in the early 1930s, Germany would be a much more likely prospect, but certainly not the only contender. Anticipating a great disaster for European Jewry in 1938, Vladimir Jabotinsky, leader of the right-wing Zionist Revisionists, called for mass evacuation. In his view, however, the source of the coming catastrophe was east European antisemitism, not that of the Nazis. The east European upheaval, he predicted, with Poland at the center, would far surpass what had already transpired in Hitler's Germany.[2]

Only a few decades before the Nazis, the map of European antisemitism looked quite different than in the 1930s or 1940s. There was certainly an antisemitic tide in Germany at the end of the nineteenth century, as there was in other European countries, but one must be cautious in assessing its relative significance. Compared to Russia or Rumania, where Jews suffered extreme poverty, intense popular hostility, and public discrimination, Germany was a *Rechtsstaat,* according fundamental legal rights to Jews.[3] There were no pogroms in the German Empire—the riotous outbreaks against Jews in which public authorities often failed to intervene or even assisted the violent assaults upon Jews and the destruction of their property. France, where there *were* pogroms at the end of the nineteenth century, became known to Jews elsewhere as the country of the Dreyfus affair and the home of very considerable popular anti-Jewish feeling. In Alsace, formerly French and annexed to Germany after the Franco-Prussian War in 1871, many local Jews extended their loyalty to the Kaiser at this time, abandoning attachments to their former country which they felt had betrayed them.[4] In Habsburg Galicia, a major Jewish population center, the Jews endearingly referred to the Austrian kaiser in Yiddish as Froyim Yossel (Franz Josef), and they looked to Imperial Vienna for protection and favor. During the First World War, when German troops entered Polish territory heavily populated by Jews, they were sometimes welcomed as liberators by a Jewish populace eager to enjoy the benefits of German civilization.[5]

Historians no longer insist with such assurance, as they undoubtedly once did, on the importance of a "Jewish question" in Imperial Germany.[6] The title of a book by Richard Levy, *The Downfall of the Antisemitic Political Parties in Imperial Germany*, tells at least part of the story: by the time of the Reichstag elections of 1898 these parties were running out of votes, numbers, money, and political energy.[7] Divided within themselves, suffering badly from the effects of a "one-issue" strategy, they went into steep decline. In the end, according to Levy, such parties never amounted to much: between 1887 and 1912 representatives from this camp constituted only 2 percent of deputies who were reelected. Yet Levy would be the first to acknowledge that political parties were not the exclusive bearers of antisemitism. In a book on a related theme, Peter Pulzer noted that "the decline in the virulence of organized party antisemitism was matched by its increasing pervasion of social life, semipolitical bodies, and ideological and economic pressure groups."[8] Opposition to Jews undoubtedly composed a low-grade consensus among many elements in German society at the time: this was especially the case among middle-class pressure groups such as the National Union of Commercial Employees, Pan-German associations, student fraternities, and the like. Shulamit Volkov has deemed antisemitism a "cultural code," a convenient abbreviation for a broad "cluster of ideas, values and norms" created in the first decade of the German Reich. This worldview opposed liberal, capitalist, democratic, and internationalist currents associated with the nineteenth-century emancipation of Jews. From the turn of the century, as a result, "antisemitism was professed by all groups and associations that propagated militant nationalism, imperial expansion, racism, anti-socialism, militarism, and support for a strong, authoritarian government."[9]

Specialists in the history of antisemitism would acknowledge that what has been said so far could apply also to many other countries and that Germany was certainly not unusual in the extent of anti-Jewish thought at the time of the First World War. Some have made a strong case, however, for the particular intensity of one current of antisemitism that emerged in the Wilhelmenian Reich. In a book first published in Hebrew in 1969, Uriel Tal argued that there were two strands of anti-Jewish thought in Germany, traditional and radical. The former was largely Christian in inspiration and rested its opposition to Jews essentially on their rejection of the religious faith of the majority; the latter was violently anti-Christian in inspiration, pagan in its models for the ideal society, and racist in its definitions of Jews. This second blend of antisemitism proved much more dynamic, virulent, and uncompromising. Relatively the weaker of the two before 1914, radical antisemitism grew much stronger in Germany and Austria in the postwar period, eventually with disastrous consequences.[10] This version, of course, became the mainspring of the Nazis' anti-Jewish ideology.

Extensive investigation of the beginnings of Hitlerian and Nazi antisemitism has failed to uncover any particular originality in this field—any new twist or turn in thinking about Jews. Virtually every commentator concludes that, despite his efforts to portray himself as an independent thinker and creative genius, Hitler expressed nothing that was not part of the popular culture of Vienna or Munich in the period of his youth.[11] And the Nazi party, similarly, offered voters no anti-Jewish plank that could not be found elsewhere in political life. Beyond this, it does not seem that antisemitism was always salient even in the Nazi camp in the period before Hitler became German chancellor. Sarah Ann Gordon notes that "surprisingly few of the top Nazi leaders were virulent antisemites before 1925," with the exceptions being Hitler himself, Alfred Rosenberg, and Julius Streicher—the latter two never becoming decision makers of the first rank.[12] Neither Goebbels, Himmler, Göring, Frank, Hess, the Strasser brothers, nor even Adolf Eichmann seems to have joined the Nazis because of antisemitism. Antisemitism was clearly a distinguishing feature of the party in the mid-1920s, and by the time Hitler made his political breakthrough in 1930, the Nazis were the most enthusiastic exponents of anti-Jewish ideology in electoral politics. But it is difficult to say how important it was for members of the party, or for their increasingly powerful following.[13]

After a careful reexamination of autobiographical statements written by 581 early Nazis and originally collected by the sociologist Theodor Abel, Peter Merkl was struck by "how little the Nazi movement was motivated by shared, constructive goals of any kind"—even antisemitic ones. A third of the sample showed no evidence of prejudice, and nearly half seemed fairly uninterested in Jews. Thirteen percent were "paranoid" antisemites, prone to violence and political action against the Jews.[14] Among voters, antisemitism is similarly less evident than one might expect as a basis for attraction to the Nazi cause. Notably, antisemitic propaganda did not do much for the party's popularity before 1930; nor, indeed, did every other effort to construct a broad, national movement. After the major success in the Reichstag elections in September of that year, when the Nazis won nearly 6.4 million votes (18.3 percent of the electorate), antisemitism played an uneven role. The Nazi leadership made a determined effort, at this point, to make the party *salonfähig*, or socially acceptable.[15] At times this could mean toning down the obvious anti-Jewish preferences of Hitler or the Nazi leadership. For example, antisemitic expression seems to have been a positive liability among big businessmen, the very group the Nazis were eagerly courting in the period immediately before Hitler's seizure of power.[16] In many localities, on the other hand, hatred of Jews was shouted from the rooftops because it was deemed politically advantageous. Looking at Lower Saxony during the *Kampfzeit*, the years of struggle before Hitler took power, Jeremy Noakes observed the very limited appeal of antisemitism among a population that was far more interested in economic and political matters. Studying Bavaria in the same period, Geoffrey Pridham felt that aggressive and "ideological" antisemitism was far stronger among party activists than among voters.[17] Both, I think, would agree with William Sheridan Allen, who concluded in an examination of one town in Lower Saxony that residents "were drawn to antisemitism because they were drawn to Nazism, and not the other way around."[18] Reviewing the literature on several localities in a substantial study of voting patterns, Richard Hamilton concludes that political opportunism took command. "If antisemitism was not a viable theme in a given area, it was played down or abandoned. If it was viable, it was given considerable play."[19]

HITLER'S ANTISEMITISM

Given the foregoing, it is reasonable to ask in what way antisemitism may be seen as "central" to Nazism. The key, I think, lies with Hitler himself. About the centrality of anti-Jewish commitment in his own worldview, there seems little doubt. The Jews not only appear in virtually everything that ever concerned Hitler, but are at the very basis of his conception of the historical process—the idea of struggle. Adopting the crudest perversion of the familiar Darwinian view, Hitler saw history as a great arena in which peoples forever engaged in ruthless competition. These confrontations were not limited, as with sporting contests or the highly ritualized warfare of the eighteenth century. Nations, like individuals, Hitler believed, had to struggle desperately for their very existence. "The idea of struggle is as old as life itself," he said in a 1928 speech, "for life is only preserved because other living things perish through struggle. . . . In this struggle the stronger, the more able, win, while the less able, the weak, lose. Struggle is the father of all things. . . . It is not by the principles of humanity that man lives or is able to preserve himself above the animal world, but solely by means of the most brutal struggle."[20] "Ultimately this struggle, which is often so hard, kills all pity," Hitler wrote in Mein Kampf, the book that was supposed to describe his personal odyssey as well as that of his people. "Our own painful struggle for existence destroys our feeling for the misery of those who have remained behind."[21]

Hitler claimed to have first discovered the Jews in Vienna, where he lived for five years before the First World War. In the pages of Mein Kampf he presented this discovery as an earth-shattering revelation. His eyes were opened to Marxism and Jewry, "whose terrible importance for the German people" he previously did not understand. "In this period there took shape within me a world picture and a philosophy which became the granite foundation of all my acts. In addition to what I then created, I have had to learn little; and I have had to alter nothing."[22]

Hitler consistently portrayed Jews as the most determined and sinister enemies of the Germans and all other nations as well. Jews constantly undermined a people's capacity for struggle, weakened and subverted its racial purity, poisoned its institutions, and corrupted its positive qualities. The Jews themselves were not a race, but an antirace; they had no culture of their own, but purveyed instead such doctrines as democracy or parliamentarianism which perverted or degenerated previously sound societies. Jews were continually mingling with other cultures, seeking to dissolve their structures and their institutions. Marxism was but one additional means by which Jewry conducted its relentless assault upon the societies and peoples of the world. Capitalism was another. In a world dominated by struggle, the Jews could be fiendishly successful and were a perpetual threat to the existence of all healthy societies.

Jews posed a particular danger to the German people, for whom Hitler claimed to be a prophetic spokesman. Indeed, as he excoriated German society and its institutions during the *Kampfzeit,* Hitler associated the degeneration of his country with the triumph of Jewry. "In Germany today," he wrote in 1928, "German interests are no longer decisive but rather Jewish interests." [23] Undermined and weakened by the Jews at home, Germany at the same time confronted world Jewry abroad. Committed in the long run to securing *Lebensraum,* or living space in the east, Germans were locked in an uncompromising conflict with Bolshevism, itself a Jewish invention. Jewry, Hitler believed, "has taken over the leadership of all areas of Russian life with the Bolshevik revolution." What emerged from that upheaval was a regime that had a single aim: "to carry over the Bolshevist poisoning to Germany." [24] Finally, according to Hitler, the situation was desperate. Germany was sunk in decay and decadence. Jewry had triumphed in 1918, with the defeat of the Wilhelmenian Reich, and was closing in for the kill. To do nothing would be to assure catastrophe. "The German people is today attacked by a pack of booty-hungry enemies from within and without. The continuation of this state of affairs is our death." [25]

Historians have made various attempts to make sense of this torrent of hatred and to answer the most puzzling of questions: Why the Jews? Eberhard Jäckel, the editor of Hitler's writings and speeches, sees the Führer's anti-Jewish obsession in the perspective of the rest of his worldview. According to Jäckel, Hitler identified three factors that were essential to a people's "racial value"—its sense of itself, its form of leadership, and its capacity to make war. These three elements—translated into nationalism, the Führer principle, and militarism—wove their way into Hitler's thought and reappear whenever he estimated a people's ability to conduct the inescapable struggle for existence. *Mein Kampf,* according to Jäckel, rails against the three opposites of these qualities—internationalism, democracy, and pacifism. Hitler's electrifying discovery, Jäckel says, was that "the originators and bearers of all three counterpositions are the Jews." Bringing these ideas together in his unpublished volume of 1928, known as his *Secret Book,* Hitler "established for the first time a logical link between his foreign policy conception and his antisemitism. They were synthesized in his view of history. With this, Hitler's *Weltanschauung* had finally achieved the kind of consistency for which he had groped for a long time." [26] Jäckel goes on to see an inherent logic of massacre—a "blueprint," as noted in the title of his book, only in this case a blueprint not for power but for mass murder: "He had to annihilate the Jews, thus restoring the meaning of history, and with the thus restored, nature-intended struggle for existence, he at the same time had to conquer new living space for the German people. Each of these tasks was inextricably linked to the other; indeed, they were the mutually necessary preconditions for each other. Unless the Jews were annihilated there would very soon no longer be any struggle for living space, nor therefore any culture, and consequently nations would die out; not just the German nation, but ultimately all nations. But if, on the other hand, the German people failed to conquer new living space, it would die out because of that and the Jews would triumph." [27]

Other historians look at the entire body of Nazi ideology, attempting to place Hitlerian antisemitism in the wider framework of Nazi social thought on a variety of issues. Drawing upon the earlier work of the German intellectual historian Ernst Nolte, Otto Dov Kulka sees an assault by National Socialism upon "the very roots of Western civilisation, its basic values and moral foundations." As such, the Nazi counterrevolution was "a revolt against the all-embracing idea of the unity of the human race." "In this context, Judaism was conceived as the historical source and the continuous driving force of this idea, which was then expanded in the course of universal history through Christianity and later in the democratic and socialist systems." [28]

Still other historians have attempted to root Hitler's anti-Jewish obsessions within his own psychology, often seeing in his personal traumas the basis for his subsequent statecraft and remarkable appeal to the German people. In the view of Rudolph Binion, Hitler's poisoning in a mustard gas attack in 1918 was linked in his own mind with the painful events accompanying the death of his mother eleven years before, while she was being treated by a Jewish physician, Dr. Bloch.[29] Following his psychic upheaval of 1918, Hitler sought to relieve the earlier trauma, projecting his own guilt feelings for his mother's death upon the Jews. Hitler's subsequent career may be seen as an effort to contend with his painful past experiences by mass murder of the Jews and by territorial expansion at the expense of Soviet Russia. Germans followed Hitler, the argument goes, because his strategy promised to assuage their own national trauma—defeat in the Great War, a defeat that was never acknowledged or accepted.[30]

Casting his net more widely, Robert Waite sifts Hitler's views on Jews and many other questions, offering what must be for the layman a dizzying array of Oedipal conflicts, projections, displacements, and other psychological mechanisms. Waite credits stories that Hitler may have believed in his own Jewish ancestry, seeing in this almost-forgotten aspect of the Führer's biography one powerful force pushing in the direction of genocide: "Since he never knew whether his own grandfather was Jewish, and no one could prove he was not, Hitler had to prove to himself beyond a shadow of a doubt that he could not possibly be 'corrupted' by Jewish blood. In order to convince himself that such a direct threat to his personal identity and life work was an impossibility, he became history's greatest scourge of the Jews."[31]

While impressed with the learning and ingenuity that have gone into analyses such as those of Binion and Waite, readers may nevertheless emerge from these analyses, like Alan Bullock, "in a state of suspended disbelief."[32] Historians usually remain unconvinced about the workings of such mechanisms as "collective trauma," agreeing with Binion that such collective mental processes can be hard to perceive. Their effects are still harder to prove—at least to most historians' satisfaction. For related reasons, the sweeping explanations offered by Eberhard Jäckel, Ernst Nolte, or Dov Kulka may also be on too high a level of generalization to command universal agreement. These assessments tend to downplay the possibility that Hitlerian objectives evolved, that his attitudes may have shifted, and that the predisposition of the German population to follow this fanatic seems not always to have been constant. Most historians remain uncomfortable with contentions of ideological consistency or a "psychological continuum" lasting almost half a century. Further, it seems even more risky to apply such theories to an entire population—north and south, Catholic and Protestant, urban and rural, educated and uneducated, upper and lower class. Specialists in recording change, historians look for evidence of evolution or transformation, rather than their opposite. Also, being professional choosers of evidence, selecting some bits and pieces to relay to readers and rejecting others, historians are often suspicious about elaborate historical structures built upon an underpinning of quotations—aware that another selection could alter the balance or even send the entire framework crashing about its foundation.

Finally, historians usually prefer to focus on the way that Hitler's personality interacted with his environment. Presumably, Hitler could easily have remained a failed art student or a lonely, embittered antisemite without power or influence. In one particular social context, however, Hitler's narcissistic and paranoid characteristics became an especially potent mixture. As Fred Weinstein reminds us, although absorbed with his own personal strivings and obsessions, the Führer was able to address himself to real problems and real people. "Hitler's actions were oriented to reality, he promised solutions to real grievances, and he was highly admired for that reason." [33] Historians seek to understand that wider "reality" and to learn how Hitler could act so effectively in it.

Having said this, I think that even the most determined skeptic could draw two conclusions about the Nazi leader from what has been said. First, Hitler had an intense hatred of Jews, lasting his entire political career, seeing their very existence as a mortal threat to his geopolitical projects. Second, Hitler was the principal driving force of antisemitism in the Nazi movement from the earliest period, not only setting the ideological tone, but raising his intense personal antipathy to an affair of state. Hitler alone defined the Jewish menace with the authority, consistency, and ruthlessness needed to fix its place for the party and later the Reich.

Whether he had a "utopian project" of a Europe free of his Jewish

enemies, or a concrete genocidal goal, or just an ill-defined commitment against Jews, agreement is widespread that the Führer set the
course.[34] Later in this book we explore decision making associated
with the Holocaust and see how historians divide on the question of
Hitler's role in this process. We also examine the place of various
state agencies and the German population, and the involvement
of collaborationist governments and peoples. For the present, however, we anticipate a conclusion that defines the centrality of antisemitism for Nazism, and by implication for the Third Reich. Antisemitism was central because Hitler determined that it should be so.
Opposition to the Jews became a leitmotif of the regime, whatever
the priority assigned to it in a tactical sense, because for Hitler ideological questions mattered and were treated with desperate serious-
ness. Beyond this, neither the existence of anti-Jewish traditions in
Germany, the commitments of Nazi party leaders, nor the beliefs of
the extensive Nazi following in the German population *required* the
murder of the Jews. Put otherwise, antisemitism in Germany may
have been a necessary condition for the Holocaust, but it was not a
sufficient one. In the end it was Hitler, and his own determination to
realize his antisemitic fantasies, that made the difference. The implication is summed up in the title of a popular article on a related
theme: "No Hitler, No Holocaust."[35]

THE UNIQUENESS OF THE HOLOCAUST

More problematic is the notion of the "uniqueness" of the Holocaust—a contention that requires careful definition. In one sense, of
course, every historical event and every individual is unique, in that
each is different from any other. Unlike social scientists, who search
for generalities, historians are especially aware of such uniqueness,
and indeed specialize in discerning those elements that make a particular event or society or individual unlike any other. Normally,
their focus is on the particular rather than the general. Historians
study a revolution, rather than revolutions; a war, rather than warfare; and the Holocaust, rather than genocide. Naturally, historians
have their ideas about the latter, but they do not usually earn their
living by such pronouncements, and I venture to say that these are
not the most valued exercises of historical scholars' time.

It is sometimes assumed that the contentions of historical unique-ness stake out some special claim for recognition of the Holo-caust—a political or theological affirmation, rather than a histori-cal evaluation. Reflecting on this problem, Geoff Eley feels that with the use of a particular terminology—*Holocaust*—he was being drawn into "an ontological statement about the Jewish predica-ment." "To insist upon the uniqueness of the event is a short step to insisting on the exclusiveness of interpretation which asserts an em-pathetic privilege and even a Jewish proprietorship in the sub-ject."[36] Historians feel uncomfortable with the implicit charge set for them by philosopher Emil Fackenheim, for example, that they respond to the Holocaust "authentically" and that they acknowl-edge prior limitations on what they can and cannot explain.[37] Limi-tations there undoubtedly are, as every sensible person will acknowl-edge. To dwell on them is likely to paralyze the historian, however, and almost certainly will prescribe the historian's conclusions.

Another claim for historical uniqueness concentrates unduly, in my opinion, on one aspect of the massacre of European Jewry—the death camps. In the opinion of George Kren and Leon Rappoport, "the uniqueness of the Holocaust . . . stands out when the focus of inquiry is shifted from historical trends to the level of personal ex-perience." Drawing upon the testimony of the survivors, they single out the netherworld of the camps as the basis for the singularity of the Holocaust. To them, the distinctive Holocaust theme is the re-moval of the camp experience from ordinary reality. Taking this as the essence of the Holocaust, these authors oppose studying it "in the cold light of normal history," feeling that in this way "there is no special challenge to critical inquiry" and that historians will conse-quently "conduct business as usual."[38]

I have three objections to this line of argument. First, historical "business as usual" does no violence to the experience of the survi-vor and is no mean or idle pursuit. To the contrary, we owe it to survivors, and to ourselves, to conduct as objective and as thorough an inquiry as we can—along with whatever commemorative or philosophical reflections may be appropriate. Second, we know that while in general the Jewish experience of the camps was the worst of any group, and while Jews made up the overwhelming majority of those killed in the gas chambers, they were not alone in suffering these horrors. People from many groups and nations could be found in the camps, and gassing also accounted for deaths among Gypsies, mentally ill Germans, Soviet prisoners of war, anti-Nazi Poles, and many others. Third, any overall assessment ought to encompass Jews who died in countless circumstances inside *and* outside the camps—each with its own private horror. It is clearly wrong to separate from the essence of the Holocaust those Jews who never survived long enough to reach the camps, or who were shot down by the Einsatzgruppen in the Soviet Union, or who starved in the ghettos of eastern Europe, or who were wasted by disease because of malnutrition and neglect, or who were killed in repisal in the west, or who died in any of the countless other, terrible ways—no less a part of the Holocaust because their final agonies do not meet some artificial standard of uniqueness.

Claiming uniqueness may, of course, simply be a way of asserting that the Holocaust was unprecedented. With this we are on more familiar historical terrain and closer to the kind of problem that historians are used to examining. After all, historians are supposed to have some idea how the events they describe compare with those that have gone before. To be sure, we are speaking in relative terms. No event occurs without antecedents, and few would assert that there were no preceding instances of massacre or anti-Jewish persecution that bear a relationship to the murder of European Jewry. The real question is: How much of a break with the past is this particular event?

Hitler's own words are sometimes adduced to demonstrate the filiation of the Holocaust with the massacre of Armenians by the Turkish government during the First World War. Before his military commanders, assembled at Obersalzberg on 22 August 1939, a few days before the German attack on Poland, Hitler urged the most savage treatment of the enemy. "I have placed my death-head formations in readiness . . . with orders to them to send to death mercilessly and without compassion, men, women and children of Polish derivation and language. Only thus shall we gain the living space [*Lebensraum*] that we need. Who, after all, speaks today of the annihilation of the Armenians?" [39] Hitler's bloodcurdling passage, originally relayed to the West by the American journalist Louis Lochner, is offered as evidence of the importance of precedent to the Nazi leader. Recent research suggests the authenticity of the quotation, which probably came to Lochner from the notes of the army intelligence chief Wilhelm Canaris, relayed by former chief of staff General Ludwig Beck.[40] But the Führer's reference is hardly a convincing case for seeing the Holocaust as simply one more instance of escalating violence toward innocent people in the twentieth century.

No serious person could detract from the horrors of the slaughter of Armenians within the Turkish Empire, beginning in the years 1894—96, when beleaguered central authorities collided with an emergent Armenian nationalism and, reaching a genocidal climax in 1915, with deportations and killings apparently designed by the Young Turk government to remove the Armenian population from Turkish Armenia and Asia Minor. Observers from Britain and the United States were shocked not only by the brutality and scale of the massacres, but also by the appalling way in which communities were victimized throughout the whole of Anatolia. Arnold Toynbee, who assisted Viscount Bryce in preparing a massive report on the massacres in 1916, made the point that the deportations and killing, which often amounted to the same thing, were carried out according to a coordinated government plan. While there was considerable local variation in practice, and while some provincial governors were not ill disposed to the Armenians, the central authorities were "directly and personally responsible without exception, from the beginning to the end, for the gigantic crime which devasted the Near East in 1915."[41]

Killing on this scale, and with this apparent objective, was what the jurist Raphael Lemkin had in mind when he coined the term *genocide* in 1943, under the impact of news about the Nazis' murder of European Jews. As Yehuda Bauer has observed, Lemkin defined the term in two different ways—sometimes meaning the literal extermination of a people, but sometimes also suggesting that the assault could be gradual—"a coordinated plan of different actions aiming at the destruction of the essential foundations of the life of national groups, with the aim of annihilating the groups themselves," as sociologist Leo Kuper puts it.[42] In the Armenian case, it is clearly the latter definition that applies. For however extensive the murder of Armenians within the Ottoman Empire, and however thorough the work of the executioners in particular localities, killing was far from universal. Although downtrodden and oppressed as a community, the fact is that many thousands of Armenians survived *within* Turkey during the period of the massacres. Armenians continued to shelter in the Turkish capital of Istanbul throughout the war, and, as Toynbee himself estimated, possibly a third of the Armenian population escaped the carnage entirely, most of them fleeing abroad. When the bloodshed ended, and after the departure of several hundred thousand Armenian refugees who fled to Transcaucasia, Europe, and the Middle East, about 140,000 Armenians were still living in the Turkish republic, about a tenth of the prewar population.[43]

Eugen Weber has suggested that technological capacity may have had something to do with the "incomplete" character of the Armenian genocide.[44] Descriptions of the slaughter make it plain that those in charge employed any and every means at their disposal, but that these were primitive indeed compared to the modern railway network, machine guns, and gas ovens used by the Nazis. Although Toynbee and others concluded that murder was directed from the center, in practice Armenians were butchered by the local gendarmerie, beaten to death by peasants, set upon by Kurdish tribesmen, left to die by roadsides, drowned in rivers, or abandoned in the desert. As Weber laconically observes, "these haphazard methods missed a lot of people." Beyond this, the primitive means available to the Young Turks also limited the horizon of what was conceivable in terms of mass murder. I have seen no indication, for example, that the Turks felt the killing ended prematurely or considered that their plans for the Armenians had *failed*. However atrocious the results, therefore, the killing process of 1915 lacked the machinelike, bureaucratic, regulated character as well as the Promethean ambition that we have come to associate with the Nazi Holocaust.

Another point about the attack on Armenians is that it occurred in the absence of the kind of all-consuming ideological obsession associated with the Nazis' detestation of Jews. As Bernard Lewis notes, the slaughter took place within the framework of genuine political conflict: "it was a struggle, however unequal, about real issues; it was never associated with demonic beliefs or the almost physical hatred which inspired and directed anti-Semitism in Europe and sometimes elsewhere."[45]

Reflecting on the differences between the two instances of genocide, Yehuda Bauer suggests that the Armenian case is much more akin to traditional massacres of helpless civilian populations in times past than it is to the attempted elimination of European Jews. Both involved stunning brutality, limitless cruelty, and disregard for human life. But, Bauer would add, the Nazi Holocaust went further. "What was unique in the Holocaust was the totality of its ideology and of its translation of abstract thought into planned, logically implemented total murder."[46] This is what Kren and Rappoport and others may have had in mind when they singled out the camp experience. For even if the camps did not encompass the whole of the Holocaust, they have been perceived as emblematic of the phenomenon as a whole. Reference to the camps may have significance as a way of evoking what are probably the most horrifying aspects of the destruction of European Jewry—the systematic dehumanization of the victims, the assembly-line process of mass murder, and the bureaucratic organization on a continental scale that brought people from every corner of Europe to be killed. These elements are certainly part of the Holocaust, and I would agree that they constitute part of its uniqueness.

It should be plain by now that uniqueness in the sense of being unprecedented does not refer to the numbers of people massacred. Massacre on the scale of the Holocaust would have been unthinkable in previous centuries, but not in our own. The twentieth century has seen a quantum leap in the numbers of people who fell victim to such man-made catastrophes as war and revolution, numbing those who assemble previously unheard-of statistics of the dead. In this gruesome context, the Jews have an important place, but not one that is unique. Some other instances of mass killing may illustrate the point. According to a recent investigation, Stalin's assault on the Soviet countryside during the 1930s took the lives of some 14.5 million—a ruthless attack on the peasantry associated with the collectivization of agriculture, and a deliberately caused "terror-famine," mainly in the Ukraine.[47] About the same time, Mussolini waged a murderous campaign in Ethiopia that involved the systematic use of mustard gas to kill masses of people; he was intending to replace the native population with Italian colonists. After the defeat of the German armies in eastern Europe in 1944 and 1945, some 12 million ethnic Germans were uprooted from parts of the Soviet Union, Poland, Hungary, Czechoslovakia, Rumania, Hungary, and Yugoslavia. Hundreds of thousands perished in the process. The partition of the Indian subcontinent in 1947 precipitated the slaughter of close to a million persons in religious strife between Muslims and Hindus. As many as 3 million Bengalis may have been massacred in 1971, with the secession of the now-independent state of Bangladesh. And genocide in Kampuchea, ruled by a cruel and despotic revolutionary government in the 1970s, killed between 1 million and 2 million among the total population of only 7 million persons.[48]

The Nazis murdered between 5 million and 6 million Jews during the Holocaust, two-thirds of European Jewry and about one-third of the entire Jewish people. But a staggering 55 million may have perished in all theaters during the Second World War—including some 20 million Soviet citizens, 15 million Chinese, 5 million Germans, and 3 million non-Jewish Poles. In what has been called "total war," the lot of civilians was sometimes even worse than that of soldiers, and the proportion of noncombatants killed certainly surpasses by far that of the First World War. In all, some 18 million European civilians may have died as a result of famine, disease, persecution, and more conventional acts of war.[49]

Awesome as they are, therefore, numbers do not in themselves prescribe the singularity of the Holocaust. But they provide a clue. For the *proportion* of European Jews killed during the Second World War, with roughly one of every three civilian deaths in Europe being that of a Jew, was undoubtedly greater than that of any other people, because of the Nazis' policy toward them. Unlike the case with any other group, and unlike the massacres before or since, *every single one* of the millions of targeted Jews was to be murdered. Eradication was to be total. In principle, no Jew was to escape. In this important respect, the Nazis' assault upon Jewry differed from the campaigns against other peoples and groups— Gypsies, Jehovah's Witnesses, homosexuals, Poles, Ukrainians, and so on. Assaults on these people could indeed be murderous; their victims number in the millions, and their ashes mingle with those of the Jews in Auschwitz and many other camps across Europe. But Nazi ideology did not require their total disappearance. In this respect, the fate of the Jews was unique.

Consistent with the Nazis' biological racism, each and every Jew was a threat, including the old, the ill, women, children, and even tiny infants. No Jewish community could be left in peace—at least, not for long. At the Wannsee Conference in January 1942, intended to set in motion the Final Solution, the minutes noted 11 million European Jews.[50] The most ambitious task involved the millions of Jews of Poland and the Soviet Union, but the listeners were also told to prepare for eliminating Jews in such widely disparate places as Finland, Ireland, Turkey, and Switzerland, where the number of Jews was derisible. The smallest community mentioned was that of Albania, where the minutes noted a Jewish community of two hundred. So vital was this campaign that the Nazis even importuned their allies and client states to turn over Jews to be murdered. The destructive urge, moreover, was not a momentary spasm. It lasted as long as there were Jews to kill, despite important evidence of wavering within the Nazi hierarchy which I shall discuss in chapter 9. In the spring of 1944, when the end could reasonably be foreseen, Joseph Goebbels's Propaganda Ministry urged the press of the Third Reich to reiterate the official line: "In the case of the Jews there are not merely a few criminals (as in every other people), but all of Jewry rose from criminal roots, and in its very nature it is criminal. The Jews are no people like any other people, but a pseudo-people welded together by hereditary criminality. . . . The annihilation of Jewry is no loss to humanity, but just as useful as capital punishment or protective custody against other criminals."[51]

TOWARD MASS MURDER

The Propaganda Ministry's definition of the Jewish foe reflects the particular virulence of Hitlerian and Nazi antisemitism, according to which the Jews were demonized—presented not only as the mortal enemies of the Reich, but as an all-powerful, pervasive, biologically defined source of evil in the world. Eliminating the Jews, therefore, became a central commitment of Hitler's regime, for which he demanded the total determination of his underlings. This became the hallmark of the massacre of European Jewry within the German bureaucracy. Officials all along the chain of command repeated that Jewish policy had the highest priority and required the most resolute fidelity to the principles of Nazism. From the Führer down, Nazis urged one another to be hard, unswerving, ruthless, determined. In a famous speech to his commanders in October

1943, SS boss Heinrich Himmler ridiculed the disposition to make exceptions: "I am referring to the evacuation of the Jews, the annihilation of the Jewish people. This is one of those things that are easily said. 'The Jewish people is going to be annihilated,' says every party member. 'Sure, it's in our program, elimination of the Jews, annihilation—we'll take care of it.' And then they all come trudging, 80 million worthy Germans, and each has his one decent Jew. Sure, the others are swine, but this one is an A-1 Jew. Of all those who talk this way, not one has seen it happen, not one has been through it. Most of you know what it means to see a hundred corpses lie side by side, or five hundred, or a thousand. To have stuck this out and— excepting cases of human weakness—to have kept our integrity, that is what has made us hard. In our history, this is an unwritten and never-to-be-written page of glory." [52]

Such Nazi declarations carry the unmistakable overtones of Hitler's own obsession with Jews and his penchant for seeing the world in terms of apocalyptic confrontations. Totality was built into Hitlerian rhetoric, as J. P. Stern has described so well. In this as in so many other contexts, Hitler drew upon the "catastrophe-mindedness" of his culture and insisted that in accomplishing goals, customary human limits were meaningless. Even simple tasks or routine operations could be transformed into earthshaking necessities and decisive confrontations. Military chiefs labored painfully under these obsessions of their leader. Frequently Hitler's commanders protested to their Führer that particular military operations were beyond the capacity of the troops. To their dismay, Hitler usually replied by accusing them of faintheartedness or a lack of fidelity to National Socialism. Told that the Hermann Göring division could not cross the straits of Messina to the Italian mainland to face the Allied invasion of 1943, for example, the Führer burst into a characteristic rage: "It is not the ferries that are decisive. What is decisive is the Will!" [53] In the same way, having determined upon the elimination of Jews from the Reich, Hitler allowed no limits to the means necessary to achieve this "never-to-be-written page of glory."

One of the arguments of this book is that the distinctive elements of the Holocaust emerged during the campaign in the Soviet Union, in the second half of 1941, when a murderous Final Solution was extended to all Jews within the grasp of German forces. Up to that point there was no consistent, European-wide plan of action. Indeed, Nazi persecution of the Jews followed an uneven path after Hitler's seizure of power in 1933.[54] From the start, there were two contradictory tendencies. Brown-shirted storm troopers and Nazi party activists lashed out at Jews on the local level, terrorizing and vandalizing Jews wherever they were to be found. On the other hand, more conservative elements in government circles and the bureaucracy preferred caution, worried that anti-Jewish actions might injure Germany's economic recovery and international reputation. Gradually, restraint got the upper hand, and persecution was directed from the center, with the Nuremberg Laws of 1935 setting the legal framework and a campaign of "Aryanization" organizing the confiscation of Jewish property. Jews were removed from government service, from most professions, and pressured to leave Germany. In the second half of the 1930s, with economic recovery and with the regime more securely established politically, there was a new round of radicalization. Following the Nazi-sponsored riots of Kristallnacht in November 1938, the Nazis' objective for the Jews centered on emigration. Reinhard Heydrich and his SS police apparatus, operating under Himmler, were placed in charge. So it remained until the Barbarossa campaign. Up to Kristallnacht about 150,000 Jews emigrated, and another 150,000 managed to flee thereafter. Even after the outbreak of war Jews continued to leave, their numbers drastically reduced, of course, by the restrictive policies of receiving countries in the West. Murderous episodes were not uncommon throughout this period, and killing came easier to the Nazis once in occupation of Polish territory. When examined closely, even the two specific emigration schemes—the Nisko Project of 1939 and the Madagascar Plan of 1940—had a murderous dimension. But Jewish emigration still remained the long-term goal.

The momentous change that occurred in the latter part of 1941 was marked by the Nazis' decision to abandon emigration, which had previously defined the "Final Solution of the Jewish Question." From this point, the Nazis were impatient. No longer did they say, as they had constantly repeated to one another when their Jewish policy seemed to be floundering, that the Final Solution would come eventually, at the end of the war. No longer did they anticipate that a peace treaty, to be signed with the vanquished enemies of the Reich, would define the terms of this solution in the form of a mass departure of Jews from the European continent. In a stunning volte-face, Berlin ordered the SS to block all exits. On 23 October 1941, registering a new policy that had revolutionized Nazi policy toward the Jews, Gestapo chief Heinrich Müller passed along an order from Himmler: apart from a few exceptions judged to be in the German interest, no more Jews were to emigrate from anywhere in the Reich or occupied Europe. A few days earlier deportations from Germany to the east began. Within days, technical teams began work on the first two death camps, at Chelmno (Kulmhof) and Belzec. At the end of November, Heydrich sent invitations to Nazi Jewish experts across Europe to participate in a planning conference at Wannsee. Gassing of Jews started at Chelmno on 8 December. Planning everywhere speeded up. It was important now to work quickly, to finish the job before the fighting ceased. As Franz Rademacher of the German Foreign Office put it, "The Jewish Question must be resolved in the course of the war, for only so can it be solved without a worldwide outcry." [55] The Holocaust had begun.

This chain of events points to what I have defined as the essence of the Holocaust—that it targeted every living Jew for murder. Massacre, of course, was a familiar part of Nazi operations before the turning point in the autumn of 1941. The starvation of tens of thousands of Jews in Polish ghettos and the mass shootings conducted by killing squads that entered the Soviet Union following the Wehrmacht in the Barbarossa campaign suggest that war and occupation provided scope before this time for murderous solutions. But only when the gates of all occupied Europe were sealed, and when the destructive machine turned impatiently to the Jews of western as well as eastern Europe, did the Holocaust emerge as we understand it. Only then did the Nazis begin their compulsive hunt for Jews that designated the two hundred Jews of Albania as well as the 3 million of Poland. This was to be no ordinary massacre, therefore; nor even the greatest massacre that the world had ever seen. "No other government and no other regime would have the strength for such a global solution of this question," Joseph Goebbels wrote admiringly in his diary on 27 March 1942. [56]

Having set their course on European-wide killing, the Nazis gave ample indication that the "radical solution" mentioned by Goebbels was no idle boast. Indeed, although the tide of war began to run against the Third Reich at the end of 1942, mass murder continued unabated, reaching a peak as the German war machine was being battered to pieces. On 15 March 1943, for example, in the wake of the Stalingrad disaster, Hitler told his propaganda minister that he should not "cease or pause until no Jew is left anywhere in Germany." [57] To the end those who followed orders knew that there should be no slowing down of the engines of destruction, even though mass murder interfered with the conduct of the war, even though Jewish labor was a valuable commodity, and even though railway transport was needed for military uses. In the spring of 1944, for example, when the Reich was being pounded by Allied air forces, with the Red Army approaching and the Western powers poised to strike in France, the Germans found time to deport the 260 Jews of Crete, among tens of thousands of others. Together with Greek hostages and Italian prisoners of war they were placed on a ship in the Aegean which was then deliberately sunk. All of them drowned. Two weeks later, on the day the Allies landed in Normandy, the Gestapo also bothered to round up 1,795 Jews on the island of Corfu, in the Adriatic. The deportees went directly to Auschwitz, where 1,500 were immediately gassed. [58] We usually know about such events, it should be noted, because the Nazis tell us about them, through the careful records that they kept, the punctilious bookkeeping of the Final Solution that chronicled details of the "radical solution." In contrast with other massacres of our time, including those that approach the scale of the Nazi Holocaust, the perpetrators convinced themselves that they were participating in a decisive, historic enterprise. Although their program was cloaked in secrecy, they ponderously counted the millions of dead, even assigning an SS actuary to the task in order to record a momentous accomplishment of the Nazi regime.

This view of the Holocaust stresses the evolution of Nazi policy, the radicalization of persecution to the point of European-wide mass murder, plotted in the latter part of 1941. As such, it suggests that both policy and the ideology behind it were subject to change, and were affected by a variety of circumstances that historians can identify and describe. Some of these, such as Hitler's sense of timing or the course of battle in the Russian campaign, had nothing to do with the Jews. Accepting the uniqueness of the Holocaust, this approach nevertheless insists upon it being a party of history, explicable as other aspects of Nazism and the Second World War. It may well be that on some profound level events such as the murder of

European Jewry will forever elude human understanding, as Isaac Deutscher suggested. But so it is also for much of recorded history, and for much of what we encounter in daily life. While historians cannot help but stand in horrified awe at the Final Solution, they have also tried to explain what brought it about. Their work on this particular issue is the subject to which we now turn.

3. THE FINAL SOLUTION

THE TERM *Final Solution* (*Endlösung*) first appeared as Nazi terminology, used by German themselves to designate their policy toward Jews. But what did the Nazis mean by these words? And what was the reality behind the phrase they employed? We must take care, in answering, lest we apply our own understanding, invariably associated with European-wide deportations and death camps. For while this undoubtedly *became* the Final Solution, this was not what those who first used these words with respect to Jews intended to convey. As we shall see, the stated objectives of the Third Reich changed over time. A look at how this particular term entered the Nazi lexicon raises the important question of why this occurred and how decisions on the Jews were made in the Third Reich.

As suggested in the last chapter, 1938 marked the intensification of persecution of Jews in Germany, with a new round of violence and a drive to expel Jews from the recently expanded Reich. In January 1939, the German Foreign Office told its representatives abroad about the "necessity for a radical solution of the Jewish question," referring also to the long-term goal as "an international solution." At the time, however, to quote the document further, "the ultimate aim of Germany's Jewish policy [was] the emigration of all Jews living on German territory." [1] By "international solution" the Foreign Office meant a negotiated settlement with receiving countries, according to which Jews would leave Germany, possibly taking a pittance of their property with them. Eight months later, just after the German conquest of Poland, Reinhard Heydrich alerted his SS Einsatzgruppen to a forthcoming "final aim" (*Endziel*), which would require extensive periods of time. Heydrich also referred to "planned total measures," which were "to be kept strictly secret." His communication indicates that some sort of vast population movement was contemplated, for one of the purposes of the instructions was to concentrate Jews in large urban areas, at rail junctions, and along railway lines.[2]

As a habitual programmatic short form, *final solution*, or *Endlösung*, may have first appeared in June 1940 in the context of a "territorial final solution" (*territoriale Endlösung*), and clearly linked with evolving schemes for massive forced emigration of Jews to the island of Madagascar, in the Indian Ocean, off the east coast of Africa. At the Jewish desk of the Foreign Office, Franz Rademacher used the phrase in this sense in September of the same year, when he was drafting concrete plans for installing the Jews in Madagascar and planning a visit to the island to map out details. The term appeared increasingly in the first half of 1941 and was mentioned notably by SS bureau chief Walter Schellenberg on 20 May, when discussing Jewish emigration priorities for the SS across Europe. As then understood, the "final solution" had to await the end of the war—the defeat of Great Britain and the definitive settlement of affairs with France through a peace treaty.[3] Early in the Russian campaign, a few months later, the language shifted once more. On 31 July 1941, there was a new, urgent reference in a telegram from Hermann Göring to Reinhard Heydrich, head of the vast SS police apparatus. Göring now instructed Heydrich to begin substantive preparations for a "total solution [*Gesamtlösung*] of the Jewish question in the German sphere of influence in Europe," considering this to be "the intended final solution of the Jewish question."[4] The pace quickened thereafter. In a letter of 28 August Adolf Eichmann referred to an "imminent final solution" as "now in preparation."[5] There was mention once again of a "final solution" at the Wannsee Conference of January 1942, with every indication that it was now under way. Calling the meeting to order, Heydrich told the assembled "Jewish experts" from across Europe that Göring had placed him in charge of preparations for "the final solution of the Jewish question" and that implementation was to be directed through Himmler's office.[6] The time for waiting was over.

Most historians agree that with this meeting, European-wide mass murder emerged as the essence of the Final Solution. I shall now examine how historians have understood the evolution of this particular "solution" to this point, given that the Nazis seemed in earlier times to lean in quite another direction, and given the frequent reference to other kinds of "solutions"—nonmurderous, at least in Pan-European terms—that were apparently taken seriously within the Nazi hierarchy.

The Nazis' own records provide little help. Typically, Hitler and his lieutenants cloaked their most criminal activities in euphemistic language, tried strenuously to keep their murderous plans secret, and were notoriously vague in delimiting lines of authority, especially on the most sensitive issues. Beyond this, Hitler had a positive aversion to orderly procedures and almost never discussed various policy options with his subordinates. As opposed to his British counterpart, Winston Churchill, who left mountains of documents, ruminating endlessly on possible courses of action, the Nazi dictator was reluctant to commit himself to paper with concrete ideas and preferred always to give orders orally, sometimes even then avoiding detailed instructions. As a result, important German officials were used to living with ambiguities and imprecisions on important issues, especially those in which the Führer had shown a special interest. At the top of the Nazi hierarchy, high-ranking Nazis were accustomed to Hitler's procrastination, particularly on the most difficult or dangerous problems. Further down, Nazi underlings avoided asking questions, especially when, as was often the case in the Third Reich, policy lines depended on ideology rather than empirical evidence, and hence could veer off in unexpected directions. On sensitive issues it was unwise to take policy initiatives before the Führer made up his mind.

In the absence of a clear record of Hitlerian decision making on the Final Solution, interpretations have varied considerably. In a book published in 1977, British writer David Irving even suggested that the Führer had nothing to do with the matter. Building his case on the inability of historians to discover written orders from Hitler to kill all the Jews of Europe, Irving contended that the Führer was not responsible for anti-Jewish policy at all, was basically uninterested in Jews, and knew nothing about their terrible fate—at least until 1943.[7] As a chorus of reviewers immediately pointed out, however, this contention not only ignored Hitler's hate-filled rhetoric about Jews, it also disregarded reports on the killings destined for him, plus the repeated statements of his underlings, including Himmler, that policy was determined at the highest level, by the Führer himself.[8]

What was particularly mischievous about Irving's argument was the notion that without explicit, written orders, it was impossible to assign responsibility for the Final Solution. Numerous critics have made clear that such orders were probably not necessary at all to begin the killing process. Authority in the Third Reich flowed not from laws and orders, issued by carefully delimited agencies, but rather from expressions of Hitler's will. Channels of government were frequently circumvented in favor of proclamations that such or so was "the Führer's wish." This is what Raul Hilberg, the dean of Holocaust historians, has called "government by announcement." In Hilberg's view, it is quite possible that a signed order to kill the Jews may never have been issued. What counted was a "mandate" from Hitler to proceed. Hitler frequently issued such mandates, and there is plenty of evidence that others understood just what the Nazi leader meant. Those in charge did not trouble with documentary niceties when the Führer expressed himself. "What he actually meant, or whether he really meant it, might have been a matter of tone as well as of language. When he spoke 'coldly' and in a 'low voice' about 'horrifying' decisions 'also at the dinner table,' then his audience knew that he was 'serious.'"[9] From one to another, Nazi leaders transmitted the latest impulse. The problem historians have is reconstructing what these signals were, and when and under what circumstances they were given.

INTENTIONALISTS: THE STRAIGHT PATH

For an important body of historical opinion, the questions asked about the emergence of the Final Solution can be answered easily with reference to Hitler's anti-Jewish rhetoric, drawn from various points in his career but seen to reflect a consistent murderous objective. In this view, Hitler is seen as the driving force of Nazi anti-semitic policy, whose views indicate a coherent line of thought from a very early point. Hitler is also seen as the sole strategist with the authority and the determination to begin the implementation of the Final Solution. In what is probably the most widely read work on this subject, Lucy Dawidowicz argues that the Führer set the stage for mass murder in September 1939, with the attack on Poland. "War and the annihilation of the Jews were interdependent," she writes. "The disorder of war would provide Hitler with the cover for the unchecked commission of murder. He needed an arena for his operations where the restraints of common codes of morality and accepted rules of warfare would not extend." September 1939, therefore, saw the beginning of "a twofold war": on the one hand there was the war of conquest for traditional goals such as raw materials and empire; on the other there was the "war against the Jews," the decisive confrontation with the greatest enemy of the Third Reich.[10] Orders to begin Europe-wide mass murder, issued in the late spring or summer of 1941, are seen as flowing directly from Hitler's idea on Jews, expressed as early as 1919. On various occasions his "program of annihilation" may have been camouflaged or downplayed. But Dawidowicz insists that it was always his intention: "Once Hitler adopted an ideological position, even a strategic one, he adhered to it with limpetlike fixity, fearful lest he be accused, if he changed his mind, of incertitude, of capriciousness on 'essential questions.' He had long-range plans to realize his ideological goals, and the destruction of the Jews was at their center."[11]

Borrowing from the British historian Tim Mason, Christopher Browning was the first to dub this interpretation "intentionalist," linking it to other historiographical themes in the history of the Third Reich. This line of thought accents the role of Hitler in initiating the murder of European Jewry, seeing a high degree of persistence, consistency, and orderly sequence in Nazi anti-Jewish policy, directed from a very early point to the goal of mass murder. Like much of the interpretative literature on Nazism, this explanation of the Final Solution rests on quotations and depends, in the final analysis, on the notion of a Hitlerian "blueprint" for future policies, set forth in *Mein Kampf* and other writings and speeches. Critics of this approach, referred to as "functionalists," are rather impressed with the evolution of Nazi goals, with the sometimes haphazard course of German policies, and with the way that these are related to the internal mechanisms of the Third Reich.[12]

Intentionalism, it may be supposed, was born at Nuremberg in 1945, when American prosecutors first presented Nazi crimes as a carefully orchestrated conspiracy, launched together with the war itself. At that time American legal experts hoped to prove that there had been a deliberate plan to commit horrendous atrocities as well as other breaches of international law; in this way they expected to designate certain German organizations and institutions as part of a criminal conspiracy, vastly simplifying the work of future prosecutions.[13] Years later, after much historical analysis, many historians still accept the notion of an unfolding Hitlerian plan. In his detailed critique of David Irving, for example, Gerald Fleming sees an "unbroken continuity of specific utterances" leading from Hitler's first manifestations of antisemitism "to the liquidation orders that Hitler personally issued during the war." A major task of Fleming's work is the collection of such utterances, which the author hopes will tear away the camouflage covering Hitler's primary responsibility.[14]

One can sympathize with an effort to remind a sometimes negligent audience of Hitler's incessant, raving hatred of Jews. And it is similarly valuable to expose the Nazis' linguistic perversions—distortions intended to conceal the killing process from the victims, from the Allies, and from the German public as well. Nevertheless, the problem of interpreting Hitlerian rhetoric still remains. For the fact is that Hitler was forever calling for the most ruthless action; for sudden, crushing blows; for the complete annihilation of his foes; or evoking his irrevocable, ironlike determination to do this or that. We cannot ignore Hitler's amply demonstrated blood lust, and there is no doubt that the contemplation of mass killing inspired him on more than one occasion.[15] In retrospect, historians have little difficulty in tracing "direct lines," but it is much more problematic to ascertain what Hitler actually intended and how he acted on such expressions at specific moments.[16] In May 1938, for example, Hitler told his generals of his "unalterable decision to destroy Czechoslovakia by military action in the foreseeable future." According to Gerhard Weinberg, the Nazi leader indeed wanted military action, but believed he could avoid a general war. When he learned in September, on the eve of his attack, that a general war threatened, that neither Mussolini nor the German public were likely to follow him, and that he could achieve a stunning success peacefully, he changed his mind.[17] So "unalterable decisions" could be altered. The implication is that Hitler's words should indeed be taken seriously, but that they must also be seen in the context of his actions and the concrete situations he faced.

This is a reasonable reply to the use made of Hitler's famous speech of 30 January 1939 by intentionalist historians such as Dawidowicz and Fleming. Adopting a characteristically "prophetic" tone in his address to the Reichstag, Hitler issued a terrible warning: "One thing I should like to say on this day which may be memorable for others as well as for us Germans: In the course of my life I have very often been a prophet, and I have usually been ridiculed for it. During the time of my struggle for power it was in the first instance the Jewish race which only received my prophecies with laughter when I said that I would one day take over the leadership of the State, and with it that of the whole nation, and that I would then among many other things settle the Jewish problem. Their laughter was uproarious, but I think that for some time now they have been laughing on the other side of their face. Today I will once more be a prophet. If the international Jewish financiers outside Europe should succeed in plunging the nations once more into a world war, then the result will not be the bolshevization of the earth, and thus the victory of Jewry, but the annihilation of the Jewish race in Europe." [18]

Fleming is certainly right to stress the importance of Hitler's self-portrayal as a "fighting prophet," and Hitler's subsequent references to this speech in the middle of the war indicate a conscious desire, once the Final Solution was under way, to assert a continuity of actions against the Jews. This is but one of many pieces of evidence that suggest Hitler insisted on a definitive solution to the Jewish question, and in this sense the speech is an important measure of his priorities. Less clear, however, is what the January speech tells us about Hitler's objectives at the time. A look at his words in context shows that Hitler spoke for several hours, but devoted only a few minutes to the Jews. Speaking in the wake of the Munich conference, Hitler focused mainly on economic matters, in an address judged by the British ambassador to be relatively conciliatory. One of the purposes of Hitler's address was likely to sow confusion and division among the Western powers. He probably did envisage war in Europe as his "prophecy" suggested; but this was likely not a world war, but rather a fight over Poland, which would be over quickly. As Uwe Dietrich Adam points out, Hitler and other Nazi leaders looked to an even more ruthless crackdown on Jews in the event of war.[19] We shall never know for certain precisely what plans lurked in Hitler's consciousness and whether his reference to "annihilation" at that particular time should be taken literally. But it is not at all plain that he had fixed upon mass murder, which presumably would have to begin once the short Polish campaign was over. And it is even less likely that Hitler thought concretely about European-wide killings, which he was not in a position to undertake until his stunning military successes in 1940–41.

In utterances such as Hitler's 30 January address, Eberhard Jäckel identifies the "universalist-missionary touch" in the Führer's antisemitism, which became an integral part of Nazi war aims. Hitler's antisemitism in Mein Kampf, according to Jäckel, "presupposes war, it demands the methods of warfare, and it is therefore not surprising that it should have reached its bloody climax during the next war, which was a part of Hitler's program from the start." Once the fighting continued into 1941 and 1942, "the extermination of the Jews became increasingly the most important aim of the war as such; as the fortunes of war turned against Germany, the destruction of the Jews became National Socialism's gift to the world." Finally, in the eery atmosphere of Hitler's bunker beneath the ruins of Berlin, antisemitism assumed supreme importance. The extermination of the Jews "now appeared to him as his central historical mission."[20] A key suggestion, I think, is that antisemitism became ever more salient. But was there a "blueprint" from a very early point, as Jäckel implies? Was extermination an inevitable outgrowth of this antisemitism? These questions remain open.

Some intentionalists link Hitler's determination to murder the Jews with other aspects of his thought and strategy. In his book The Three Faces of Fascism, first published in German in 1963, intellectual historian Ernst Nolte presented National Socialism as part of a European-wide opposition to modern ideas and development, of which the Jews were a principal symbol in the eyes of antisemites.[21] In Hitler's thinking, said Nolte, the Jew came to stand for "the historical process itself." Unlike some of his followers, Hitler and

Himmler were "logically consistent" in their thought and practice. Assuming that everything they detested in the world derived ultimately from this mainspring of modernity, annihilation made sense. "In Hitler's extermination of the Jews it was not a case of criminals committing criminal deeds, but of a uniquely monstrous action in which principles ran riot in a frenzy of self-destruction." [22] For Andreas Hillgruber, on the other hand, the key lies in the Barbarossa campaign and the struggle against the Soviet regime. The Final Solution, he argues, derived from the ideological fixation with Bolshevism and the east, seen as inseparable in Hitler's mind from "international Judaism." Killing on a mass scale emerged from the ideological mobilization for the onslaught on the Soviet Union that began on 22 June 1941.[23]

In the absence of reliable guides to Hitler's plans for the Jews, apart from his murky "prophecies," intentionalists differ among themselves as to when precisely Hitler's intentions became fixed. In his most recent book, Jäckel rules out the idea that there was "a single killing order." Rather, "extermination was divided into several phases and covered a wide variety of methods and victims." [24] The weight of opinion about a turning point falls on the war against the Soviet Union. According to Helmut Krausnick, there was a wartime decision of the Führer, but its timing remains obscure. "What is certain is that the nearer Hitler's plan to overthrow Russia as the last possible enemy on the continent of Europe approached maturity, the more he became obsessed with an idea—with which he had been toying as a 'final solution' for a long time—of wiping out the Jews in the territories under his control. It cannot have been later than March 1941, when he openly declared his intention of having the political commissars of the Red Army shot that he issued his secret decree—which never appeared in writing though it was mentioned verbally on several occasions—that the Jews should be eliminated." [25] Together with a colleague, Hans-Heinrich Wilhelm, Krausnick has pored over the activity of the murderous Einsatzgruppen, the killing teams of motorized SS troops who followed in the van of the Wehrmacht when they swept into the Soviet Union in the summer of 1941. Ultimately these and related units are responsible for more than 2 million deaths, one of the greatest orgies of mass killing in the history of mankind. Krausnick and Wilhelm have documented the genocidal character of the campaign, which Hitler referred to as a *Vernichtungskrieg,* a war of destruction, and they have incidentally demonstrated the extensive support and assistance given to their slaughters by the regular army. In their view the extermination of the Jews was included in the Barbarossa planning process.[26] This assessment has been contested, however, with other authorities arguing rather that the killing evolved into genocidal proportions during the early course of the fighting. But of genocide itself there is no doubt. Christian Streit and others have documented the active participation of the Wehrmacht in a whole complex of killing orders and massacres—including Jews, Communists, and prisoners of war.[27]

FUNCTIONALISTS: THE TWISTED ROAD

Against this interpretation, so-called functionalist historians present a picture of the Third Reich as a maze of competing power groups, rival bureaucracies, forceful personalities, and diametrically opposed interests engaged in ceaseless clashes with each other. They see Hitler as a brooding and sometimes distant leader, who intervened only spasmodically, sending orders crashing through the system like bolts of lightning. While in theory the power of the Führer was without limit, in practice he preferred the role of arbiter, according legitimacy to one or another favorite or line of conduct. Add to this Hitler's curious leadership style—his inability to mount a sustained effort, his procrastination, his frequent hesitation—and one can understand the reluctance of many to accept the idea of a far-reaching scheme or ideological imperative necessitating the Final Solution. Few historians of this school doubt that Hitler was murderously obsessed with Jews; they question, however, whether he was capable of long-term planning on this or any other matter, and they tend to look within the chaotic system itself for at least some of the explanation for the killing of European Jews.

Reflecting this perspective, Martin Broszat's 1977 critique of David Irving's *Hitler's War* presented to a wide public a serious interpretation of the origins of the Final Solution in which Hitler did not have full operational responsibility.[28] Broszat's approach was hardly an exculpation of the Nazi leader. On the contrary, he took Irving to task for his "normalization" of Hitler and pointed to dangerous forces within the German Federal Republic that utilized the apologetic drift in the British historian's work. Broszat reasserted Hitler's "fanatical, destructive will to annihilate" that traditional historiography has always seen at the core of the Führer's personality. He stressed Hitler's "totally irresponsible, self-deceiving, destructive and evilly misanthropic egocentricity and his lunatic fanaticism." As the author of a 1969 work, *Der Staat Hitlers,* Broszat had no doubt about who was in charge and what kind of a person he was.

Nevertheless, the heart of Broszat's argument was that the Final Solution was not begun after a single Hitlerian decision, but arose "bit by bit." He suggested that deportations and systematic killings outside the sphere of the Einsatzgruppen in Russia started through local Nazi initiatives, rather than a directive from the Führer. According to this view, Hitler set the objective of Nazism: "to get rid of the Jews, and above all to make the territory of the Reich *judenfrei,* i.e., clear of Jews"—but without specifying how this was to be achieved. In a vague way, the top Nazi leadership hoped to see the Jews pushed off to the east, and uprooted large masses of people with this in mind. Top Nazi officials had "no clear aims . . . with respect to the subsequent fate of the deportees," however. Their policy was "governed by the concept that the enormous spaces to be occupied in the Soviet Union would . . . offer a possibility for getting rid of the Jews of Germany and of the allied and occupied countries," but they also toyed with other schemes, such as the Madagascar Plan, to achieve their objectives. Expectations of an early resolution heightened during the Russian campaign, which was supposed to finish in a matter of weeks. Deportation trains carrying Jews from the Reich began to roll eastward. Yet by the autumn these plans were upset. Military operations slowed, and then came to a standstill. Transportation facilities were overloaded. Nazi officers in the occupied east, receiving shipments of Jews from the Reich, now complained that they had no more room in the teeming, disease-ridden ghettos. It was then, in Broszat's view, that Nazi officials on the spot started sporadically to murder the Jews who arrived from the west. Killing, therefore, "began not solely as the result of an ostensible will for extermination but also as a 'way out' of a blind alley into which the Nazis had manoeuvered themselves." In its early stages, annihilation was improvised, and its execution was marked by confusion and misunderstanding. Only gradually, in early 1942, did Himmler and the SS establish the coherent structures of the Final Solution, coordinated on a European-wide basis.[29]

Among functionalists, Hans Mommsen has presented the most forceful case for a Führer uninvolved in and perhaps incapable of administration, concerned rather with his personal standing and striking propaganda postures. Mommsen goes even further than Broszat in suggesting that Hitler had little directly to do with anti-Jewish policy. While not denying his intense hatred of Jews, Mommsen sees the Nazi leader as thinking about the Jews mainly in propagandistic terms, without bothering to chart a course of action. The Final Solution, he observes, resulted from the interaction of this fanatical but distant leader with the chaotic structure of the Nazi regime. In the Third Reich, office was piled upon office, and underlings were left to find their way in a bureaucratic and administrative jungle. The only guide to success, and a compelling one, was fidelity to the Hitlerian vision. Underlings competed for the favor of this ideologically obsessed, but essentially lazy leader. Given the Führer's mad compulsions, this competition programmed the regime for "cumulative radicalization," a process that ended ultimately, of course, in its self-destruction. Hitler's heightened rhetoric prompted others to realize his "utopian" ravings about Jews and undoubtedly stimulated murderous excesses. But he issued no order for the Final Solution and had nothing to do with its implementation.[30]

"Hitler's precise role remains hidden in the shadows," says Ian Kershaw, reviewing this literature recently.[31] Given the paucity of documentation, this issue may forever remain obscure, without disputing either the importance of the Führer in the process or the demonic potency of his antisemitism. Whatever their view of Hitler, however, functionalist historians agree that the Final Solution emerged through improvisation, rather than deliberate planning. In his survey of Nazi policy toward the Jews, Karl Schleunes suggested that there was a "twisted road to Auschwitz." The paths that led to the extermination camps, he elaborates, "were by no means direct or, for that matter, charted far in advance."[32] Unlike Broszat, Uwe Adam posits a distinct Hitlerian decision to murder the Jews as occurring sometime "between September and November 1941" and assumes there was an order from the Führer to this effect. But he too considers that there was no course set from a very early point for European-wide mass murder. Instead, one decision led to another piecemeal, with mass murder emerging as a way to resolve a hopeless contradiction. Having set in motion deportations from the west, the Nazis had to do something with the Jews accumulating in Poland. When the "territorial" option in Russia was foreclosed, the Führer decided on the Final Solution. Hitler and his relentless anti-Jewish ideology were the dynamic element, pressing for a solution to the "Jewish Question"; policy evolved, however, in the chaotic institutional environment of the Third Reich, where planlessness and internal contradictions were the norm.[33]

In the most recent scholarly analysis of this issue, Browning settles upon a position that he terms "moderate functionalist."[34] He finds it implausible that Hitler was merely "awaiting the opportune moment" to realize his murderous intentions, since the Nazi leader allowed nearly three years to pass between the conquest of Poland and the onset of European-wide mass murder. If the outbreak of war simply provided Hitler with a "cover" for mass murder, "why were the millions of Polish Jews in his hands since the fall of 1939 granted a thirty-month 'stay of execution'? They were subjected to sporadic massacre and murderous living conditions but not to systematic extermination until 1942." During this time there was no "blueprint" for mass destruction, but rather an ideological imperative that called for some sort of ultimate reckoning with the Jews in a manner that would satisfy Nazi racial preoccupations. Competing Nazi agencies put forward one proposal after the next, schemes that continually shattered against practical obstacles. Nazi activists appealed to a Führer whose mind was sometimes elsewhere, who was worried about tactical issues of many sorts, and who often delayed making up his mind about important matters.

The crisis came with Barbarossa, not only because of the apocalyptic character of the campaign, but also because it promised to bring hundreds of thousands more Jews within the hegemony of the Reich. What were the Germans to do with them? During the early course of the campaign Hitler tipped the scales for mass murder. The decision to massacre the Soviet Jews was probably taken in March, as part of the Barbarossa planning process. Before the end of July, Hitler, buoyed up by the spectacular successes of the Wehrmacht in the early part of the Russian campaign, probably issued his order for European-wide mass murder. At that point, the

Führer likely felt, everything was possible. On 31 July, Göring authorized Heydrich to prepare a "total solution" (*Gesamtlösung*) of the Jewish question in the territories under the Nazis' control. Before long, work began on the first two death camps—at Belzec and Chelmno, where construction started in the autumn. On 23 October, Himmler issued a fateful order that passed along the Nazi chain of command: henceforth there would be no Jewish emigration permitted anywhere from German-held territory. On 29 November, invitations went out to the Wannsee Conference, intended to coordinate deportations from across Europe. The Final Solution was about to begin.

Browning and others have criticized the work of various functionalists on three grounds.[35] First, they challenge Adam's notion that pushing great masses of Jews off "to the east" was still an option for the Nazis in the summer of 1941. No concrete preparations for such a massive deportation have ever been discovered, and it is unlikely that serious planning for it could have been under way without leaving a trace in the historical record. Göring's authorization to Heydrich on 31 July to prepare a "total solution" could hardly have referred to such expulsions, they say, since Heydrich already had such authority and had been expelling Jews on a smaller scale since the beginning of 1939. Seen in the context of the furious killings then under way by the Einsatzgruppen, Göring's communication appears rather like a warrant for genocide. Like many, Klaus Hildebrand finds it difficult to distinguish between the gigantic operations of the killing teams in Russia and the other aspects of the Final Solution. "In qualitative terms the executions by shooting were no different from the technically more efficient accomplishment of the 'physical final solution' by gassing, of which they were a prelude."[36] Second, historians have challenged Broszat's idea of locally initiated mass murders. Not only does it seem unlikely that the systematic killing of Jews from the Reich, for example, could have been undertaken without the Führer's agreement, there is also too little evidence of local initiatives with which to sustain this theory. As Eberhard Jäckel noted recently, there is rather "a great deal of evidence that some [local officials] were shocked or even appalled when the final solution came into effect. To be sure, they did not disagree with it. But they agreed only reluctantly, referring again to an order given by Hitler. This is a strong indication that the idea did not originate with them." [37]

Third, Browning contends that the decision for European-wide mass murder was taken in the summer of 1941, in the euphoria of the first victories in the Barbarossa campaign, and not a few months later. He draws upon postwar evidence from Rudolf Höss, the commandant of Auschwitz, and Adolf Eichmann, from the start a key official in the bureaucracy of the Final Solution, to the effect that the Führer's mind was made up during the summer. This sense of timing differs notably from functionalists who conclude that the Final Solution arose from disappointment with the outcome of the fighting in Russia. Adam, for example, sees the Nazis depressed by the prospect of having to spend another winter with the Jews; the journalist Sebastian Haffner imagines, much less plausibly, that Hitler saw as early as the end of 1941 that the European war could not be won and that the other contest, "the war against the Jews," could at least be pursued to its final conclusion. [38]

Outsiders to these disputes may well suspect that some of the sharp edges of the controversy are wearing off and that there is more agreement among these historians than meets the eye. Opinion is widespread that there was some Hitlerian decision to initiate Europe-wide killing. The range of difference over timing extends across only a few months, with intentionalists positing a Führer order sometime in March 1941, with Browning and others opting for the summer, and with a few, such as Adam, looking toward the early autumn. What finally precipitated this decision, however, is likely to remain a mystery. Military historians tell us that, despite the extraordinary successes of the Wehrmacht in the first weeks of the Barbarossa campaign, the Germans found the going difficult as early as mid-July 1941. Although their forces advanced great distances and destroyed much of their opposition, they were surprised at the extent and efficacy of Soviet resistance and were greatly slowed by faulty intelligence, poor roads and bridges, and marshes. Chief of the army general staff Franz Halder portrayed an exasperated Führer after only six weeks of fighting, and it seems likely that by late August Hitler already knew that the war would continue well into 1942. This was a major setback, even though the Germans did not taste real defeat until December. [39] Whether euphoria or disappointment prompted the decision is therefore difficult to say. On the other hand, the idea of Hitler breaking the logjam caused by an ill-defined policy rings true, given what we know of his leadership style. Students of Hitler's behavior in other areas have been struck by his preference for sudden, unexpected, spectacular coups. His was the method of the supreme gambler, "forever looking for short cuts." [40] For someone as ruthless and fanatical as Hitler, a decision for the Final Solution can well be imagined in the apocalyptic atmosphere of Barbarossa, the war to settle once and for all the fate of the thousand-year Reich.

"La guerre révolutionna la Révolution," French historian Marcel Reinhard once wrote about the revolutionary impact of the war of 1792 on the revolutionaries in Paris. So it has been observed that the war against the Soviet Union revolutionized the Third Reich, and it is not surprising that this campaign transformed Nazi Jewish policy as well. It is difficult to follow the process of political and ideological radicalization in detail, for this was a period of extensive fluidity—even for a regime that, as Karl Dietrich Bracher has said, "remained in a state of permanent improvisation." [41] Ian Kershaw observes that "the summer and autumn of 1941 were characterized by a high degree of confusion and contradictory interpretations of the aims of anti-Jewish policy by the Nazi authorities." [42] It seems useful, however, to understand Jewish policy in this period as evolving within a genocidal framework—extending beyond Jews to include the incurably ill, Soviet intelligentsia, prisoners of war, and others as well. In this fevered atmosphere, incredible as it may seem, an "order" to send millions of people to their deaths may have been no more than a "nod" from Hitler to one of his lieutenants. [43]

FUNCTIONARIES OF THE FINAL SOLUTION

For historians of the Holocaust, the greatest challenge has not been making sense of Hitler, but rather understanding why so many followed him down his murderous path. Given the state of the evidence, this difficulty may seem curious. For while documentation of Hitler's acts is relatively scarce, material on the rest of the regime is available in great abundance, including much of what happened during the Holocaust. Nevertheless, the mystery remains. And in seeking their answer, students of the Final Solution simply join with other historians of the Third Reich and the Second World War who confront similar issues. Why did so many politicians and statesmen fail to get the full measure of Adolf Hitler? Why did the cream of German generals, renowned for their professionalism, permit themselves to be led to ruin by a criminal maniac? Why did the structures of the Reich remain under his spell for so long in 1944–45, when by all objective standards the adventure of Nazism was finished? All of these questions are related.

Having depreciated the operational importance of the Führer, functionalist historians tend to broaden the range of culpability associated with the Final Solution. To them, blame extends across the German elite, especially in the military and the civil service, for having performed the manifold tasks of mass murder and having done so without complaint. Martin Broszat describes the evolution of a huge apparatus represented by the security police and the SS, operating entirely outside the framework of law and state administration. By 1942 this Nazi elite could direct various branches of the bureaucracy to carry out portions of the murderous operation, designated in euphemistic administrative language as "removals," "evacuations," "cleansing actions," and so on.[44] With regard to the Wehrmacht, several historians' demonstration of the complicity of high-ranking officers with the annihilation policy of the Barbarossa campaign shows conclusively that direct involvement in genocide was not limited to the SS. Omer Bartov has come to similar conclusions about junior Wehrmacht officers as well.[45] Hans Mommsen poses the issue of what accounts for the widespread elimination of inhibitions to mass murder. Antisemitic indoctrination is plainly an insufficient answer, for we know that many of the officials involved in the administration of mass murder did not come to their tasks displaying intense antisemitism. In some cases, indeed, they appear to have had no history of anti-Jewish hatred and to have been coldly uninvolved with their victims.[46] Motivation seems to have varied considerably. As students of the Holocaust have long understood, the extensive division of labor associated with the killing process helped perpetrators diffuse their own responsibility. In Mommsen's view, a "technocratic-hierarchical mentality" accounts for a great deal, and he suggests that the political-psychological structure of this process is the real problem for the historical explanation of the Holocaust.[47]

It is on this issue, posed as the how rather than the why of Nazi genocide, that Raul Hilberg has made a signal contribution to the study of the Final Solution. The product of painstaking and wide-ranging research, Hilberg's book offers a magisterial synthesis, on a scale that no one has matched before or since. First published in 1961, and now reissued in a "revised and definitive edition," Hilberg's *Destruction of the European Jews* remains the most important work that has ever been written on the subject. Of breathtaking scope, with a description of the destruction process extending across the entire European continent, his book provided the first detailed and systematic combing of German materials on the Holocaust.

Interestingly, Hilberg does not address the debate on the origins of the Final Solution. In his new edition, he remains on another level, faithful to the objective he outlined more than a quarter of a century ago. "I wanted to explore the sheer mechanism of destruction, and as I delved into the problem I saw that I was studying an administrative process carried out by bureaucrats in a network of offices spanning a continent. Understanding the components of this apparatus, with all the facets of its activities, became the principal task of my life."[48] A political scientist, heavily influenced by his Columbia University mentor Franz Neumann, Hilberg developed the notion of "the machinery of destruction," the description of which is the core of his analysis. This machinery, with awesome power, grinds on ineluctably—not only to destroy its victims, but also to engage an ever-wider circle of perpetrators in the murderous task.

How was the Nazis' project realized? In Hilberg's view the destruction of the Jews proceeded by stages—"sequential steps that were taken at the initiative of countless decision makers in a farflung bureaucratic machine." First came the definition of the Jews, then their expropriation, concentration, deportation, and finally their murder. The machine remains his controlling image, and his leitmotif is the gigantic scale of its work. Nazi genocide was a truly monumental task, requiring great exertion throughout the whole of the German empire, bureaucratic ingenuity, countless administrative decisions, the continuous cooperation of widely diverse agencies, and many thousands of officials. In hundreds of pages, Hilberg recounts an officialdom across Europe working together in mechanized fashion. Significantly, the perpetrators themselves had no special characteristics; the essential element was the structure into which they fit. "To grasp the full significance of what these men did we have to understand that we are not dealing with individuals who had their own separate moral standards. The bureaucrats who were drawn into the destruction process were not different in their moral makeup from the rest of the population." [49] Faced with its enormous task, to do away with the Jews, the Nazis discovered a remarkable new administrative process that set the machinery of destruction "on its track of self-assertion." At a certain point, the machine needed no operator. It required no master plan or blueprint. "In the final analysis the destruction of the Jews was not so much a product of laws and commands as it was a matter of spirit, of shared comprehension, of consonance and syncronization." This human machine generated its own momentum, "operating with accelerating speed and an ever-widening destructive effect." Efficiency was its hallmark. "With an unfailing sense of direction and with an uncanny pathfinding ability, the German bureaucracy found the shortest path to the final goal." [50]

As with most historians, Hilberg sees Hitler's role in the Final Solution as "salient," but he does little beyond implying that the Führer activated the machinery already programmed for murder in 1941. "For years, the administrative machine had taken its initiatives and engaged in its forays one step at a time. In the course of that evolution, a direction had been charted and a course established. By the middle of 1941 the dividing line had been reached, and beyond it lay a field of unprecedented actions unhindered by the limits of the past." While there can be no doubt about the Nazi leader's inspiration of mass murder, he seems an even more distant figure in the new edition than the first. Passages that considered or speculated about his decisions have been removed, and the role of the machine and its destructive logic are thereby enhanced. At the bottom of a footnote reference to the evidence of Adolf Eichmann and Rudolf Höss, we find Hilberg's sole comment on an issue that has been so widely disputed: "Chronology and circumstances point to a Hitler decision before the summer [of 1941] ended." [51]

Detailed study of particular components of the "machinery of destruction" is likely to help us understand how it worked and how it acted on the impulses of its demented Führer.[52] In his 1978 book on the Jewish section of the German Foreign Office, for example, Christopher Browning portrayed a group of Nazi bureaucrats eagerly pursuing the directions that came from their superiors, but also capable of their own initiatives when opportunities arose. Martin Luther, chief of this section, was an archcareerist with a talent for organization, but no pressing anti-Jewish vocation. Luther "was not a doctrinaire racist like Heinrich Himmler, dreaming of fantasies of a future Aryan heaven-on-earth. Nor was he an *Altkämpfer* like Goebbels, wallowing in nostalgia and ready to stick by Hitler to the end. . . . Primarily, Luther was an amoral technician of power."[53] Strikingly, with the shift toward the Final Solution in the latter part of 1941, these officials sensed a new direction and acted upon it. Browning notes: "when zealous administrators like Luther were desperately trying to anticipate the will of the Führer in the Jewish question . . . a chain of command requiring obedience to the Führer's orders was superfluous. Initiative from below obviated the necessity for orders from above."[54]

It was similar with the development and production of the gas van, a Nazi invention for killing, first utilized in the so-called euthanasia program against mental patients. By early 1942 these machines were in use at Chelmno, in German-incorporated Poland, and with the Einsatzgruppen in captured Soviet territory. There was no Führer order for the gas vans, and it is not clear if Hitler was ever informed about them. According to Browning, the impetus for development came with the problems encountered by killing teams in Russia. Complaints flowed from the field, where murder squads were being demoralized by the inefficient and gruesome process of mass shooting. Ideas flowed from Berlin, where scientists attached to the Führer's Chancellery received directives from Heydrich to design a vehicle using exhaust gas for killing people. All along the line individuals made their contributions. During 1942, with the Final Solution having been deemed an urgent priority, and for want of any better way to do the job, the gas vans were pressed into service to speed the killing process. Who was responsible for the gas van? Hitler set the killing priority but left the details to others. Among the high-ranking dignitaries of the Third Reich, Himmler and Heydrich both had their role. But we are now able to glimpse more humble contributors to the Final Solution—in the machine shops where the vans were assembled and repaired, in the procurement offices and dispatching agencies that sent them on their lethal missions. Officials there loathed bottlenecks and set about to make their work more effective. "Kept fully abreast of the problems arising in the field, they strove for ingenious technical adjustments to make their product more efficient and acceptable to its operators. What could not be remedied had to be blamed on someone else. . . . Their greatest concern seemed to be that they might be deemed inadequate to their assigned task."[55]

According to George Mosse, the heavy reliance upon technology in the Final Solution—the use of gas, railways, controls, and movement of vast numbers of people—"interacted with the dehumanization of the victims."[56] Those involved in the process could take refuge in their professional specialty, banishing all humane considerations. These perpetrators hardly thought of themselves as anything other than skilled technicians, and often seemed genuinely surprised when, years later, they were branded accomplices to mass murder.

ASPECTS OF NAZI POPULATION POLICY

Just as the examination of particular aspects of the Final Solution assists historians in understanding the process as a whole, so the study of related themes casts light on the destruction of European Jews.[57] A good example is the Nazis' so-called euthanasia campaign, which reflects, as one student of the matter has recently argued, a much wider involvement by doctors in the racial engineering of the Third Reich. According to psychiatrist Robert Jay Lifton, there was a special affinity between Nazism and a perverted medical outlook, yielding what he calls the "Nazi biomedical vision." Drawing heavily upon eugenic ideas common in much of the Western world in the 1920s, this was a view of the entire German nation as a biological organism, which was threatened by a kind of collective illness—a potentially fatal threat to a formerly healthy society. The task of Nazism was to cure the German *Volk* by eliminating all sources of corruption—carried mainly by the Jews, but evident also in the feebleminded, the incurably ill, and the insane. The goal, Lifton says, was "biocracy," built on the model of theocracy—a state committed to purification and revitalization, applied as if through divine commandment.[58]

These ideas did not remain the province of theory. Beginning with little children, the Nazis encouraged and directed a program of systematic killing of the physically and mentally impaired, eventually using gas chambers, to rid the Reich of those deemed "unworthy of life." It is difficult to establish the death toll in this campaign, partly because many doctors and institutions were allowed to proceed on their own after the campaign was officially stopped; it is generally believed, however, that the total killed was between 80,000 and 100,000 people.[59] All who have examined this killing have noted a link with the Final Solution—in the particular propensity to murder Jews as part of its operation, but also in the development of killing methods and the training of personnel who would eventually find their place within the death camps of eastern Europe.[60]

Another example is the Nazi population policy for eastern Europe, which has been addressed recently in the work of several scholars. Seen from this angle, Nazi Jewish policy was part of a vast German project for the demographic reordering of eastern Europe, to be undertaken in a manner consistent with Nazi principles. In a word, the Nazis encouraged vast population movements throughout the region: non-Germans had to be ruthlessly excluded from the territory of the Reich; at the same time, pure Germans or *Volksdeutsche* were to be taken into the fold, particularly in the new eastern marches.[61] In the autumn of 1939, Heinrich Himmler, head of the SS and master of the gargantuan police apparatus known as the Central Office for Reich Security (Reichsicherheitshauptamt, or RSHA), brought under his control a series of agencies devoted to racial and settlement matters. In October, as soon as the Polish campaign was successfully completed, Hitler authorized Himmler to institute a Reich Commission for the Consolidation of Germandom (Reichskommissariat für die Festigung des deutschen Volkstums, or RKFDV), a powerful bureaucracy to coordinate the Nazis' vast population schemes. Under Himmler's direction, vast numbers of people, Jews and non-Jews, began to move in Nazi-held eastern Europe.[62]

Nazi population policy in the east, it becomes clear, was governed by the same lack of planning and well-ordered priorities as Jewish policy in the period before the Final Solution. Gigantic projects were set in motion, often with the slimmest preparation or appreciation of the constraints of wartime conditions. According to Robert Koehl, "the chaos created by the lack of conformity between theory and reality, and especially by top-level decisions out of touch with reality, led to violent and brutal measures, to fantasy and more false logic, and to cynicism."[63] Gangsterism took command. Officials fought bitterly with each other; Nazi agencies staked out grandiose claims for jurisdiction; and the entire program, deemed of the highest ideological significance, suffered from Hitler's failure to make decisive choices.[64] As with the Final Solution, the climax came with Barbarossa. With his ambitions apparently fed by conquest, Himmler stirred the imagination of his underlings to build a vast SS empire in European Russia. The possibilities seemed limitless. A *Generalplan Ost*, a draft of which emerged from Himmler's bureaucracy at the end of 1941, envisaged the deportation of no fewer than 31 million non-Germans from eastern areas, which would eventually be settled by *Volksdeutsche*. German colonists would hold thirty-six "strong points" in former Soviet territory, and settlement areas would extend to Lithuania, the Leningrad area, and the Crimea.[65]

Killing was an important tool for the achievement of this Nazi utopia. In the end the slaughter was awesome, as we know, with the murder of many millions of Poles, Russians, Ukrainians, Belorussians, and others. In terms of the numbers murdered the bloodbath may have surpassed even the Final Solution, although the grim distinction of *Holocaust* is usually reserved for the massacre of Jews alone.[66] Unlike the Final Solution, the extravagant schemes for the conquered east did not involve murder on a universal scale, as was being simultaneously decreed for the Jews. National entities among such people were to be eradicated, it is true, but some individuals would live. Notably "Nordic" elements among the newly occupied Slavic peoples were to be identified by a complicated racial survey, and there was to be extensive Germanization of the most valued elements among them. Himmler's experts acknowledged that it was impossible to kill the entire Russian population in any event, and Nazi plans referred to a large proportion that were to be enslaved.[67]

Closer examination of Nazi population policy in the east helps put the Final Solution into perspective and may suggest new connections. An East German historian, for example, considers that expansion into the Soviet Union brought home to the Nazi leadership that they now had a limitless reservoir of labor and could finally dispose of the Jews without serious cost.[68] A look at Nazi settlement policy, requiring vast energy and transport for the movement of *Volksdeutsche,* makes more understandable the priorities set for Jews in Poland, the rhythms of ghettoization, and the procrastination regarding the Final Solution.[69] One comes away from this material with the sense that the destruction of European Jewry should not be studied in isolation from other aspects of Nazi policy. Though different in kind from other massacres, it nevertheless fits into patterns we can find elsewhere. Identifying such patterns is likely to enlighten us even further.

4. GERMANY'S ALLIES, VANQUISHED STATES, AND COLLABORATIONIST GOVERNMENTS

ACCORDING TO RAUL HILBERG, more Jewish deaths occurred in 1942—about 2.7 million—than in all the other years of the Third Reich together.[1] The Nazis murdered fewer than 100,000 Jews in the period between their seizure of power and the end of 1940, when SS and Wehrmacht units were shifting masses of Jews about the newly occupied Polish territories. The death toll soared to 1.1 million the following year, as a result of ghettoization, periodic massacres in Poland, and the murderous assault of the Einsatzgruppen and other units. The year 1942 saw the coordination of the Final Solution across Europe and also its greatest impact. Following the Wannsee Conference in January, trains began to roll from east and west, bringing Jews to specially constructed death camps in Poland. Operation Reinhard, code name for the elimination of the Jews of the *Generalgouvernement* of Poland, started in March. That summer, convoys of Jews left various European countries occupied by the Germans, bringing their human cargo to be killed. In 1943, the toll dropped to 500,000. The great Polish reservoir of east European Jewry was practically emptied. With east European Jewry decimated, the Nazi bureaucracy sent its tentacles elsewhere for Jewish victims. New demands for deportees rained down on western Europe. Evidently, the task strained the resources of the Third Reich, now battered by heavy attacks in the Mediterranean theater, the Soviet Union, and the skies over Germany. Alert to changing fortunes on the battlefield, both Axis allies and collaborating states proved less cooperative. Also, the worsening military situation put pressure on railway traffic. Yet the trains continued to roll. In 1944 it was the turn of Hungarian Jewry, who made up a substantial part of the 600,000 swept away that year. In 1945, Allied victories severely disrupted the machinery of destruction, and the Red Army engulfed the ghettos and camps where so many had died. Even so, Jews continued to perish in great numbers. More than 100,000 met their end on death marches and in the chaos of the camps at the very end of the war, in a cataclysm that went undocumented by the previously attentive Nazi statisticians.[2]

This brief sketch is a reminder of the unparalleled scope of the Holocaust and the importance of seeing it in a chronological sequence. As the sequence suggests, the murder of European Jewry proceeded unevenly, conditioned by factors over which the Nazis had only limited control. Moreover, the annual tolls suggest a paradoxical weak point in the murderous enterprise. In a word, the Nazis were heavily dependent on foreign help in carrying out the declared purpose of the Final Solution—the murder of each and every Jew within their sphere of influence in Europe. The machinery of destruction worked with awful efficiency in Poland and occupied parts of the Soviet Union, where hundreds of thousands of Jews were close at hand and where German forces were firmly in control. Elsewhere, the Nazis had to rely on many thousands of local police and foreign bureaucrats to hasten the Jews on their final journey. Men were needed not only to run the trains and guard the camps, but also to keep track of the Jews, to separate them from their possessions, and to process the considerable paperwork associated with the deportations. Across Europe, collaborationist governments and officials provided the essential personnel virtually without hesitation in 1942. Thereafter, they sometimes slackened and dragged their feet. The Jews were also harder to find, and the task of dispatching them to the east became more taxing. Hence the steep falling off in the number of deportees and an even greater decline in the numbers murdered. True, killing still proceeded on a horrendous scale. To some degree the Germans even intensified their efforts. But in this as in other spheres, the Third Reich discovered that it was not invincible.

Historians can learn about the Holocaust by pondering these limitations of the machinery of destruction as well as its awesome capacity to kill. This is what moved political sociologist Helen Fein to examine the varying extent of Jewish victimization across the continent in a volume published in 1979. Fein drew attention to a remarkable failure of the Final Solution: "in almost half (nine of twenty-two) of the states and regions occupied by or allied to Germany, fewer than half of the Jews counted there were killed." [3] With the aid of a computer, she set out to ascertain the reasons for wide variations in the proportions of Jews murdered in the European countries. Her search involved the assembly and coding of such diverse variables as the extent of SS control, the amount of warning time permitted the Jews, the character of native government response, the prewar size and visibility of the Jewish community, the accessibility of havens, the intensity of prewar antisemitism, and the kinds of Jewish defense strategy. Testing their relative importance, her work cast into relief important differences and similarities between countries and regions.

But Fein's results were inconclusive. In my view the approach was misguided, despite the suggestive material and analysis contained in her book, because the author did not take sufficient account of Nazi policy—the power and inclination of the Germans to carry mass murder to such different places as, for example, Poland with over 3 million Jews or Finland with 2 thousand. In the implementation of the Final Solution, the crucial factor was always the extent to which the Nazis determined to do the job. In Poland, the heart of European Jewry, they were indeed determined; in Finland, an ally reluctant to deport its own Jews, and with a mere handful at stake, the Germans felt they could wait. Beyond this, the most decisive influence on the extent of killing was the course of the fighting in Europe. For the Nazis' will to destroy the Jews weakened only toward the end, among certain top leaders, in the face of impending defeat. In the end, the murders stopped and the Final Solution did not succeed because the Nazi empire collapsed in ruins in 1945. Had the war ended a year earlier, for example, Hungarian Jewry might have survived; had it continued for another year or so, there would have been too few Jews left alive anywhere in Europe to constitute significant "national differences." What is really measured in Fein's work, therefore, is the *pace* of victimization in various places, something determined at least as much by the German's own priorities and the fortunes of war as by the variables she examined.[4]

EASTERN EUROPE: THE FINAL SOLUTION IN THE GERMAN *LEBENSRAUM*

Few historians of the Holocaust have been so ambitious as Fein, attempting to encompass the entire continent within an analytical framework. (Interestingly, one of the few to do so has been Hilberg, a political scientist.) Quite properly, most have concentrated on eastern Europe. Here the Jewish losses were catastrophic—approaching 100 percent in many regions. Over three-quarters of the Jews killed during the Holocaust were from Poland and territory taken from the Soviet Union. Here, moreover, the Germans were all-powerful for most of the occupation period. The Nazis certainly employed local auxiliaries in formerly Soviet territory, as they did in the death camps where Jews were killed. In places, the work of the Final Solution was heavily dependent on aid from violently antisemitic elements in the local population. But there were no collaborationist governments in the Nazi-occupied east to facilitate the Final Solution, and no native bureaucracies to administer the orderly removal of Jews from their homes. The Germans set their own timetable and determined their own priorities in the territory destined to be the *Lebensraum* of the Third Reich.

Race was the principal foundation upon which the Nazis built their imperial control in eastern Europe. Here the Führer defined the greatest threat to the Germanic empire, and also its greatest opportunity for future growth. Populated by inferior racial breeds, dominated in part by Jews, the area destined for the German *Lebensraum* was a region in which the imaginations of Nazi planners roamed freely. All previous political structures were to be swept away. All centralized forms of government were to be eliminated. In a memorandum to Hitler in May 1940 Himmler explained that the

Germans were to comb the entire population of the east to weed out the racially impure elements; these would be brought to the Reich and assimilated. As for the rest, Nazi programs were never precise, but all signs pointed toward the total elimination of all national consciousness, staggering mortality, enslavement, and dispersion.[5]

How did Nazi policy toward Jews evolve in these eastern regions? Strikingly, the Jewish issue figured hardly at all in the opening of the war against Poland in 1939. Fall Weiss, code name for the attack on Germany's eastern neighbor, indicated no concern with the Jews—in marked contrast to Barbarossa, the attack on the Soviet Union almost two years later. There were no elaborate instructions to deal with Jews in a special way, and much of German policy toward the Jews was improvised after the Polish campaign. If this was indeed the start of the "war against the Jews," to use Dawidowicz's phrase, it was an odd way to begin. In the event, different courses of action were followed at once—prompting Hilberg's remark that newly conquered Polish territory was a field for experimentation.[6] On 21 September Heydrich ordered his Einsatzgruppen chiefs to clear the Jews from the countryside and concentrate them in a few large cities "with all speed." To the contrary, however, ghettoization proceeded very unevenly, with local military and SS commanders taking initiatives as they saw fit. The first ghetto was set up in Poland in October 1939, but the last were still being established in 1943. Directions to concentrate the Jews of Lodz went out in December 1939, but the ghetto was not closed until the following spring; work on the Warsaw ghetto proceeded by fits and starts, with the gates being sealed only in November 1940.[7]

As functionalist historians have suggested, improvisation was the hallmark of Nazi Jewish policy for at least a year and a half after the Polish defeat. Heydrich's order of 21 September indicated that Polish Jews were being concentrated as a short-term measure, pending the implementation of a "final aim"—intended as a mass resettlement of Jews. Nazi occupation authorities had considerable leeway in dealing with the Jews at the time, however—even greater than that implied in the SS security chief's communication. This leeway is particularly noteworthy in the regimen established for ghettos in Poland. In some, communication with the outside was quickly severed; in others, contact remained for many months. Examining the records of the ghetto masters in the important ghettos of Lodz and

Warsaw, Christopher Browning identifies two alternative courses of action followed in the absence of fixed German policy. "Attritionists" zealously pursued a goal of eliminating ghettoized Jews, who began to perish in great numbers from starvation and disease when links with the outside were cut; "productionists," on the other hand, favored the enslavement of the ghetto population, which would be put to work for the Third Reich. According to Browning, the short-term result in both cities was the same: after protracted controversy and appalling mortality on the part of the ghetto inmates, the "productionists" prevailed and the ghettos were allowed "to create viable, self-sustaining ghetto economies."[8]

Improvisation also set the tone for the Nazis' demographic program, the context in which Jewish policies were usually set. As we discussed in the previous chapter, the basic idea was to fortify the racial foundation of the new Reich by eliminating "undesirables" and by "repatriating" ethnic Germans, or *Volksdeutsche,* wherever they lived. Pursuing these objectives, the Nazis divided German-held Poland in two: northern and western regions were incorporated into the Reich, most of which formed the new *Reichsgaue* of Danzig-Westpreussen and the Wartheland; the rest, known as the *Generalgouvernement,* was placed under the direct authority of a German governor, Hans Frank, responsible directly to Hitler. The incorporated provinces were to be subjected to intense Germanization to remove all alien elements; the *Generalgouvernement,* to which the latter were to be sent, was to become a vast work camp, an immense repository of unskilled labor to serve the needs of the enlarged German state. SS chief Heinrich Himmler was put in charge of the great population shift, and a vast new bureaucratic apparatus was placed at his disposal for the purpose—the Reich Commission for the Consolidation of Germandom (Reichskommissariat für die Festigung deutschen Volkstums, or RKFDV). Robert Koehl's book on the RKFDV provides an excellent picture of the Nazis' wildly ambitious program for the demographic reordering of Europe. As he illustrates, the Jews had an important, but by no means predominant place in these plans.[9]

Seen from the standpoint of German policy in Poland, the Nazis appear to many historians to be far less preoccupied with the Jews than might be expected given their ideology or previous antisemitic persecutions. The Jews, of course, figured prominently among the

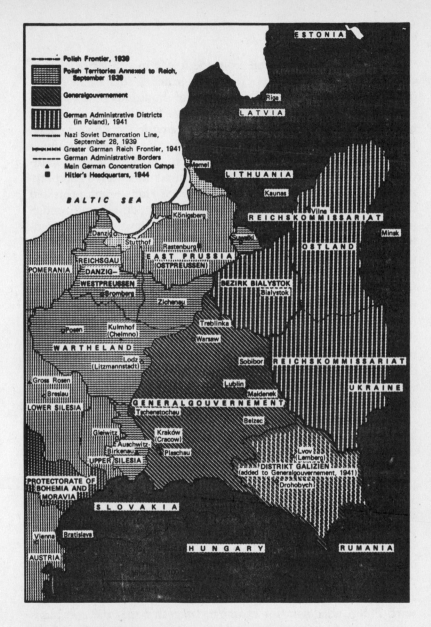

1. Poland under Nazi occupation (From *The Unwanted: European Refugees in the Twentieth Century,* by Michael R. Marrus. Copyright © 1985 by Oxford University Press. Reprinted by permission.)

"undesirables" to be cleared from the newly incorporated territories as well as from the rest of the Reich. Schemes such as the Lublin or Nisko Plan, which actually saw tens of thousands of Jews transported eastward, were but a foretaste of the expulsions that were to occur. The earliest program for Poland envisioned 600,000 Jews being moved en masse to the *Generalgouvernement*. Almost immediately, however, the Germans' objective of expelling Jews from incorporated Polish territory ran up against administrative and practical obstacles. In the *Generalgouvernement* Hans Frank protested the status of "dumping ground" for his domain, developing a much more ambitious standing for his miniempire. Beyond this, Himmler's eagerness to consolidate the newly acquired *Lebensraum* in the east suggested new priorities. "As usual in Nazi theory," Norman Rich points out, "the main emphasis was on agriculture." [10] Faced with the problem of settling the *Volksdeutsche* on homesteads in the Polish countryside, the Nazis shifted their deportation strategy to the removal eastward of Polish peasants so as to accommodate the incoming Germans. The largely urban Jewish population did not, for the moment, fit into Nazi priorities. Most Jews who had escaped the earliest "wild" deportations of 1939, therefore, stayed where they were—many of them to die of starvation or typhus in ghettos over the winter. [11]

As the geopolitical ambitions of Himmler and his colleagues escalated, their planning eventually involved tens of millions of people in conquered lands. And of these, the masters of the Third Reich knew well, many millions would perish. [12] The task was immense, and the Jews were simply too few to dominate the concerns of agencies such as the RKFDV. To be sure, the Jews were not forgotten. Other schemes proposing to solve the "Jewish problem" materialized from various parts of the Nazi bureaucracy, notably the proposal to ship Jews to the Nisko region of Poland or to the island of Madagascar, in the Indian Ocean. Intentionalist historians tend not to take these proposals seriously as real "solutions," believing instead that Hitler, and perhaps also his lieutenants, had their eyes on murder from the start. Philip Friedman, for example, suggested that the two plans were largely efforts to fool the public and camouflage the Nazis' objective of extermination. [13] Lucy Dawidowicz concludes that "everything we know of National Socialist ideology precludes our accepting the idea of a Jewish reservation as the last stage of the Final

Solution."[14] Such critics introduce as evidence the lack of careful preparation for settlement or the differentiation the Nazis sometimes made between Slavs (most to be allowed a slavelike existence) and Jews (set even lower in the racial hierarchy). Yet in view of what other historians tell us about chaotic and often inconsistent Nazi planning in the east, it seems entirely possible that Nazi decision makers seriously intended such schemes and were prepared to live with insufficiencies that have been subsequently identified. One can never be certain what Hitler thought of these proposals, it is true. Certainly no one can claim that these were to be "humane" alternatives to mass slaughter, for even in the most sanguine view the deportation of Jews to these places was supposed to involve "attrition" by various means. But internal evidence and the context of these plans suggest that they were genuine efforts to deal with a Nazi-defined "problem." Browning, for example, is persuaded that Madagascar was eagerly seized upon by the German leadership, and was similarly viewed on a lower level, at the Jewish desk of the Foreign Office.[15]

Once under way, the Europe-wide Final Solution conformed easily to Nazi policy in the east—the construction of a vast Pan-German empire in which inferior human types would be reduced to a serflike status and from which the Jews would be removed. German administrators in Poland demanded that their jurisdiction be cleared first. In early 1942 Hans Frank's domain had nearly 2.3 million Jews—the greatest concentration anywhere under Nazi rule. Historians have often reported Frank's unhappiness with the lesser status of the *Generalgouvernement,* and his displeasure at having to receive Jews deported from German borderlands to the west. At the Wannsee Conference, Frank's deputy Josef Bühler made a special appeal that the Jewish question there be solved as soon as possible. Apparently, the planners in Berlin agreed. Four of the six principal extermination centers were located in the *Generalgouvernement*— Treblinka, Sobibor, Belzec, and Majdanek. The first three of these were put to work in 1942. According to the historian of Operation Reinhard, code name for the liquidation of the Jews in the *Generalgouvernement,* the task was virtually complete by the end of the year.[16]

Elsewhere in the occupied east the Nazis' intentions were less clearly defined than in Poland, and their objectives shifted and even became more grandiose as the war progressed. But throughout these regions, it was wartime conditions rather than demographic engineering that set the framework for the Final Solution. Mass killing began earlier than in eastern Poland, as part of the Barbarossa attack on 22 June 1941. The slaughter started as soon as the Germans arrived: as we have already seen, a fearsome and deliberately planned "war of extermination" accompanied the invasion of the Soviet Union, a country that Hitler once told his intimates was "our India." Against what has been the prevailing view in West Germany until fairly recently, responsibility for the killings extends far beyond the Einsatzgruppen and the SS. Regular army units were also heavily involved; they provided logistical support and participated directly in shootings as well.[17]

Hilberg divides the killing into two "sweeps," extending beyond European Russia into the former Baltic countries, the Ukraine, the Caucasus, and the Crimea.[18] Several kinds of administration were involved. Behind the battle lines on the east, a great swath of territory remained a military zone, under the control of the Wehrmacht. The remainder was divided into several jurisdictions: two huge provinces, known as the Reichskommissariate Ostland (including White Russia and the Baltic states), and the Ukraine were ruled by colonial governors, Gauleiters Hinrich Lohse and Erich Koch, respectively, under the jurisdiction of Alfred Rosenberg's Ostministerium, the Ministry for the Eastern Occupied Territories; the rest was divided among the Rumanians (Northern Bukovina, Bessarabia, and the newly defined province of Transnistria, between the Dniester and the Bug rivers) and Hans Frank's *Generalgouvernement* (the province of Galicia); or partly incorporated into the Reich (the Białystok region). Pursuing the killings in their various jurisdictions, German commanders regularly enlisted the services of White Russian, Baltic, and Ukrainian personnel to assist SS, army, and police formations conducting massacres. Antipartisan units from local nationalities performed similar functions. In Bessarabia and the southern Ukraine the Germans received help from their Rumanian allies, who operated in liason with the southernmost Einsatzgruppe D. Where Jews escaped the first killing wave, they managed to survive for a time in Nazi-imposed ghettos. After a few months' hiatus, however, the shootings resumed in force in 1942. Gas vans were also used, both to facilitate the work of mobile shooting squads and to eliminate inmates in stationary camp settings such as Trostinez, near Minsk.[19] Untold thousands also perished in ghettos, work gangs, and camps. The job was practically done in 1942, although in a few ghettos pathetic remnants remained alive, often because of demands for labor.

Thousands had a hand in these murders—military personnel, police, native auxiliaries, civilian administrators in the various districts, and representatives of Rosenberg's Ostministerium. In contrast to the exterminations in Poland, ordered by the regimen of the death camps and dedicated to efficient operation, this was a primitive bloodbath—with the widest circle of complicity anywhere in Europe. In 1953, summing up his chronicle of these massacres, Gerald Reitlinger observed that their naked savagery was unsurpassed even in the history of the Final Solution.[20]

WESTERN AND CENTRAL EUROPE: MURDER IMPROVISED

However devastating, the Holocaust in western and central Europe was of an entirely different character from that in the east. Although the impact was catastrophic, the Nazis operated outside Russia and Poland with a certain restraint. Much of the destruction process was hidden from the surrounding populations and even from the Jews themselves. Some reasons for this are obvious. First, the racial composition of the eastern territories justified to the Nazis the most brutal and cruel policies. In a subhuman environment, Nazis told themselves, scruples were both unnecessary and dangerous. Second, in Poland and the Soviet Union the great density of Jewish population precluded the removal of those destined to be killed. There were simply too many Jews to be sent on long journeys to their massacre, even if this would have lightened the task of the executioners and appeased the local populations. Third, the Nazis were all-powerful in these regions and had no need to take account of hostile local sensibilities or, for that matter, international opinion. Outside the territory destined for the German *Lebensraum*, however, none of these conditions prevailed. Although the Nazis sometimes despised indigenous western populations, they nevertheless deemed them to be of a higher racial order than the peoples of the east and believed they should be treated accordingly. Also in the west the Jews were relatively few and could be removed from their homes and transported to killing centers. And finally, the German forces were never so strong as in the east; consequently in the west they needed the more or less willing collaboration of local authorities.

In a memorable image—the semicircular arc—Hilberg encompassed the entire geographic scope of the Holocaust outside of the occupied east and the Reich itself—"a vast semicircular arc, extending counterclockwise from Norway to Rumania." At the center of this great arc was the camp of Auschwitz, to which most of the Jews in these places would be sent to be killed.[21] Along the rim were countries with the most divergent of regimes and statuses of occupation—allies, puppet states, satellites, annexed regions, zones of military control, and those under German civilian rule through the Foreign Office. In this vast area, with over 2 million Jews, the architects of the Final Solution faced their greatest challenge. For although there were fewer Jews than in the east, they were far more integrated into the societies in which they lived; often they had the respect and support of their non-Jewish fellow citizens; and they lived in societies committed to liberal and democratic values. Prying Jews loose from this environment sorely taxed the administrative and political skills of the Nazi officials placed in charge. Historians working on the application of the Final Solution within the semicircular arc have focused on three kinds of issues—the workings of the German bureaucracy, the relationship between the local authorities and the Nazis' machinery of destruction, and the strategies of independent or semi-independent states when faced with German demands to yield up their Jews. In the remainder of this chapter we examine each of these in turn.

The German Administration

A remarkable aspect of Nazi policy in the "semicircular arc" is the hesitation and slowness with which officials concerned with Jewish matters moved against their victims. Jewish policy, in this respect, simply reflected the lack of planning in other domains. In mid-1940, western Europe lay at Hitler's feet. Significantly, the German leader seems to have had no clear idea of what kind of a settlement he

2. Europe under Nazi occupation (before 22 June 1941) (From *The Unwanted: European Refugees in the Twentieth Century*, by Michael R. Marrus. Copyright © 1985 by Oxford University Press. Reprinted by permission.)

wanted in the region. Pending a final resolution, the Germans imposed a complex grid of armistice and occupation arrangements, leaving to a final settlement the delineation of new boundaries of the Reich and the status of the conquered countries. All occupation structures were held to be provisional. Meanwhile, Hitler's mind increasingly turned toward the east, contemplating an attack on the Soviet Union. By the end of 1940, when the Luftwaffe failed to clear the way for an invasion of England, he became absorbed with planning for what eventually became Operation Barbarossa.[22]

Jews in western Europe were not plunged into the abyss, in 1940, as were their coreligionists in eastern Europe in 1939 or 1941. True, the Germans imposed discriminatory ordinances where they could. But there were no massacres and no massive shifting of the Jewish population. Nor were the Jews rounded up and assembled into work battalions as was happening simultaneously in the east. For some time, much of Jewish policy remained in the hands of several agencies at once—the Foreign Office and its representatives, military and civilian occupation authorities, and various arms of the SS. Each branch of the Nazi administration, moreover, operated cautiously, with a high degree of autonomy. German officials built their own routines, looked to their own aggrandizement, and awaited instructions.[23]

Of all these agencies, the Central Office for Reich Security of the SS (Reichsicherheitshauptamt or RSHA) was the most important and claimed preeminence in Jewish affairs. Although jurisidictional conflicts plagued the Nazi bureaucracy in this as in so many other areas, the role of the SS could be challenged only with the greatest difficulty. As if to stake out the Jewish field, Eichmann's Gestapo office dispatched representatives to Paris, Brussels, and The Hague very shortly after German troops arrived. Significantly, however, the SS and its police formations remained in the background in western Europe. They had no authority to monopolize Jewish policy. In addition to other demands made on SS personnel, the resistance of the army, party, and Foreign Office explains why this was so. As Robert Koehl has pointed out, Himmler's rivals were reluctant to see him given a free hand in such places as France, the Low Countries, Norway, and Denmark. Notably, in 1940 the military put up a stiff resistance to the SS boss, insisting for example that no *Einsatzkommandos* were to set up shop in Belgium and France. In Greece and

Serbia, conquered the following year, the Wehrmacht jealously guarded its own jurisdiction against the SS as well.[24]

Given that racial policy was not a central concern of the other branches of the Nazi bureaucracy, the result in western Europe was caution and delay. Berlin had little to suggest beyond a promise of some future, European-wide "solution." Therefore, there were no innovations in anti-Jewish policy. Sealed ghettos such as those in eastern Europe were never contemplated. Occupation authorities encouraged emigration, though without much success, and on a few occasions actually dumped Jews into unoccupied territory. Confiscation of Jewish property began, but was not pursued with energy except for the most valuable prizes. All measures were considered "preliminary," with the final resolution to depend upon the expected peace settlement. German soldiers and diplomats had to contend with the SS on Jewish matters, but until mid-1942 the former were firmly in control.[25]

Serbia, where the Wehrmacht was in charge, was an exception to this lassitude. Having conquered Yugoslavia in the spring of 1941, the Germans faced a small but desperate Communist uprising that began on 22 June, with the Nazi attack on the Soviet Union. As the insurgency spread, the Wehrmacht imposed an ever more draconian reprisal policy, spreading terror throughout the Serbian countryside. Doubtless the ruthlessness of the repression flowed in part from the occupation troops' contempt for the local population, often assimilated in the Nazis' minds with the savage inhabitants of eastern Europe. But the specific terms of reprisal came from Berlin. Concerned at the extent of the disturbances, armed forces chief of staff Wilhelm Keitel sent strict instructions to shoot large numbers of hostages. Given that Jews and Gypsies were stigmatized as primary enemies of the Reich, it was but a short step to feeding them to the firing squads, once the pool of prominent Communists was exhausted. Christopher Browning's research into Wehrmacht reprisal policy shows how this slid easily into a "final solution" for local Jews—or at least the males among them. "As long as the anti-Jewish measures in Serbia were perceived and construed as military measures against Germany's enemies," he observes, "it did not require Nazified zealots (though such were not lacking), merely conscientious and politically obtuse professional soldiers to carry them out."[26] On the strength of such conscientiousness and obtuseness, the number of reprisal shootings approached twelve thousand by the end of 1941.

Browning's investigation of the German Foreign Office bureau charged with Jewish affairs suggests that it provided a professional and bureaucratic momentum. The Foreign Office had a significant impact on Jewish policy in countries that were not under direct military or civilian administration—part of France, Denmark, Slovakia, Croatia, and the countries of southeastern Europe. Here too, rivalries with other Nazi agencies played a role. Taking its cue from Foreign Minister Joachim von Ribbentrop, never one to concede important areas of National Socialist policy to others, the Foreign Office had its own vision of the Jewish Question, tending to see it within the framework of an eventual European political settlement—to be arranged by diplomats, of course. Foreign Office officials had their own version of the Madagascar Plan, in which the Wilhelmstrasse had an important part to play. But this is only part of the story. The Abteilung Deutschland, which occupied itself with Jewish questions, was not inspired by antisemitic fanaticism, but rather by concerns for professional competence. Its officials conscientiously applied themselves to their tasks, instinctively sensing the change in Nazi policy during the Barbarossa campaign. Careerism drove officials forward. Eager to demonstrate his indispensability, the head of the Jewish desk took initiatives to help speed the Jews on their way.[27]

Wherever possible outside eastern Europe, the Nazis relied on local agencies to prepare the Jews for their own destruction. Remarkably few Germans were available for such work. Berlin sent fewer than three thousand civilians to manage occupied France in August 1941, for example, and not many more for the Netherlands.[28] Throughout western Europe the Nazis could never assign many men for this purpose and always preferred to see native police and bureaucrats remain at their posts and carry on with their jobs. One of the first tasks of occupation, indeed, was to make security arrangements with local authorities and to weed out unsatisfactory elements among them. In consequence, indigenous police remained a significant force. In France, the complement was about 100,000 men, some of them well armed, with 30,000 for the city of Paris alone.[29]

Local Authorities and the Machinery of Destruction

Once deportations from western Europe began, in the summer of 1942, the Germans relied heavily upon native police and administrative personnel. While the degree of cooperation varied, it existed practically everywhere. In Norway, a puppet state effectively controlled by a German *Reichskommisar,* such collaboration was practically unnecessary, for the Germans could easily move on their own against the tiny Jewish community. In France, however, cooperation was indispensable. For the first wave of deportations, mainly involving foreign Jews, the French police participated on a massive scale—not only in the northern, occupied zone, under Nazi scrutiny, but in the south, in the unoccupied zone as well. Elsewhere too the Germans had few problems with the police at this stage. Moreover, in every occupied country, homegrown fascists organized into militias that stiffened the resolve of the local gendarmerie or assisted them in rounding up their victims. Jacques Doriot's Parti populaire français, Rexists and Flemish bands in Belgium, and Anton Mussert's National Socialist Movement in the Netherlands all became small cogs in the machinery of destruction. Less dramatically, civil servants also provided crucial help. Government agencies helped snap the links that attached Jews to the structures of ordinary life—welfare organizations, professions, schools, and so forth—while civil registries kept track of their addresses and personal backgrounds. Having worked with the Germans for nearly two years, most native officials hardly thought twice about maintaining the pattern of collaboration when it came to assembling Jews to be sent eastward.[30]

Collaboration went particularly far in France, Robert Paxton and I have argued, because the autonomously inspired antisemitic program launched by the Vichy regime had already given the persecution of the Jews such momentum. Vichy leaders began their own anti-Jewish campaign immediately after the constitution of a new French government in the summer of 1940. This was not in response to a German *Diktat,* but was launched by French politicians pursuing longstanding antisemitic priorities. For a time, the French operated independently against the Jews, fully integrating their antisemitic measures with Vichy's program of "National Revolution," trumpeted by the head of state Marshal Philippe Pétain. Action against the Jews was held to be a French objective, part of a broad campaign against excessive "foreign" influence, corruption, licentiousness, and materialism. Gradually the Germans enticed Vichy even further, stimulating the French to confiscate Jewish businesses and to go beyond what they had intended in their own anti-Jewish legislation. By 1942 Vichy had not only effectively outlawed the Jews, but had taken much of their property and interned many in special camps. Scores of bureaucrats were accustomed, as a matter of official routine, to harassing Jews, marking their documents with special stamps, and sending them to internment camps. For many French officials the roundups and deportations of 1942 were simply a continuation of a program deemed by the highest authorities in the land to be in the French national interest.[31]

Yet in France and elsewhere in the west trouble arose when it came to shipping western European natives off to some "unknown destination." Historians have noted how, in 1943, when foreign Jews could no longer be found so easily to fill the deportation quotas, even formerly collaborationist officials began to drag their feet. Across western Europe, the local engines of support for deportation began to misfire. Police forces in France and the Netherlands started to lose their taste for rounding up Jews once the manhunts turned to local citizens in addition to outsiders. In Belgium, the particularly high proportion of foreign Jews may have facilitated the task of the Nazis in that country in 1942; close to 30 percent of the Jews living in Belgium were swept away in the first three months of deportations. When a group of Belgian Jews were rounded up in 1943, however, there were loud public protests. Brigadier General Eggert von Reeder was forced to concede, releasing some Belgian Jews from internment.[32] Hoping to ease the situation, the German Foreign Office proposed the automatic denationalization of deportees in mid-1943, thereby offering a fig leaf to protect native sensibilities. But this was too much even for Pierre Laval, then head of the French government at Vichy. Having first agreed to the Germans' proposal for massive denationalization, Laval suddenly retracted in August, attempting to cover his action with a cloud of excuses. To be sure, this reversal was not prompted by any sudden remorse for previous deportations or by solicitude for native French Jews. Vichy's stance was affected far more by the military punishment now being meted out to the Germans and a feeling that French bargaining power had correspondingly improved. Laval was also moved by a sense that the deportations were unpopular, particularly when they affected French citizens. The summer of 1943, therefore, was a good time to back away from some of the nastier responsibilities of the policy of collaboration.[33]

To what extent were collaborationists like Laval in a position to say no to the Germans on a Jewish issue? Debate on this question continues, taking up many of the arguments made in postwar trials, when the accused invariably protested: "Without me, it would have been worse." There is no doubt that such protestations have a certain plausibility. For France, a few historians still suggest that subverting German plans would have provoked the Nazis, bringing about a situation akin to German terror in Poland. The Nazis might have proceeded even more energetically against the Jews on their own, it is said, and might have replaced people such as Laval and Pétain with fanatical antisemites who would have wreaked even greater havoc.[34] Yet everything we have learned about German occupation policies suggests otherwise. Occupation authorities as well as their superiors in Berlin invariably preferred to work with popular conservatives—Pétain, for them, was a model custodian—who could keep order at home and could be bullied from time to time, rather than with pro-Nazi zealots whose views were shared by only tiny minorities and who were too unpredictable. These conservatives could be made to serve the Reich and would do so without causing serious disruption. Moreover, the Germans were much more hard pressed to act on their own than we might think. It is unlikely that they could have spared the men and the resources needed to achieve a significantly higher level of repression in France. Besides, there is no evidence that Laval or his colleagues ever believed, *at the time,* that they were acting in the Jews' interest; on the contrary, there is every indication that they cared nothing for the fate of the Jews, had no qualms about working with the Germans on this issue, and had no "protective" strategy in mind.

Nazi policy ran into significant obstacles in two countries—Fascist Italy, the closest ally of the Reich, and the puppet state of Denmark, believed by Nazi administrators to be a "model protectorate." In each case, thousands of Jews were rescued. The most famous instance is that of the Danes, who spirited a good part of the eight thousand Jews in their country across a narrow stretch of water to Sweden in the autumn of 1943. But Italian soldiers and police probably saved many more, providing protection for the Jews wherever Italian forces were in Europe. In both societies, Danish and Italian, there was genuine popular opposition to Nazi antisemitism and a particular set of reasons for opposing Nazi policy toward Jews. In Denmark, a country that surrendered in 1940 to the Germans practically without firing a shot, the implementation of the Final Solution coincided with a broad crackdown on the entire Danish nation in the second half of 1943—a time when resistance everywhere was taking heart from the repeated blows delivered against the Reich by the Allied military forces. Moreover, the Germans in Denmark were weaker than elsewhere: the Danish Nazis were hopelessly divided among themselves and politically incompetent; at the same time, German occupation authorities fought with each other, causing them to mishandle their negotiations with the Danish government and to bungle their proposed deportation of the Jews. Finally, the path to safety was short. Mostly concentrated in Copenhagen, the Jews had only a few miles of open water to cross and found a welcome haven in Sweden.[35] In Italy, as a recent book by Meir Michaelis argues, antisemitism struck a dissonant cultural note from the start because the emancipation of Italian Jewry was remarkably successful and the Jews were relatively few and fully integrated. Mussolini adopted an official anti-Jewish line in 1938 as part of a rapprochement with the Reich, but he obviously did so without conviction or a commitment to extensive anti-Jewish action. Persecution of the Jews in Italy was therefore serious, but limited. And like much of Fascism, it was riven by corruption and incompetence, which significantly reduced its effectiveness. With the advent of war emerged the Italians' detestation of the Germans and their distrust of Nazi-style racism that only thinly disguised German feelings of superiority. Italian war weariness in 1942 helped discredit German policy further. The result was repeated obstruction of persecution and deportations by Italians everywhere in Europe—in Italy, of course, but also in Italian-occupied parts of France, Croatia, and Greece.[36]

Once Mussolini's attack on Greece collapsed in the autumn of 1940, necessitating vast infusions of German aid, the Italians lost much of their former freedom of action. Yet interestingly, the Germans seemed to have been unwilling or unable thereafter to bring their Axis partner to heel on the Jewish question. Possibly some of this can be attributed to Hitler's curious admiration for the Duce, chronologically his senior as a European fascist. Possibly in Berlin's calculation there were simply too few Jews at stake to bother with at the time. For whatever reason, the Germans obtained only promises from the Italians, despite persistent evidence of Fascist protection of Jews. After the Italian surrender to the Allies in September 1943, the Germans salvaged the wreckage of Fascism, eventually reassembled under Mussolini in a puppet state, the Salò Republic. In some places, as in southeastern France, the SS took its revenge and rounded up formerly protected Jews. In Italy itself, manhunts against Jews began. Yet even then it was obvious that if the Germans really wanted to move against Jews still nominally under Italian Fascist authority, they had to do so on their own.

German Satellites

In one form or another, the debate over responsibility for the Final Solution echoes through the literature on Germany's satellites—Slovakia, Croatia, Rumania, Hungary, and Bulgaria. In each case there were German demands to participate in the Final Solution. Each satellite responded differently, sometimes with dramatically different results. Of course, one must be aware of the time and circumstances under which the demands were made. Slovakia and Croatia were small, weak, semi-independent states, with clearly less margin for maneuver than Germany's allies and cobelligerents Rumania and Hungary. In both Slovakia and Croatia, countries that owed their very existence to the Third Reich, the Germans set up aggressive, extreme right-wing conservatives—the clerical corporatist father Jozef Tiso in Bratislava in 1939, and the terrorist Ustasha leader Ante Pavelić in Zagreb in 1941. Each was bent on establishing a strongly authoritarian, nationalist regime in which there was no place for Jews. Both countries had a German military presence, with Croatia nominally under Italian patronage. Hungary and Rumania had far more independence, and both gained much from the German alliance—Hungary at the expense of Rumania, and Rumania at the expense of the Soviet Union. In Hungary, the regent, Admiral Miklós Horthy, presided over a pro-German, authoritarian government that continued an extensive anti-Jewish drive begun in the late 1930s. And in Rumania, the overthrow of

King Carol II in September 1940 brought to power a military leader, Marshal Ion Antonescu, associated with the fascist and highly antisemitic Iron Guard. Bulgaria was different yet again—an ally on the periphery of the Nazi empire, with insignificant antisemitic traditions, and determined more than other satellites to keep the Germans at arm's length. Only in Bulgaria did official antisemitism lack enthusiasm and commitment. Bulgaria joined the Axis for purely opportunistic reasons, and the Bulgarian political community seems to have been sharply divided on whether the government should accede to German wishes. Significantly, Sofia did not follow the Rumanians and Hungarians in going to war with the Soviet Union. Persecution of the Bulgarian Jews began in early 1941, but it was far milder than elsewhere and included many exemptions.[37]

All five satellites moved against the Jews on their own, issuing definitions and discriminatory legislation and confiscating Jewish property during the period 1939 to 1941. Antisemitic officials patterned many of their laws and decrees on the model set by the Third Reich. Evidently, these anti-Jewish campaigns were undertaken with an eye to Berlin, a mighty and demanding patron. But they also derived from genuine pressures at home. With the exception of Bulgaria, there seems little doubt that powerful indigenous forces accounted almost entirely for the wave of anti-Jewish measures that continued up to the German attack on the Soviet Union. But this is not to say that opinion was uniformly hostile to the Jews and that everyone shared the Nazis' vision. The overall level of violence was highest in Croatia, where Pavelić's Ustasha movement devised the most thoroughly totalitarian state of any satellite and pursued a merciless, bloody assault on the country's 2 million Serbs. With this exception, however, each of the regimes had radical rivals ready to impose an even more zealous anti-Jewish program as well as policies more closely attuned to the Third Reich. Vojtech Tuka and the activists of the Hlinka Guard played this role in Slovakia, as did the Iron Guard in Rumania, the Arrow Cross in Hungary, and the Ratnitsi in Bulgaria. Throughout the war, such radicals looked to Berlin for assistance, and the Germans, in turn, attempted to use their presence to squeeze an ever more radical antisemitic policy from their satellites.[38]

At various times the Germans pressured all of the satellites for

Jewish deportees, usually using the language of forced labor. In every case, historians must try to assess the extent to which the local governments knew about the destination of the deportation convoys—usually the camp of Auschwitz, in Upper Silesia, where most of the deportees were immediately gassed. After the war, of course, collaborators at the highest levels protested their ignorance. Tiso suggested, for example, that the Germans' cover story about the Jews' being mobilized as forced laborers was highly plausible, given that non-Jewish Slovaks were being sent to work in Germany at the same time. But the evidence speaks strongly against the defense based on ignorance. We know that rumors about death camps for Jews were rife almost from the time they began operation. By mid-1942, foreign radio broadcasts included extensive reports on the murder of Jews. That summer, details of systematic extermination appeared in the Swiss press.[39] In the case of Slovakia, the Vatican sounded the alarm at the beginning of the 1942 deportations, telling Tiso, a Catholic priest, that the Jews were being killed. Giuseppe Burzio, the Vatican representative in Bratislava, warned Prime Minister Tuka in March of that year that deportation meant "certain death" for most of the deportees.[40] Further, the character of the deportations themselves ought to have been warning enough. No provision was made for work parties, as with labor conscription; the convoys eventually included women, children, the very young, and the infirm. The victims were jammed into cattle cars, and nothing was ever heard of them after departure. There seems little doubt: even if some of the stories were dismissed as exaggerations, or ignored as propaganda, or simply disbelieved, the defense of ignorance cannot be seriously maintained. Many of the details were unknown, but of mass murder there was no serious question.

In any event, ignorance of the meaning of deportations can have had little bearing in the cases of Croatia and Hungary, for reasons peculiar to the Final Solution in those countries. In Croatia, many thousands of Jews were marked for annihilation within the country—part of the vicious war against Serbs, Gypsies, and others deemed outsiders. Camps run by the Ustasha worked thousands to death; others perished from typhus and terrible abuse. Shooting parties roamed the country, killing presumed enemies of the new Croatian state. A third of the Jewish population of about thirty thousand may thus have been killed before the end of 1941. There were already many thousands of victims of the Ustasha regime when Zagreb agreed to deportations in the summer of 1942, and the Final Solution had already been in effect for some time.[41] With Hungary, the delay of deportations until 1944 gave Jews and non-Jews extensive opportunities to learn about the massacres. According to Randolph Braham, there is convincing evidence that Hungarian leaders knew the nature of the Nazis' intentions for the Jews long before convoys of Jews left their country for Auschwitz. Jewish refugees fleeing Poland entered Hungary throughout the war, often bearing tales of frightful killings.[42] At Horthy's meetings with Hitler and Ribbentrop at Schloss Klessheim in April 1943, the Nazi leaders seem to have been remarkably unguarded in their language. And if, conceivably, they had managed to forget what they had learned when the trains began to roll northward, the papal nuncio in Budapest, Angelo Rocca, reminded them in his protest of May 1944 that "the whole world knows what the deportation means in practice."[43]

Could the satellites have resisted specific German demands for deportees? Assessments of the role of government leaders sometimes return to this question. The accusations against Slovakia are powerful, pressed by the postwar testimony of the Nazi "expert" on Jewish matters, SS Hauptsturmführer Dieter Wisliceny. Having survived the war, and having testified at several war criminals' trials, Wisliceny contended that the Slovak government willingly agreed to the deportation of the country's eighty-nine thousand Jews. Contemporary German documents also suggest the Slovaks' eagerness to see the Jews deported in early 1942.[44] The Slovak authorities were eager to demonstrate their cooperation in the building of a Nazi-dominated Europe and hoped to benefit from the confiscation of Jewish property. Beyond this, it seems likely that a struggle within the ruling Slovak People's party played a role. Yeshayahu Jelinek suggests that head of state Tiso was successfully pursuing his goal of establishing a clerical-authoritarian society in Slovakia; against him was a strong opposition group associated with the ultranationalist Hlinka Guard and headed by Prime Minister Vojtech Tuka, which was much more pro-Nazi. The suggestion is that Tiso badly needed German support in early 1942 and may well have curried favor with Berlin over Jewish deportations for this reason.[45]

In the summer of 1942, after a majority of the Jews had been deported, Berlin learned that the Slovaks were losing heart: pressure against the deportations was mounting, and, in this strongly Catholic country, particular difficulties were caused by extensive Jewish conversions to seek exemptions. The Vatican, we know, protested the measures against the Jews. The government's ability to organize the transports was clearly affected, and before long Bratislava actually suspended deportations altogether. Did these moves reflect serious second thoughts? Among some, including possibly Tiso himself, this may have been the case. Tuka, on the other hand, with what Hilberg understands as a typical "satellite mentality," apparently requested German pressure on Bratislava in order to overcome the opposition to deportations at home.[46]

Aided by their strategic position in Nazi-dominated Europe, both Rumania and Bulgaria resisted Nazi demands for deportees, although in each case these allies helped the Final Solution in other ways. The Rumanians controlled the destiny of an extremely large Jewish population—some 757,000 in 1939. As in Hungary, an antisemitic campaign begun before the war continued under the dictatorship of Antonescu. The Jews suffered a barrage of anti-Jewish legislation in 1940, including the forcible seizure of Jewish property. Joining the Nazi attack upon the Soviet Union in the following year, Rumanian troops participated in massacres associated with the Einsatzgruppen in the Crimea and southern Ukraine and massacred about 26,000 Jews in Odessa.[47] The killings continued unabated through the summer of 1941, with the Rumanians moving masses of Jews into the killing areas on forced marches, drowning them in the Dniester River, and forcing others into the German zone. "No other country, besides Germany," concludes Hilberg, "was involved in massacres of Jews on such a scale."[48]

At home, however, it was different. Apart from some pogroms in which soldiers and Iron Guardsmen had a hand, the authorities distinguished between the acculturated Jews of Old Rumania, the heart of the country, and the unassimilated, non-Rumanian-speaking Jews of Bukovina and Bessarabia, taken from the Russians in 1941. Moving ruthlessly against these provinces in a broad program of Rumanianization, Bucharest had many killed directly and dispatched the rest to the newly acquired province of Transnistria, between the rivers Bug and Dniester. Some 146,000 Jews were sent there to be packed in camps and ghettos and periodically murdered. The mortality was colossal, and only 50,000 of these deportees

seem to have survived. In all, some 75 percent of the Jews of Transnistria perished.[49] Yet although no friend of the Jews, Antonescu
would not go along with German demands to send Rumanian Jews
to Poland to be killed in the latter half of 1942. By this point, having
won all the territory they could be expected to digest, and clearly
wearying of the war, the authorities in Bucharest were trying to dis-
tance themselves from Berlin. In the end, most of the Rumanian
Jews were not deported.

Bulgaria is of special interest since, as the author of a study of
that country observes, there were more Jews alive there after the
war than before.[50] Unlike other states of southeastern Europe, antisemitism seems to have played only a small part in local politics,
and the small Jewish community of under fifty thousand, mainly
Sephardic in origin and well integrated into the country, was not
widely perceived as a threat. There was considerable opposition to
the anti-Jewish regimen of 1941, and little interest in surrendering
the country's Jews to the Nazis when the latter applied pressure to
this end in 1942. Jewish refugees even managed to trickle into Bulgaria. Like their Rumanian neighbors, the Bulgarians dithered and
delayed, holding the Germans off. In early 1943 the Germans sent
an SS expert, Hauptsturmführer Theodor Dannecker, to Sofia to try
to speed things up. By that point, however, the Bulgarians too were
tiring of the war and cooled their affections for their Axis ally. To
appease Berlin, the government did deport some eleven thousand
Jews from newly occupied Macedonia and Thrace, territories that
were being forcibly integrated into their country. At home, however,
the feeling against deporting Bulgarian Jews strengthened. Metropolitan Stefan of Sofia, the Bulgarian patriarch, spoke out, together
with other prominent Bulgarians. Allied victories now strengthened
the Bulgarians' hand. Finally, the deportations were halted. By the
spring of 1943 the Germans doubtless realized they could achieve
no more, and they abandoned their efforts to pressure their erst-
while cooperative ally.[51]

The Hungarian case is particularly dramatic because so many
Jews survived for so long and because the final result was so catastrophic. Hungarian authorities counted some 825,000 persons as
Jews in 1941, including many who were in fact non-Jews and many
who were counted as Rumanian inhabitants in 1939. More than
437,000 were deported to Auschwitz, beginning in the spring of

1944. Others were murdered on the spot or sent elsewhere on transports or forced marches, for a total mortality of over 600,000.[52] Up to the last year of the war Hungarian Jewry lived a tenuous existence, persecuted at home, but protected from repeated German requests for their deportation. Hungarian troops participated in massacres of Jews—notably at Novi Sad (Ujvidék) in January 1942, and possibly at Kamenets-Podolsk in August 1941—and Jewish males suffered grievously in specially defined forced labor batallions, responsible for tens of thousands of deaths.[53] But toward the end of the war, it seemed that the bulk of Hungarian Jewry might survive. Then, on 19 March 1944, the Germans swept into the country, fearing that the Hungarians were about to break away from the Axis and eager to implement the Final Solution in a previously untouched country heavily populated with Jews. A pro-German government, led by General Döme Sztójay, was set in place, and a new round of persecutions began. In May, convoys of Jews started to roll toward Auschwitz, where the ovens incinerated as many as twelve thousand persons a day. After almost two months of this pitiless operation, punctuated by protests from around the world, Admiral Horthy finally suspended the deportations in July. For Horthy and his associates, the end came a few months later, on 15 October, when the Germans arrested the regent and helped set up a pro-Nazi government headed by Ferenc Szálasi and his Arrow Cross fanatics. The result was mayhem, more slaughter of Jews, and further deportations—many of them now on foot, to Mauthausen. The Soviets put an end to this grotesque regime with the advance of the Red Army in early 1945. The Russians captured Budapest in February and drove the last Germans out of the country a few weeks later.

Braham credits the government of Miklós Kállay, prime minister from March 1942 until the German occupation of 1944, with having prevented the imposition of the Final Solution in Hungary for two years, through a policy of fence-sitting, verbal support of the Nazis, and a nominal anti-Jewish program. What collapsed this house of cards, in Braham's view, was the provocative diplomatic effort to disengage the Hungarians from the German alliance in 1944.[54] Sympathetic though he may be to the government of Kállay, however, Braham judges Horthy's role harshly, seeing the regent as preferring a Nazi takeover to a possible Russian invasion. With Germans swarming through his country, including Eichmann's two-hundred-man unit, Horthy refused to abdicate, lent legitimacy to a viciously antisemitic regime, and helped thereby to mesh the Hungarian police and administration with the Final Solution. Braham extensively documents official Hungarian involvement in the deportations and massacres of 1944—both before and after the toppling of Horthy. He supports the postwar testimony of German officials, such as the Reich plenipotentiary Edmund Veesenmayer, that the Hungarians bore a heavy responsibility for what followed. "The record clearly shows that the German demands could have been refused or sabotaged—they were in Bulgaria and Rumania as well as in the case of the Budapest Jews in July 1944—had Horthy and the Hungarian authorities really been concerned with their citizens of the Jewish faith. The Germans would have been quite helpless . . . without the wholehearted and effective cooperation of the Hungarian authorities." [55]

Can we draw a balance sheet on collaboration with the Holocaust in Europe? Given the traditions at work in the region, it is not surprising that anti-Jewish forces came to the fore under the impact of the Third Reich. It is striking, nevertheless, to see so many governments, not all of them subservient, joining the bandwagon of persecution in the wake of German victories, with countries as different as France in the west and Rumania in the east imposing comprehensive anti-Jewish laws. Even more shocking is the involvement of governments, for their own purposes, in the deportation and murder of Jews. The identification of Jews with former hegemonies, thrown off by the Germans, was a particularly powerful force in Slovakia, Croatia, Poland, the Baltic states, and the Ukraine, and generated an ugly reaction. On the other hand, there is no doubt that Germany's allies as well as collaborationist states made some effort on behalf of native Jews and resisted demands to participate fully in the Final Solution. National pride, apprehension about public opinion at home, distaste for the Germans' killing program, and fear of Allied retribution all played a part in their recalcitrance. While generally ruthless against foreign-born or unassimiliated Jews, governments in Rumania, Hungary, and Bulgaria used their bargaining power to hold the Germans at bay. As a result, the Jews of Bulgaria survived, as did most of the Jews of the Regat, the core of the Rumanian state. More Hungarian Jews might have also been spared, had the Hungarian leadership not acceded to German demands after the Nazis occupied the country in 1944. The French apparently believed they lacked such bargaining power; there is little evidence, moreover, that they were prepared to use the leverage they did have before it was too late.

To be sure, every one of these governments could have done far more for the Jews. But a real question is how much was possible. In eastern Europe, a region of critical importance for the German *Lebensraum*, it is unlikely that the Nazis would have suffered a disobedient ally or subject state for long. In western Europe, with fewer Jews and fewer Germans in occupation, the prospects were probably better. Except in Denmark and with the Italians, however, the question was never put to the test. In most cases it never even occurred to leaders to try.

So much for speculation. More certain is the other side to this coin, and the theme of this chapter: across Europe, the Germans needed help to achieve their objective, the murder of the Jews. As Hilberg pointed out long ago, the apparatus of destruction was thinly spread across the European continent. The Germans enlisted legions of helpers: in governments, ministries, police, private industry, the railways—virtually everywhere, in short. And all of it was important—whether the "green police" in Holland or the local gendarmerie in Hungary. To achieve the task of comprehensive mass murder the machine called not only upon the cold-blooded killers in the SS, but also upon remote officials of postal ministries, tax and insurance adjustors, bankers and clergymen, mechanics and accountants, municipal officials and stenographers. The clear implication is that murder on such a colossal scale involved the entire organized society to one degree or another and depended on a measure of support everywhere.

5. PUBLIC OPINION IN NAZI EUROPE

POPULAR PERCEPTIONS of what Europeans thought about Jews during the Holocaust differ remarkably from the findings of historical research in the past decade or so. I have the impression that assessments of such attitudes during the Nazi era often prompt sweeping generalizations, defining the dispositions of an entire society in a manner that few of us would consider reasonable for any other set of convictions. One hears that "antisemitism was practically universal" or that there was a "particular virulence" to German antisemitism—or Polish, or Ukrainian, or Hungarian, or whatever. Similarly, common generalizations often involve diametrically opposed views about basic facts. We are told that "knowledge about the Holocaust was widespread from the moment killing began," or, alternatively, that "no one knew about the scale of mass murder until the end of the war." Clearly not all of these statements can be correct. Pointing a way out of these difficulties, historians of public opinion have defined fundamental questions: Are there not degrees of antisemitism? Does it make sense to identify "German" or other national varieties of anti-Jewish feeling? What do we mean by "knowing" about the Holocaust? How did opinions about Jews evolve during the course of the war? The answers historians provide permit us to talk more substantially about public opinion—specifying by whom, when, and where particular views were held.

GERMANS

Evaluations of German opinion, particularly in the immediate postwar period, were heavily conditioned by moral or political judgments rather than careful historical analysis.[1] Despite some Allied disclaimers, there was widespread sentiment in the West that the German people as a whole were implicated in Nazi criminality. During the summer of 1945 posters were hung in towns and villages across Germany with pictures of Bergen-Belsen and the words "You are guilty." Allied troops marched columns of German civilians past decaying corpses of concentration camp victims in order to drive the point home. Writers sweepingly identified criminality with "the Germans," assuming the profound Nazification of society under the Third Reich. "The guilt belongs not to Nazism but to Germany," declared the former French resistance fighter Justin Godart in 1949.[2] And in a related view the eminent German historian Friedrich Meinecke described the demoralization of the German people under Nazism, which permitted Hitler and his cohorts to do their will. "The Third Reich was not only the greatest misfortune that the German people have suffered in their existence," he wrote, "it was also their greatest shame."[3]

More specifically, some historians posited extensive support for the goals of Nazism among the German population even when the anti-Jewish project was assumed to have been hatched by a Nazi minority. They defined a special deformity in German history, one of the consequences of which was that the German people as a whole shared the perverted goals of Nazism. "The German enigma is not Hitler," wrote Peter Viereck in a book first published in 1941. "Nor is it the behavior of either frauds or police-sadists. . . . The real enigma is the honest, unsadistic German majority that unleashes them rather than throwing them in jail."[4] Identifying a major fault line that runs through German history, others have referred to a tradition of abstention from politics on the part of a large segment of the population, opening the way to authoritarianism and the ruthless persecution of a small minority. In his discussion of this issue, Karl Dietrich Bracher of the University of Bonn referred to his countrymen's "readiness for acclamatory agreement and pseudo-military obedience to a strong authoritarian state," which outweighed in their minds the negative aspects of National Socialism.[5] Many historians continue to see Nazism as combining strands of popular disposition and charismatic leadership, difficult to untangle from one another. Martin Broszat, for example, has criticized the view that Nazi ideology is simply a reflection of Hitler's *Weltanschauung*, seeing the Führer himself as often expressing preexisting popular views—of which people may not even have been fully conscious.[6]

Challenging these notions, other writers have alluded to terroristic controls on the German public in the Nazi period, and the forcible association of the German people and the ideals of the Third Reich. Ordinary Germans, the implication is, could not be blamed for anything that happened after 1933, and certainly should not be presumed to have endorsed Hitler's repressive apparatus. Coercion, indeed, affected everyone. The philosopher Karl Jaspers put this succinctly: "Germany under the Nazi regime was a prison. The guilt of getting into it is a political guilt. Once the gates were shut, however, a prison break from within was no longer possible."[7] For much the same reason, some historians have denied that one could ever know what the German people thought under such circumstances. The Jewish activist Eva Reichmann therefore ended her social analysis of German antisemitism with the advent of Hitler, feeling that evaluations of the Holocaust period could be made "only indirectly and with great caution."[8]

Necessarily, the earliest references to this subject in the historical literature were impressionistic or based on evidence collected in harrowing circumstances, hardly likely to inspire confidence. In one of the first historical surveys of the Holocaust, French historian Léon Poliakov adopted the strongly judgmental tone of many of his countrymen at the time. Even if many Germans did not agree with the massacres of Jews, he wrote, they were "tacitly accepted by the popular will [*volonté populaire*].[9] But interestingly, German émigrés and opponents of Nazism were often reluctant to associate the German people with a murderous antisemitism. Hermann Rauschning's *Revolution of Nihilism*, published as a "warning to the West" in 1939, considered antisemitism as a product of Nazi propaganda and manipulation of opinion. The despised figure of the Jew, he wrote, "can always be made to serve as fuel for the fighting spirit, and at the same time to keep alive the happy feeling of belonging to the company of the elect." [10] Further, some observers felt that Nazi anti-Jewish propaganda fell far short of its goals. Eva Reichmann, whose entire career was associated with opposition to antisemitism, observed that there was no genuine opposition of Germans and Jews. The Nazis' success was not due to antisemitism, in her view, although their campaign against the Jews did win some adherents. While it was true that a larger number of people could be persuaded that the Jews were responsible for their nation's problems, the average German disapproved of the severe antisemitic measures of the first years of the regime. Beyond this, Reichmann denied a direct link between popular anti-Jewish feeling and mass murder. "Antisemitism," she concluded, "does not account for the catastrophe of the Jews." [11]

Anti-Nazi Germans frequently protested that others had exaggerated the importance of German antisemitism. The German democrat Michael Müller-Claudius carried out a private survey of German opinion in 1942, claiming that only 5 percent of his sample supported Nazi policy toward Jews and over two-thirds were indifferent. [12] In Behemoth, a masterful study of the Third Reich first published in the same year, the German émigré Franz Neumann contended that "spontaneous, popular antisemitism was still weak in Germany," and that "the German people are the least antisemitic of all." Neumann noted the absence of spontaneous attacks on Jews by the German public—in marked contrast to other countries— and suggested that this was all the more remarkable because of the intensity of vicious anti-Jewish propaganda beamed at the German public during the Nazi years. [13]

The first systematic examinations of German attitudes toward persecution and the Final Solution have come only recently, using documentary evidence coming from the Nazi period. Most of this information derived from the SS security service or SD, which was responsible for keeping watch over the German population. [14] Historians have also utilized the underground reports of the outlawed German Social Democratic party, even while acknowledging their tendency to highlight opposition to the regime. [15] Both kinds of source have marked biases, but it is the job of historians to evaluate such material as best they can. With an evaluation of this documentation, the debate has descended from the lofty heights of some of the writers mentioned above and has gone in some unexpected directions. The most obvious result was to make distinctions, whatever the final conclusion.

In a study of German attitudes published in 1973, Lawrence Stokes considered the extent to which ordinary Germans grasped the essence of the murder process and concluded that "much, although not all of the terror and destruction inflicted upon the Jews of Europe by the Nazis was generally known among the German people." Stokes acknowledged that the Nazis kept the extermination camps like Auschwitz hidden from the German public. It was impossible to prevent leaks about the grisly work of the Einsatzgruppen, however, and there were frequent rumors about other massacres and atrocities. Most people understood the awesome implications of the "very severe measures" taken against Jews, he concluded, even if they did not know details.[16]

The German scholar Marliss Steinert discussed this issue in a 1977 book on public opinion during the Second World War.[17] She recognized that there was indifference and lack of reaction on the Jewish issue during the period of Nazi persecutions. However, she also noted extensive examples of "non-conformist behavior," suggesting a much more positive attitude. It is important to remember that as late as January 1942 there were still more than 131,000 Jews in Germany, mainly in Frankfurt and Berlin. Most Germans found themselves cut off from Jews, but some did not. While the SS often drew satisfaction from evidence of popular antisemitism, they also reported instances where opposition evidently existed. To be sure, only a very few Germans were willing to assist the beleaguered Jews. Steinert also asked what was known about the Final Solution. In her judgment, "only a very few people knew about the monstrous scope of the crimes," and "many were befuddled by propaganda." Although rumors, fragmentary reports, and other clues to mass murder existed, for most people these were incomprehensible. Concluding her discussion, she suggested that the Jewish issue was of modest importance for most Germans at the time. Hitler was obsessed by Jews, but the German people, evidently, were not.

The studies mentioned so far draw upon SD reports on the national level; other works, as we saw briefly in chapter 2, have examined attitudes in specific German localities. As might be predicted, the result of these investigations is often to highlight regional variations. In Lower Saxony, for example, antisemitism apparently had relatively little appeal as an electoral instrument during the *Kampfzeit*. Across Germany, it was much more evident in Protestant than in Catholic areas and was stronger in the countryside than in large towns. In much the same way, studies of particular aspects of the society in the Third Reich suggest differences: anti-Jewish feeling seems to have been relatively weak among workers, for example, but more pronounced among small shopkeepers, who in some localities felt threatened by Jewish-owned department stores.[18] Looking at the year 1935, in the period immediately preceding the issuing of the Nuremberg Laws, Werner Angress stresses the differences between party zealots, who were pressing for action against Jews, and state authorities, who were much more cautious.[19]

These investigations still leave important questions unanswered, however. For the most part, they focus on the pre-1933 period, with some studies going up to the outbreak of war. There is considerably less information on the war years and on reactions during the time of systematic mass murder. Also, these investigations treat the Jewish issue incidentally, or in a short period, without tracking evidence on the character, substance, and evolution of opinion on Jews. Beyond this, one has to look very closely indeed to assess the *quality* of anti-Jewish views—to know when and under what circumstances, for example, what Müller-Claudius called "static hatred" could be transformed into "dynamic hatred," or to evaluate just how important attitudes toward Jews were at all.

The British historian Ian Kershaw has undertaken one of the few investigations of such issues in his study of Bavarian opinion from 1933 to 1945.[20] His quarry is the ordinary Germans behind the scenes—"the muddled majority, neither full-hearted Nazis nor outright opponents, whose attitudes at one and the same time betray signs of Nazi ideological penetration and yet show the clear limits of propaganda manipulation." Kershaw limits his description to the largely Catholic province of Bavaria, the cradle of Nazism and for many years the base of the movement. His conclusions are qualified, but suggest nevertheless that the ideological conformity to which Propaganda Minister Goebbels aspired was never realized. Germans remained divided by Nazism and never gave themselves entirely to the regime. At the same time, they were seldom preoccupied with public affairs or the deeper issues posed by a criminal society. Kershaw's Germans, indeed, will appear to many disturbingly normal—a point the author himself noted when he reflected sensitively in his preface: "I should like to think that had I been around at the time I would have been a convinced anti-Nazi engaged in the underground resistance fight. However, I know really that I would have been as confused and felt as helpless as most of the people I am writing about."

What did these Bavarians think about Jews? The first answer is not much. Indifference is the main impression. There were relatively few Jews in the province, about forty-two thousand in 1933 or 0.55 percent of the total population, proportionately many fewer than in the Reich as a whole. There were some centers of antisemitism, notably Protestant Middle Franconia, under the influence of the rabble-rousing Julius Streicher and his pornographic newspaper *Der Stürmer*. But activity against Jews—arson, violence, boycotts, discrimination—was overwhelmingly the work of zealous party men and their agents, rather than the general population. Although called upon to sever their relations with Jews, the local citizenry continued to deal with them in defiance of government policy. Culminating in a violent anti-Jewish campaign in 1938, the riots of Kristallnacht were widely disapproved of, mainly because of their hooligan, lawless character, with such wasteful destruction of property. No one believed Goebbels's boast that the German people had risen "spontaneously" against the Jews, and Nazi leaders were plainly disappointed with the lack of enthusiasm for the pogrom. Thereafter they attempted carefully to shield their murderous policy from popular scrutiny in Germany.

Although very few Bavarians knew details about the Final Solution, and information about extermination camps was virtually nonexistent, there were certainly rumors about mass shootings and other atrocities, not to mention the physical disappearance of the Jews from many localities. Remarkable as it may appear, opinion does not seem to have occupied itself with the Jews. Far more important were the worsening of conditions of life at home, the gloomy news from the front, and the fear of Allied retribution should the Reich be defeated. Churchmen were generally silent, reflecting the extensive lack of concern about the issue. Sometimes antisemitism showed up in reports on local attitudes to Nazi policies, suggesting that latent hostility toward Jews was widespread and that

Nazi propaganda had had some effect at home. But these were exceptions. So although the Nazis succeeded in murdering the Jews largely without German resistance, they failed significantly to mobilize the population on behalf of antisemitism. "The road to Auschwitz," Kershaw concludes, "was built by hate, but paved with indifference."

Bavaria, of course, may not be "representative." Unlike others, Bavarians had little direct contact with Jews, and indeed the predominantly rural character of the province may have insulated the population, to some degree, from the Nazis' ideological obsessions. Largely Catholic, the cradle of Nazism, and for years the base of the movement, the province was by no means solidly pro-Nazi. Between 15,000 and 20,000 Bavarians were interned in 1933 alone—mainly Socialist and Communist workers—and the danger of being sent to Dachau increased following Goebbels's declaration of "Total War" in 1943. Thousands paid for their grumblings in concentration camps or even worse, but others were either ignored, intimidated into silence, or bought off by Nazi functionairies. Generally, discontent did not produce active *opposition*. Some have raised questions about the tendency of the SS reports to accent resistance. Studying the Düsseldorf district, Sarah Gordon was struck, like Kershaw, by "the number of ordinary Germans who actually did something for Jews in the face of Hitler's police state." But her research raises serious methodological questions about the use of particular SS and Nazi sources to assess the extent of opposition.[21] Certainly the Gestapo accusations of *Rassenschande* or *Judenfreundlichkeit* (sexual relations with Jews and being friendly with Jews), the basis for her judgments, seem a highly questionable foundation upon which to make statements about German society as a whole.

While respecting Kershaw's findings, several historians have come away from this material with much harsher views of German opinion. Almost all observers have been struck by the durability of the Reich and the discipline of its population—despite the great trials of the latter part of the war, when bombs rained down on Germany and the achievements of Nazism lay in ruins. To have withstood so much for so long and to have remained at their posts suggest that Germans considered themselves bound with their Führer in a community of fate. Hitler's success in maintaining the outward allegiance of Germans in so many other areas can hardly be ignored in evaluating public opinion toward Jews. Michael Kater, the author of an important study of the Nazi party, has argued that Kershaw and others have underplayed the genuinely spontaneous expressions of popular antisemitism that erupted in prewar Germany.[22] "After January 30, 1933," he writes, "Nazi policy against the Jews came to resemble a pattern of interactions between private or personal initiative, semilegal activities . . . and, finally, government legislation." There are indications that the Nazis counted on an anti-Jewish disposition before promulgating specific anti-Jewish decrees. And while "spontaneous" expressions of antisemitism were often staged exercises, substantial numbers were involved in such manipulations. Immediately after Hitler took power the SA comprised about 2 million men over the age of seventeen, about 10 percent of the entire German population in corresponding age-groups. Together with other Nazi formations, this certainly constituted a popular mass disposed to active anti-Jewish campaigning. And finally, while it was true that official anti-Jewish policy was out of popular hands, its implementation through the state and the party allowed for very wide participation in the persecution of Jews.

Interestingly, antisemitism seems even to have had its place in the German opposition to Hitler that existed within the Reich. The German historian Christof Dipper has gone over this ground and offers some sobering conclusions. Among most of the conservative opponents of Nazism, "the bureaucratic, pseudo-legal deprivation of the Jews practiced until 1938 was still considered acceptable." To be sure, no one within the resistance movement supported massacre. But, for example, the group around mayor of Leipzig Carl Goerdeler, probably the most important within the German resistance, favored a special diminished status for Jews, segregating them as outsiders in German society. Drawing on this evidence, Dipper concludes that "a large part of the German people . . . believed that a 'Jewish Question' existed and had to be solved."[23]

In a similar vein, the Israeli scholar Otto Dov Kulka contends that before the outbreak of war one sees a tendency to "depersonalize" Jews, effectively isolating them throughout German society.[24] Kulka has also looked in detail at anti-Jewish opinion at the time of the Nuremberg Laws, noting that, while the range of opinion varied considerably, there was considerable popular initiative for anti-Jewish action.[25] According to Kulka the "indifference" which lies at the hart of Kershaw's argument may not be an accurate representation of German views. In particular, the concept is misleading if it suggests a lack of interest in the Jews; certainly it does not convey what he feels is the widespread conviction that "something, one way or another, had to be done to 'solve the Jewish Question.'" Here, it may be argued, is an echo of Hitler's insistent call for a solution—*so oder so.* Kulka contends that "the population of Germany was generally aware of what became of the Jews deported to the East," and he judges German reaction to be "a kind of national conspiracy of silence." "Indifference," he argues with a colleague in a recent review, might better be termed "passive complicity."[26]

Not every historian will be happy with the term *complicity,* suggesting as it does a legalistic determination of guilt for an entire population rather than a basis for historical understanding. In the end, research on German public opinion points out the difficulty of characterizing the society as a whole. Kershaw's work, however criticized, shows convincingly that the Nazis failed to dragoon the German public into complete conformity. Antisemitism was undoubtedly widespread, but we should be cautious in defining its extent. In this respect, biological metaphors seem to me particularly perilous. We are accustomed to hearing about antisemitism that was "rabid," "malignant," or "virulent"—suggesting both that it spread easily among a population and that it had a decisive effect on an organism. Neither assumption is necessarily correct. It is difficult enough to sort out views of "the workers," "traditional elites," "the church," and so on; much care is needed in going beyond this. Moreover, the link between longstanding anti-Jewish sentiment and Nazi-style antisemitism is also not entirely clear. Shulamit Volkov, among others, makes an important distinction between traditional German antisemitism and the murderous enterprise of Adolf Hitler and the Third Reich, thereby drawing attention away from the "antisemitic background" to the Holocaust. After all, one can easily trace the importance of antisemitism in other European countries east and west, and it is highly unlikely, by any scale of judgment, that Germany would be deemed the most antisemitic country in Europe. For Volkov, therefore, Nazism must be understood as a dynamic force, and its genocidal project must be seen in the context of its own evolving qualities rather than through its ideological "origins." [27]

Finally, we have only the vaguest idea of the relationship of Nazi anti-Jewish policy and public opinion. Although it is widely believed that antisemitism was part of the ideological glue of the Third Reich, binding together warring elements in German society, historians have been unable to identify a murderous impulse outside the Nazi leadership. [28] I have argued elsewhere that popular strains of antisemitism were never strong enough on their own to support violent persecution in the modern period. [29] In the case of certain groups, such as the Wehrmacht high command, it seems very likely that anti-Jewish predispositions facilitated their willing collaboration in genocide. [30] In the case of others, indifference or shallow-mindedness seems more commonly at work—shocking enough when one contemplates the horrors of the Holocaust, but nevertheless quite different from incitement to mass murder. The Nazi leadership rang down a curtain of secrecy between extermination in the east and the German people, well aware that there were limits to popular support for anti-Jewish measures. Hitler himself sensed that the Germans did not share his perspicacity on racial matters; in the last days of the Reich he seems to have despised them for this, raining a frightful orgy of destruction upon his countrymen as if in punishment for their shortcomings.

EAST EUROPEANS

Outside the Reich, there were similarly wide variations in popular reactions to the persecution and slaughter of Jews. Here too, precision is difficult. Evidence exists, often in abundance, but it must be read with a keen eye for context. The Nazis reported sporadically on opinion in conquered territory, but their views were heavily colored by their occupation role and their racist preconceptions. Broadly speaking, German officials were preoccupied with maintaining order and were eager to exploit and to draw comfort from the slightest manifestation of local antisemitism. Resistance groups and the Jews themselves also commented on grass roots responses to the Nazis' anti-Jewish program, but less frequently than one might expect. The assessments of each—especially those that were publicly expressed—were often shaped by the pursuit of desperate political strategies.

To facilitate their task, the Nazis strove to isolate Jews from non-Jews, to create physical and moral barriers that reduced communication to a minimum. When the Nazis succeeded in this segregation, which was usually the case, rumors and stereotypes often created an even worse relationship between Jews and non-Jews than might otherwise have been the case. Throughout much of eastern Europe this was achieved by ghettos, the walls of which were sometimes impenetrable, except for smugglers, black marketeers, segregated work gangs—and the dead. Ordinary civilians had no access to the camps, of course, although it was impossible to seal them off: there were tens of thousands of non-Jewish inmates in some camps and their satellites; rail and road traffic was open; and stories about what happened in these places circulated without constraint. As in the west, a barrage of laws and decrees cut Jews off from their environment, preparing the way for their ultimate internment and deportation. Outlawed Jewish refugees often found themselves living furtively in unfamiliar places. Longstanding inhabitants resented outsiders, particularly in the countryside where such antagonism was a hoary tradition and where it was assumed that the newcomers were rich, thriving on the black market, and draining local food supplies. In such circumstances, antisemitism invariably intensified. Nazi-imposed conditions therefore, in both east and west, stimulated anti-Jewish attitudes.

Throughout the Nazi-occupied east, opinion was heavily conditioned by anti-Jewish traditions that long predated the rise of Nazism.[31] During the depression era of the 1930s, popular antisemitism was a conspicuous fact of life for Jews in the independent states of east central Europe. Around 4.5 million Jews lived between Germany and the Soviet Union at the end of the interwar period, vastly outnumbering the community of 525,000 in Germany. Jews in this part of Europe constituted a significant minority—some 10 percent of the population of Poland, for example—often with a disproportionately important role in certain professions and some parts of the economy. While traditional Jewish culture still set the rhythms of life for much of the Jewish population, acculturation was proceeding rapidly. In the best survey of Jewish life in this region between the world wars, Ezra Mendelsohn concludes that Jews faced a crisis by 1939.[32] The economic basis of Jewish existence was severely eroded. Liberalism and democracy were in sharp decline throughout the region. A significant segment of the political world struck out at Jews for a variety of reasons, chipping away at Jewish emancipation. While important differences existed between states— there was much less antisemitism in the Baltic states, and very little in Yugoslavia and Bulgaria—the large Jewish populations of Poland, Rumania, and Hungary experienced great difficulties.[33]

Under Nazi domination, many of the prewar tensions were exacerbated. Much of the discussion among historians as to the nature of public reactions centers on Poland, the most populous Jewish community and the locus of Nazi extermination policy. Polish Jewry, close to 3.3 million at the outbreak of the war, bore the brunt of Nazi ghettoization policies during the first two years of Nazi occupation, before the implementation of the Final Solution. During this period, local Nazi officials proceeded at their own pace to construct ghettos, cutting the Jews off from the rest of the population and beginning a catastrophic mortality among the inmates—eventually costing the Jews a half million deaths, according to Hilberg, mainly through starvation, disease, and exposure.[34] Locked in these urban prisons, sealed off from the rest of the population, Jews communicated with Poles mainly through smuggling—hardly an activity conducive to mutual understanding. Massive deportations to death camps began in 1942 and continued for as long as the Nazis could find Jews to murder. While tens of thousands escaped—by fleeing to the Soviet Union, by hiding in the forests, and in a few cases by living underground in Poland itself—the Nazis considered their task in Poland practically complete within a year and a half. The toll was over 3 million. The few instances of armed resistance— notably the uprising of the Warsaw ghetto in the spring of 1943— were feeble if heroic affairs, undertaken with the puniest of means, without the assistance of the substantial Polish underground. For the most part, Polish Jewry suffered alone.

To this day Jewish and Polish historians conduct a *dialogue des sourdes* over the issue of relations between Jews and other Poles during the Holocaust, with the latter often denying any significant popular opposition to Jews within Polish society.[35] Jewish historians have presented a range of assessments, while agreeing on the central theme—widespread antipathy toward Jews, who were never completely accepted as part of the Polish nation. Even at the time, the question of Polish antisemitism was a matter of dispute among the Jews themselves. Many Jews in the ghettos argued that hostility toward them had increased during the Nazi occupation. Yet some disagreed, sensing that the tide of Polish opinion was turning against antisemitism, with a Polish tendency to see Jews and Poles together as victims of the Third Reich. This view was held for a time among Bundists, anti-Zionist Jewish socialists committed to struggle together with the Polish working class.[36] Each side had evidence to adduce. In one of the first surveys of this question, the Jewish historian Emmanuel Ringelblum wrote an important volume on Polish-Jewish relations as part of an underground research enterprise conducted in the Warsaw ghetto, known by its code name Oneg Shabbat. Ringelblum's book was completed after the liquidation of the ghetto, when its author was in hiding on the Aryan side, in the latter half of 1943. Ringelblum, who had previously examined the issue in historical terms, with studies of eighteenth-century Poland, strained mightily to be objective—a heroic effort under the circumstances. He insisted that "the attitude of the Polish population towards the Jews has not been uniform." Polish workers, he felt, were much less disposed to antisemitism than their more educated and affluent counterparts, who were highly susceptible to the appeals from the Polish Right. Poles had certainly rescued Jews. Close to thirty thousand, he estimated, were hiding from the Nazis in Poland, about half of them in non-Jewish Warsaw. Poles sheltered these Jews at great risk to themselves, and Ringelblum saluted their heroic gesture, which "is exceptionally noble and accords with the tradition of tolerance in Poland's history." But the Poles could have done far more, he felt. His conclusion was grim, if not without nuance: "the majority of the Polish people have been passive spectators of the mass murder of Jews by the Germans," he observed. As a collectivity, the Poles "have not been able to bring themselves to take a single step in defence of their fellow-citizens. Some elements of the Polish community have even actively taken measures against the Jews. . . . On the whole, there has been no collective reaction on the part of the Poles while the common enemy was murdering millions of Jews."[37]

Similar assessments are available from the Polish side. Jan Karski was a brave young courier from the Polish underground who criss-crossed Europe bringing messages and information from the Polish capital to the Polish government in exile—first in Angers, France, and then in London. He was unusually well placed to report on Jew-ish matters, having friendly relations with Jews and having traveled widely throughout Poland, including the Soviet-occupied zone. In a 1940 report, Karski noted that there were "wide segements of the Polish populace among whom antisemitism has by no means de-creased." He told his superiors that Nazi Jewish policy posed a grave danger to the Polish resistance because "a large portion of Polish society" appreciated Nazi anti-Jewish policies, and a nar-row bridge was thus created between Germans and Poles. The Pol-ish authorities in France were plainly embarrassed by their courier's evaluation and seem to have repressed his harsh judgments about Polish antisemitism in order to present Polish opinion in a more favorable light.[38]

From across the divide, a new study by Richard Lukas of Poland under the German occupation energetically argues the Polish case.[39] Written in a spirit of revisionism, intended to "lift the veil of myth and distortion about what actually transpired in Poland during the German occupation," his book seems heavily preoccupied with the Jews. Lukas's argument is that Poles did not receive antisemitism sympathetically, were not generally hostile to Jews, and did their best to help them. More convincingly, he presents reasons other than antisemitism that help explain why Polish-Jewish interests and mutual perceptions were so divergent. Poles and Jews had little real sense of each others' lives, separated as they were by the walls of the ghettos. Poles, Lukas argues, believed that their own situation was even worse than that of the Jews, that the latter were craven in their response to the Germans and were pro-Russian or pro-Soviet.[40] The Polish Home Army, or Armia Krajowa, he suggests, had under-standable if exaggerated fears of Communist influence within the Jewish resistance in Warsaw and had a completely different strategic objective from that of the Jews. The Home Army saw its task as the preservation of the Polish nation against Nazi depredations and the preparation for liberation under the most propitious circumstances; one of its important concerns, therefore, was to prevent "pre-mature" uprisings that would cost the population dearly and would weaken resistance forces unnecessarily.[41] For Jews, of course, *pre-*

mature was a word infused with bitter irony. The Jewish underground increasingly realized that the Jews would not survive the war and finally decided to lash out at their tormentors, even at the cost of what remained of their communities. Nevertheless, according to this view, the Home Army undertook diversionary attacks to help the Jewish fighters.

As the Jews saw it, the Polish reaction was a crowning betrayal. Forty years later, outrage at this rebuke infuses the careful scholarly monograph on Warsaw Jewry by Yisrael Gutman, a survivor of the ghetto and a participant in its uprising. Like Ringelblum, Gutman argues that there was much that the Poles could have done during the massive deportations of 1942 that preceded the preparation of the revolt of the following year. The Home Army was certainly in a position to sabotage rail links to Treblinka or to smuggle weapons into Jewish Warsaw. Gutman challenges the often-repeated claim of Home Army commander Tadeuz (Bór) Komorowski that the Poles were willing to help Jews during that period.[42] Once the uprising began in the spring of 1943 the Jews received support from the relatively weak and poorly armed Communist resistance, the Armia Ludowa, and were brutally opposed by the Polish Right. As for the Home Army, two attacks did take place in an effort to demonstrate solidarity with Jewish fighters, but there was no serious military commitment to these efforts. And, in Gutman's view, Polish opinion "was permeated with deep-seated prejudice that surpassed even the sentiments of the various forces in the underground."[43]

Outside Poland, we have few systematic studies of popular attitudes toward Jews or the responses of local inhabitants to the Holocaust. Memoirs of Jewish survivors, and their testimony to this day, refer to intense hostility in certain regions—notably ethnically Ukrainian territory, divided in 1939 between the Soviet Union, Poland, Czechoslovakia, and Rumania. Under German occupation, these lands were inhabited by over 36 million Ukrainians and 3 million Jews.[44] Typically, the pattern in such parts of eastern Europe, where local nationalities had been submerged by Soviet oppression or by the domination of other national groups, was for antisemitism to be woven into the fabric of popular national consciousness. At times, nationalist forces in eastern Europe collaborated, with varying degrees of commitment, with the Nazi invader—seen as a liberating force, in the early stages at least.[45] Cooperation with the Germans in anti-Jewish persecution and even the occasional slaughter of Jews was sometimes a result.

Having established their presence in such areas, the Nazis poured in anti-Jewish propaganda. Themes varied with the state of nationalist forces, but everywhere Jews were linked with former hegemonies, now overthrown thanks to Hitler and the Wehrmacht. In German-occupied regions of the Soviet Union, Jews were pictured as tools of Moscow and the Soviet secret police; in Croatia, Jews were denounced as agents of Serbian domination from Belgrade; in Slovakia, Jews were associated with the Czechs and the control of their country from Prague. Occupation troops and the Einsatzgruppen orchestrated pogroms and strove whenever possible to present their massacres as spontaneous, local "uprisings" against Jews. Paramilitary and police formations assembled locally by the Germans frequently took part in massacres, and did so even outside the ethnic homelands. Ukrainian auxiliaries, for example, turned up in the ghetto of Warsaw and elsewhere to round up and repress the Jewish population. Other units were formed into battalions of so-called Hiwis (Hilfswillige, or "ready to help") that ended up in concentration camps, killing squads, and other anti-Jewish units.[46]

Any investigation of popular reactions becomes a complex exercise in detecting nationalist, ethnic, and political opinion, all of which could be expressed in the idiom of traditional anti-Jewish culture. Here too it is important to make distinctions. Yehuda Bauer implies that elements of the local population who were themselves minorities may have been disposed to support Jews. An example of this would be Volhynia, in eastern Poland, where Poles who felt victimized by the Ukrainian majority extended aid.[47] There were moderate nationalist groups among Ukrainians and others who refused to join the antisemitic current, and of course there were many who wanted no part of any political involvement. In addition, one must remember that the Nazis' reign of terror systematically turned upon any open expression of pro-Jewish views and savagely punished anyone suspected of providing assistance. In the Protectorate of Bohemia and Moravia, for example, the Germans simply shot any Jew found in hiding, together with their accomplices. Anyone not reporting persons sheltering Jews was similarly liable to the death penalty.[48] Time also played an important role. Support for the Germans cooled notably in the latter part of the war, as a result of Nazi defeats and also the self-defeating racism of Nazi occupation policies which revealed a layer of contempt toward local nationalities unanticipated in 1941. Occasionally, there was a greater willingness to accept Jews as fellow victims. In Belorussia, the year 1944 brought a better relationship between Jews and local partisans who had previously refused to accept them.[49] Certainly there is evidence virtually everywhere of some pro-Jewish response. Some Ukrainians followed the lead of the nationalist head of the Ukrainian Catholic church in Galicia, Metropolitan Andreas Sheptytsky of Lvov, who defended Jews and hid many from the Germans. The Nazis executed scores of Ukrainians and others for what they called *Judenbegünstigung* ("helping Jews"), an extremely dangerous mode of resistance since the Nazis took reprisals for this crime not only against individuals but against other villagers and family members as well.

WEST EUROPEANS

Popular reactions to the Jewish catastrophe in western Europe occurred in a radically different context. In the east, even though the Nazis screened the death camps from the general population, Nazi brutalities were overt and mass death was an ever-present reality. To be sure, circumstances differed there as well; regions combed by the Einsatzgruppen or other death squads usually knew Nazi policies more intimately than those regions occupied in 1939; territory annexed to the Reich was spared the orgy of destruction and violence visited upon land that the Nazis considered the dumping ground for the "ethnic mush" of Europe. But all such conditions differed markedly from the relatively decorous towns and countryside of western Europe, where much of the terror of the Hitlerian occupation was unknown until 1944.

One consequence of this relative tranquillity was that many could go about their business without being reminded of the agonies of the Jews and unaware of the devastation of Jewish existence in eastern Europe. Poland, after all, was far away. At home, harsh realities of Jewish life could be explained, when explanation was necessary, as part of the costs of occupation, as the harsh retribution meted out to foreigners, or as a necessary preliminary to the national recovery of countries defeated by the Nazis. Systematic deportations "to the east" began throughout western Europe in the summer of 1942, and with them people could no longer shield themselves from the cruelties of anti-Jewish policies. At first, deportation trains were made up almost entirely of foreigners—widely despised in the countries to which refugees had flocked in the 1930s. But deportations gradually included local citizens as well. The roundups tore families apart, sometimes involved stunning brutalities, and often occurred in broad daylight, under the eyes of some who would spread the first wave of popular protest against anti-Jewish measures. Nevertheless, opinion was slow to mobilize on behalf of the Jews.

Information on the Jews' fate, as we have noted before, was widely available by mid-1942. Yet people could easily ignore it, or choose to ignore it. Political leaders and habitual skeptics, particularly those who came to resent the British or Americans for prolonging the war, could easily dismiss reports of the killings as anti-German propaganda, no better than the lurid distortions commonly spread during the First World War. For some, the jacket of indifference that encased them remained intact even in the face of the deportations to the east. Occurring simultaneously with widespread roundups of young men to work in the Reich, observers often associated "deportation" of Jews with forced labor, rather than with the Final Solution. To this day, many west Europeans understand the term *deportation* in this sense. Beyond these reasons, a substantial reservoir of anti-Jewish sentiment stifled expressions of sympathy and remained in place, remarkably, to the end of the war.

Working on France, Robert Paxton and I discovered in prefectoral reports on public opinion widespread indifference to the Jews' fate until the latter half of 1942. Broadly speaking, while the antisemitic campaign of the collaborationist Vichy regime left most Frenchmen unmoved, their protests against it were few and far between. Anti-Jewish feeling was widespread, and the public seemed to follow the lead of right-wing politicians at Vichy who built an antisemitic program into the "National Revolution" they prescribed for France. A common (and quite mistaken) assumption was that persecution affected mainly foreign Jews and that, to some degree at least, this was justified, given the "perponderant influence" Jews were supposed to have had in French society.[50] In a recent investigation of the region about Clermont-Ferrand, John Sweets provides evidence for the contrary interpretation, suggesting that Vichy had much more difficulty than has been assumed in selling its anti-Jewish policy.[51] There is no doubt that Vichy's anti-Jewish project was heavily discredited after the Germans moved into the formerly unoccupied zone of France in November 1942, and the regime's subservience to the Nazis in this as in other respects drew increasing criticism. Many Jews went into hiding at this point, and a substantial number found refuge among the local population.

As in the east, there were shifts in opinion, with support for the Jews tending to grow with opposition to the Nazi occupiers. During the summer and autumn of 1942, deportations "to the east," occurring everywhere in western Europe, prompted some sympathy for the Jews.[52] Throughout the west, early 1943 marked an important turning point toward resistance, when the impact of the great German defeat at Stalingrad registered in occupied Europe and when German labor boss Fritz Sauckel intensified his drive to bring foreign workers to the Reich. The conscription of young men for this purpose prompted many to break openly with collaboration and was accompanied by a wave of public sympathy for the Jews, however evanescent.

SUPPORT FOR JEWS

Across Europe, thousands took great risks to feed, hide, shelter, and provide cover or passage for Jews. Material interests sometimes brought rescuers and rescued together, and there is extensive testimony by survivors that bribery played a vital role in their escape. The guides who escorted Jews across the Pyrenees to Spain were commonly known as *passeurs;* while some were honest, others charged exorbitant sums for the service and were known to abandon their charges in the middle of their journey. Some assistance was motivated simply by opposition to the Nazis. Even antisemites extended aid on occasion, setting a higher priority on resistance to the invader than on punishing Jews. There is a story, perhaps apocryphal, of graffiti on a wall in Amsterdam: "Hitler, keep your dirty hands off our dirty Jews!" But there is ample evidence that most of this help derived from a principled opposition to Nazi persecution and that it was extended practically everywhere. In a great sea of indifference, these islands of support are remarkable. According to Leonard Gross, some forty thousand Jews still survived in Berlin in the spring of 1942, in the very heart of the Nazi empire. Despite periodic sweeps by the Gestapo, several hundred managed to hide there throughout the war—most protected, at one point or another, by non-Jewish friends and even strangers.[53] Similarly, about sixteen thousand Jews escaped in the Netherlands, many in Amsterdam, sheltered in apartments and other buildings under the noses of the German occupiers and the Dutch "green police."[54] In one outstanding case in France, the entire village of Chambon-sur-Lignon, dominated by two charismatic Protestant pastors, constituted itself as a kind of underground railway to assist hunted Jews and others to escape the Nazi and Vichy police.[55] Organized networks of resisters throughout the west harbored Jews as an integral part of their struggle against Nazism.

Much depended on the public positions of local churchmen. Prominent ecclesiastics could give moral support to resistance, as with the anti-Nazi appeals in Belgium of Joseph-Ernst Cardinal van Roey. In some places church leaders stoutly denounced the mistreatment of Jews by Nazis and their local agents, breaking the pattern of indifference and setting an example in rescue activity. Cardinal Gerlier of Lyon, a former enthusiast for Marshal Pétain, condemned the deportations and encouraged the sheltering of Jews throughout his archdiocese. In the Netherlands Archbishop de Jonge of Utrecht forbade his countrymen to assist the Germans in roundups of Jews. The protests of the Protestant bishops of Norway, in November 1942, as deportations were being prepared, may have mobilized support for the rescue of substantial numbers of Norwegian Jews.[56] Opinion could also be moved by calls from abroad. The BBC, as well as national voices such as the Dutch Radio Oranje, beamed information to occupied Europe on Nazi extermination policies, with details on the massacres in Poland. While at times excessively restrained, such broadcasts included exhortations to shelter Jews and warnings of punishment for their tormentors.[57] Did such sermons, broadcasts, and other appeals affect public opinion? It is impossible to be sure. There are grounds for skepticism, at least, as to whether they affected people's behavior. In the face of overwhelming German power, almost all calls to resistance action—whether to save

Jews or for other purposes—went largely unheeded, at least until the very end of the war.[58]

As noted in the previous chapter, Catholic Italy and Protestant Denmark are the two cases in which Nazi Jewish policy encountered significant popular opposition. There has been little specific investigation of opinion toward Jews in these two countries. Along with the issues discussed in chapter 4, one should mention Leni Yahil's contention that, in the case of the Danes, there existed a deep-seated democratic tradition, according to them a "special character and moral standing."[59] In the same vein, some have posited an Italian disposition toward tolerance and philosemitism.[60] But such generalizations are as difficult to substantiate as are opposite characterizations of certain societies as antisemitic. Interestingly, religious factors do not seem to have been significant in either case. Lutheran theologians in Denmark may well have been in the forefront of opposition to the persecution in their country, but this was decidedly not the case with their coreligionists in Germany. The Italian people, on the other hand, seem to have exhibited a spontaneous distrust of antisemitism without any religious lead, and certainly without instruction from the Vatican, which remained notably silent on the specific issue of anti-Jewish persecutions. On the other hand, religious influences seem to have stirred charitable responses in other situations—such as the French village of Chambon-sur-Lignon.

Recently, the study of rescue activity by threatened populations inside Nazi Europe has become more systematic, with several researchers attempting to identify patterns that help explain the persistence of altruism amid cruelty, hatred, and indifference.[61] Preliminary results for Holland, where 80 percent of the country's 140,000 Jews were murdered, suggest that support for Jews was widespread among Dutch Calvinists, in whose tradition is a pronounced philosemitism.[62] Yet the Dutch case is instructive in demonstrating the strategic limits of resistance. Holland saw the first public protest against Nazi Jewish policies anywhere—a two-day general strike in Amsterdam in February 1941, originally called by Communists after widespread arrests of Jews and riotous outbursts against them by local Nazis. Not only did the Nazis succeed in crushing this demonstration of solidarity, in retaliation they smothered the local resistance, setting back its development for two years, and took other measures that drastically worsened the situation of Jews throughout the Netherlands.[63]

Support for Jews is especially noteworthy when it occurred within a distinctly anti-Jewish framework, as was generally the case in occupied eastern Europe. Nechama Tec, who has conducted extensive interviews with both rescued and rescuers in Poland, was struck by how those who helped Jews swam against a powerful antisemitic current in the Polish population, a current churned by Nazism to some degree of course, but also moved by longstanding Polish traditions.[64] It is all the more important, therefore, to discover what prompted those who did offer help. In what seems to me a circular argument, Tec concludes that rescuers were noted for their "individuality or separateness," "independence or self-reliance," and a "broad and long-ranging commitment to stand up for the helpless and needy"; at the same time she noted that they perceived Jews "in a matter-of-fact unassuming way," did not begin their rescue activity with much planning or premeditation, and thought of Jews in univeralistic terms.[65] One would be surprised if politics had not also played its role. This was evidently the case with the Council for Aid to Jews, known as Żegota, established in the autumn of 1942 by left-of-center political parties and with the support of local representatives of the Polish government in exile, or Delegatura. Like almost everything else associated with Polish-Jewish relations, the role of this organization is a matter of controversy: Poles contend that it reflects a widespread willingness in Poland to help Jews; Jewish critics argue that Żegota's help was too little, too late, and they differ among themselves as to the place of the organization in the Polish political spectrum.[66]

In the complicated politics of the Polish resistance to the Nazi occupation, there is no doubt that a small number of Jews had their place. There were two Jewish representatives on the Polish National Council in London, Shmuel Zygielbojm of the Bund and the Zionist Ignacy Schwartzbart. Through them, and through the channels provided by the Home Army, much of the information about the Holocaust was conveyed to the West. Couriers brought detailed reports; underground radios broadcast detail; and accounts from the Jews themselves were relayed to London. To be sure, the Polish authorities and the underground did not always communicate material on the Jews with appropriate emphasis and dispatch. Moreover, the Poles usually packaged information for public distribution in such a way as to highlight the common suffering of the entire Polish nation—essentially, the official Polish view to this day. The record was far from perfect. Nevertheless, this critical channel remained open. Zygielbojm, whom Walter Laqueur describes as "not by nature the most trusting of men," never complained that the Polish authorities had withheld information from him. Yet he was not reluctant to cast blame—on the free world, for abandoning the Jews, and on himself, for leaving his family behind in Warsaw. When he finally ended his personal nightmare, taking his own life in 1943 as news of the Warsaw ghetto uprising confirmed the very worst, he left a note to the Polish leaders in London protesting against the inaction of "the people and the governments of the Allied states." But he did not single out the Poles.[67]

Laqueur's conclusion is that Polish aid and support should be seen in relation to prewar Polish anti-Jewish opinion and activity. Compared with west European countries, the Poles showed less sympathy and solidarity with the Jews. But compared to some other east Europeans, their record is probably better. Given the extent of the preceding anti-Jewish climate, "it is not surprising that there was so little help, but that there was so much."[68] Perhaps this comment may apply to other European countries as well.

6. THE VICTIMS

THERE ARE FEW more durable generalizations about the history of the Holocaust than the characterization of Jewish passivity in the face of mortal threat. "The Jews," it has often been said, "went to their deaths like sheep to the slaughter." While the Nazis certainly commented in this sense at the time and subsequently, this most famous of analogies, with its overtones of biblical sacrifice, came in the first instance from the Jews themselves as a call to arms and a refusal to acquiesce in German policies. At the beginning of 1942, young Zionists in the ghetto of Vilna issued a manifesto in Hebrew and Yiddish, composed by Abba Kovner and entitled "Let Us Not Be Led Like Sheep to the Slaughter," that helped spark the formation of a united front of resistance. A year later, in Warsaw, in an effort to goad their hesitant or resigned compatriots to a suicidal revolt, the mainstream Jewish Fighting Organization issued a proclamation: "Jewish masses, the hour is drawing near. You must be prepared to resist, not to give yourselves up to slaughter like sheep." Another manifesto, attributed to the right-wing Jewish Military Union, declared: "Know that deliverance is not to be found in going to your death impassively, like sheep to the slaughter." And again, the Warsaw ghetto diary of Emmanuel Ringelblum contains this anguished entry for 15 October 1942, after the massive deportations of that year: "Why didn't we resist when they began to resettle

300,000 Jews from Warsaw? Why did we allow ourselves to be led like sheep to the slaughter?"[1]

Raul Hilberg argued powerfully for this assessment in his magisterial *Destruction of the European Jews,* which first appeared in 1961. Only a few pages of Hilberg's work concerned Jewish reactions, but these lines were undoubtedly the most controversial and passionately contested. They were also the product of firm conviction, for almost a quarter of a century later his contention reappears without change or modification in the new and definitive edition. Hilberg is unsparing in his critique of Jewish passivity. "The reaction pattern of the Jews is characterized by almost complete lack of resistance," he writes. "The Jews attempted to tame the Germans as one would attempt to tame a wild beast. They avoided 'provocations' and complied instantly with decrees and orders. They hoped somehow that the German drive would spend itself." At times, in efforts to curry favor with the oppressor or simply to prevent unnecessary suffering, Jews even moved ahead of the Germans, in what the author calls "anticipatory compliance." Hilberg sees this pattern, moreover, not only in the behavior of Jewish leaders, but in the responses of the masses as well. The death camps, he notes, were thinly guarded—by as few as four thousand men. Everything depended upon the Jews moving along an assembly line, the product of which was murder. For the most part, the Jews were incapable of acting otherwise. Outbreaks did happen, he acknowledges, but these were almost always "local occurrences that transpired at the last moment." How does he explain this reaction? Hilberg assumes that this response was peculiarly Jewish and can be traced to "a 2,000-year old experience." Throughout their long period of exile, "the Jews had always been a minority, always in danger, but had learned that they could avert or survive destruction by placating and appeasing their enemies." Having responded in this manner for so many centuries, the Jews could not act otherwise when confronted by Nazism. "A 2,000-year old lesson could not be unlearned; the Jews could not make the switch. They were helpless."[2]

Against a firestorm of criticism, Hilberg insisted that his few pages treating the Jews were essential to the argument of his massive work.[3] As he candidly explained, "I had to delve into the ques-

tion of Jewish behavior by the sheer force of logic of my own outline of the process of destruction." That outline, as we have seen,
involved a relentless description of *how* the Jews were destroyed.
Hilberg's unsparing conclusion was that the "process of destruction, though initiated and planned by the Germans, ultimately depended upon certain kinds of behavior by the victims." Prompted
by their traditions, Jews too became part of the machine. Brooding
on the results, Hilberg cited the description of his victims by death
camp commandant Franz Stangl, facing trial, in a West German
prison. "He said that only recently he had read a book about lem-
mings. It reminded him of Treblinka."[4]

Hilberg referred to the Jews' tendency for "automatic compliance" with Nazi orders. And as he made clear, this disposition was
not only the response of beaten, starved, abandoned people. Emblematic of this response were the Jewish councils or *Judenräte,* set
up by the Nazis throughout occupied Europe, but having particular
importance in the ghettos of eastern Europe. Their policy was "institutional compliance." Drawing almost entirely upon German
sources, Hilberg stressed the basic sameness in the history of the
councils, despite differences in detail. All were linked to some German or satellite control organ. All became "implements of German
will," moving the Jews through the various phases of the destruction process—"registrations for housing or ghettoization, statistical
and other informational reports, taxation or sequestration for German uses, wall building, notification of victims to report for labor
or 'evacuation,' even the compiling of transport lists, as well as
roundups conducted by the German police."[5] Certainly, one detects
in much of the German documentation a tendency to portray Jews
according to the Nazi stereotype—cringing, acquiescent, and easily
manipulated by crude appeals to individual interest. Undoubtedly
this is how the councils appeared from the SS Gettoverwaltung and
other Nazi control agencies. But is this picture accurate? And did
"Jewish traditions" somehow determine passive Jewish responses?
As subsequent critics pointed out, Hilberg was remarkably thin in
his discussion of the inner world of diverse Jewish communities. It
remained unclear whether other source material, coming from the
Jewish side, would help resolve these questions.

Reporting on the Eichmann trial, which opened in the spring of
1961 in Jerusalem, the German-Jewish political philosopher Hannah

Arendt drew heavily on Hilberg's interpretation. In a wide-ranging discussion of the significance of the trial itself and the role of the accused in the destruction process, she returned again and again to the Jews themselves. Her target was the Jewish leadership, whose behavior, she said, Hilberg had for the first time exposed "in all its pathetic and sordid detail." "The role of these leaders in the destruction of their own people," claimed Arendt, "is undoubtedly the darkest chapter of the whole dark story." Her accusation was even more sweeping than the principal source on which she relied. Whether in eastern or western Europe, Jewish leaders performed vital tasks for their Nazi masters, directly facilitating their murderous objective. "In Amsterdam as in Warsaw, in Berlin as in Budapest, Jewish officials could be trusted to compile the lists of persons and of their property, to secure money from the deportees to defray the expenses of their deportation and extermination, to keep track of vacated apartments, to supply police forces to help seize Jews and get them on trains, until, as a last gesture, they handed over the assets of the Jewish community in good order for the final confiscation." Previously ignored, this complicity was a crucial piece in the puzzle of the Holocaust. "The whole truth was," she said in typically categorical fashion, "that if the Jewish people had really been unorganized and leaderless, there would have been chaos and plenty of misery but the total number of victims would hardly have been between four and a half and six million people."[6]

To Arendt, the Jerusalem court's failure to make this indictment was a grave omission, and she carried the burden of denouncing this Jewish leadership as though no one but herself would undertake the task. On this point, she spoke with the innocence of a recent convert, for in the Jewish world at least, charges and countercharges of "Jewish collaboration" were common in the immediate postwar period, and "courts of honor" debated dozens of times the kinds of questions she raised. Much less noticed in her argument, however, likely because she did not stress it herself, was an attempt to situate this Jewish "cooperation" in a wider context of European culture—something that preoccupied her at the time, as she was completing her somber *Origins of Totalitarianism*. For Arendt, there was no special Jewish predilection for passivity. Rather, she claimed that the Jews' reaction "offers the most striking insight into the totality of the moral collapse the Nazis caused in respectable

European society—not only in Germany but in almost all countries, not only among the persecutors but also among the victims."[7] Arendt wrote as a moralist, and her historical judgments were meant to hammer home some fundamental truths about human behavior and responsibilities in a world of powerful bureaucracies. Her intended message was universal. Although it was the Jews who were murdered in the Holocaust, the victims could have been any group; presumably there would have been no difficulty recruiting both perpetrators and collaborators. The real problem lay in a process of dehumanization plaguing modern societies, which it was the task of political philosophers to analyze and evaluate. On this level, Arendt's discourse cut loose from ordinary experience and left most readers far behind. What they remembered, and remember to this day, is a historical assessment that was deeply flawed and oddly unconcerned with the specific events she described.[8]

Before the publication of Arendt's work, historical discussion of the Jews under Nazism was primarily concerned with martyrology—described as "the obligation to preserve and memorialize the tragic events of the war, if only in their bare detail, in their heartrending repetitiveness."[9] From this point, however, we can discern a different trend. To respond to what many felt an irresponsible slight upon the victims of Nazism, some historians now launched serious historical analyses of Jewish responses to Hitlerian persecution in particular circumstances. Monographic research, much of it undertaken by Israeli scholars using Jewish sources, now spoke with greater authority than ever before on how Jews reacted. In addition, the long-suppressed sensibilities of survivors broke through the surface in the form of concrete reflections on Jewish behavior that had hitherto not seen the light of day. Outstanding ghetto diaries and other first-hand accounts, some of which appeared earlier in limited editions, were now much more widely published.

As such works accumulated, appreciation of the extended agonies of Jewish communities deepened. No longer was all attention riveted, as in the works of Arendt and Hilberg, on the destruction process alone and the dreadful moments of killing. Instead, more intimate study of particular Jewish communities suggested a long, drawn-out process of attrition, in which the victims had no knowledge of, and no way of knowing, the final outcome. In a word, the historical sense has been enhanced. Historians continue to judge, as historians will, but the edge has worn off some of the pronouncements on Jewish leaders and followers. Meanwhile, as understanding of their excruciating dilemmas deepens, studies appear that broaden our perspective on Jewish responses by looking at a variety of Jewish communities and by venturing comparisons with other groups of threatened civilians.

EAST EUROPEAN GHETTOS

Discussion of the Jewish leadership moved to a new plane with the publication in 1972 of Isaiah Trunk's *Judenrat,* devoted to the study of the Jewish councils set up by the Nazis in occupied eastern Europe. Trunk's work was painstakingly researched and anchored in extensive archival sources embracing every aspect of the activities of these *Judenräte.* Unlike Arendt, who was quick to generalize, Trunk overwhelmed the reader with detail, showing how many different paths were taken by Jewish leaders. At the very least, one must conclude from his exposition that there was a variety of Jewish responses. Beyond this, Trunk emphasized that the Jews were *forced* to establish the councils, that individuals were *forced* to serve on them, and that the councils were *forced* to provide services for the Germans. The ghettos' widely detested Jewish police, who often participated in the "resettlements" of Jews for deportation, were subjected to the most cruel forms of blackmail to induce them to do so. Almost invariably they were told that only through such actions could they and their families be spared a similar fate. While in retrospect it seems plain that the *Judenräte* did assist the Nazis, at the time most of their members felt they had little choice. Illustrating the difficulty of generalizing beyond a few basic issues, Trunk discussed the councils thematically, considering such issues as their organization, personnel, finance, public welfare, medical facilities, police, religion, and so forth. Seen this way, it becomes apparent that Berlin set few guidelines for the *Judenräte* and that their circumstances differed enormously. "Utter lawlessness and virtual anarchy prevailed in the territories under German occupation during World War II." [10] This is the apt, first sentence of the book, the constant backdrop of which is the terror, degradation, and spoliation that the Nazis wrought in eastern Europe. Trunk noted that some councils supported resistance activities—some violent, and some not—and that others opposed them; some ran corrupt and class-ridden ghettos, and others strove for equality. One might, of course, still make harsh judgments on the basis of this evidence; interestingly, Trunk's survey of the attitudes of survivors suggests that with the passage of time their own evaluations of the Jewish councils were increasingly positive.[11]

The increasing recourse to Jewish sources has by no means guaranteed a sympathetic view of ghetto leadership. Hilberg found confirmation of his views in the diary of the head of the Warsaw *Judenrat*, Adam Czerniakow, published in English in 1979.[12] An industrial engineer and Polish patriot, Czerniakow was an assimilationist Jew active in communal affairs, named by the mayor of Warsaw to lead the Jewish community in that city after its previous chairman fled. When the Germans arrived, Czerniakow was summoned to Gestapo headquarters and told to organize a Jewish council. Czerniakow, Hilberg notes, "was a caretaker, not so much of a community, as of its countless afflictions, and his entire official life was much less a singular daily effort to save a people than a whole series of efforts to save people every day."[13] He constantly intervened with the German authorities to obtain concessions, alleviate shortages, and suspend the most cruel of regulations. His daily notes portray Czerniakow as a courageous man of little vision, crushed by the terrible burdens he faced, and unable to break out of his imposed task. In the end, when faced in the summer of 1942 with the Nazis' demands for deportees, he swallowed cyanide and killed himself. For Hilberg, leaders like Czerniakow became "psychological captives of the perpetrator," lulled into a state of "institutional subservience." Almost always his efforts were stamped with failure. His diary "gives voice to an overwhelming sense of powerlessness and futility."[14]

Others, however, see nobility in the engineer turned community leader, who sacrificed himself for what he believed to be a historic task. They see Czerniaków as struggling valiantly to maintain Jewish communal existence—no mean achievement in the face of escalating German pressures and demands. They stress his evasive responses to the authorities, his exploitation of differences among the Germans, his constant playing for time. Of course, such strategies may not fit our heroic model and may not have been the wisest in the long run. So it appears in hindsight. Yet at the time of Czerniakow's suicide, as Yisrael Gutman pertinently points out, even the Jewish underground hesitated, was unsure of the best path to follow, and was uncertain about the ghetto's fate.[15]

Opinions on Jewish leadership as a whole are sometimes shaped by the most colorful or articulate of *Judenrat* leaders, those who maintained their position for the longest period or made the deepest impact on their communities. But although striking figures—sometimes larger than life—these are not necessarily representative. Notably, several adapted to the bizarre circumstances of Nazi demands with a heightened sense of their own indispensability. Rather than buckling under the Nazis' pressures, Chaim Rumkowski in Lodz and Jacob Gens in Vilna developed intensely authoritarian styles of leadership, coming to believe that they alone could save a portion of the ghetto inmates. In both cases the Germans gave reason to believe that a productive ghetto might be saved. Both leaders negotiated to save lives in exchange for Jewish labor. Prying loose favors from an implacable foe, both of these men riveted upon the bargaining process. Lives indeed hung on their every move. Both developed illusions about their own achievements, inflated their own self-image to megalomanaical proportions, and developed regal styles of personal rule. Rumkowski rode about the ghetto in a horse-drawn carriage, issued banknotes with his portrait, and was known as King Chaim. While less flamboyant, Gens too assumed dictatorial authority and ruled as Jacob the First. Opinion on these leaders differs, even today. To some the outstanding fact about such *Judenrat* chiefs is their arrogant, single-minded, ruthless style of rule. From the leader's standpoint, however, things looked different. Attacked from every quarter at once, increasingly isolated at the top, facing impossible demands, they often felt that they were the only hope for a squabbling, bitterly divided Jewish community. Both leaders, one should add, understood the charges of collaboration that were made against them at the time and declared their willingness to face courts of honor after the war. Both argued that theirs was the only way to save Jews and confidently expected postwar vindication for what they did. And neither survived to face such judgment.[16]

The main impression conveyed by the Jewish sources, however, is of the diversity of Jewish responses.[17] There are literally scores of ghetto leaders, and it is important to remember that the Germans tolerated only those who satisfied or appeared to satisfy their demands. The others usually did not last long. *Judenrat* leaders were subjected to beatings, direct intimidation, and threats to their families; some were simply shot. Among those who did the Germans' work, it should be added, there were virtually none who "collaborated" in the sense of identifying with wider Nazi aims—such as are found in every occupied society in Europe.[18] Some Jews opposed the formation of the *Judenräte,* and sometimes the Germans simply dragooned Jewish representatives on their own. Once in place, leaders faced the excruciating dilemmas of "collective responsibility": in reprisal for opposition, or even recalcitrance in the executions of their demands, the Germans kidnapped for forced labor or simply massacred ghetto inmates. It is hardly surprising then that those leaders who remained at their posts demonstrated "compliance" with Nazi orders and called for "order" within the ghetto. Beneath the surface, at times, there was other activity. Trunk notes the ambivalence of certain *Judenrat* chiefs: "They were afraid that resistance activities might hinder their carefully contrived strategies to gain time and postpone the liquidation of their ghettos for as long as possible. On the other hand, they favored the idea of physical resistance when the end came." In Białystok, Efraim Barash maintained links with the Jewish resistance, but insisted that any uprising be delayed until just before liberation by the Red Army. In the end, no such opportunity presented itself, the rebels tried to break out of the ghetto, and Barash himself was deported to a death camp.[19]

Researching the ghettos of Galicia, in eastern Poland, Aharon Weiss has demonstrated convincingly that there were many different patterns of behavior, from automatic compliance, through suicide and resistance. This region, held by the Soviets until the summer of 1941, did not have the protracted experience of Nazi occupation as in western Poland, and it underwent a far more rapid process of ghettoization. Jews there had more reason than others to believe in the impermanence of Nazi rule and hence the importance of holding out, preserving Jewish existence until the Germans were driven back. Weiss also noted that there were distinct phases of *Judenrat* activity—with a second tier of leaders having drastically less margin for maneuver than the first. Notably, most of the earliest chairmen came from the ranks of Jewish communal agencies and were often prominent prewar leaders; among the second group the proportion of former communal leaders fell significantly. Most of the original *Judenrat* leaders did not cross what Yehuda Bauer has called "the last moral barrier"—handing over Jews to be murdered; comparing these with the second group, Weiss noted a "steep rise in submissiveness and yielding." Moreover, "yielding" itself involved degrees; some *Judenrat* leaders believed that in sacrificing part of the community they could save the rest; others seem to have abandoned all concern for their fellow Jews and became totally subservient to the Germans.[20]

From a variety of investigations, individual ghettos now appear to us in all their particularity, forcing us to think harder about the strategies Jews adopted under specific circumstances. As Christopher Browning suggests, the German expectation in 1939–40 seems to have been that the Jews would suffer a great "decimation" in the ghettos—precisely what did occur, of course, with the death of nearly one-fifth of Polish Jewry from starvation and disease.[21] This is also what happened, for the most part, to Soviet prisoners of war. Under such conditions, the determination of the Jewish councils to keep the Jews alive under German hegemony was in direct opposition to the Nazis and need not suggest some inappropriate, traditional instinct for compliance. Individuals, moreover, could make a difference—for a time, at least. In Belorussia an interesting case is the important ghetto of Minsk, where the *Judenrat* chairman Ilya Moshkin helped coordinate resistance activity. According to one researcher, the *Judenrat* under Moshkin functioned effectively "as the executive arm of the underground." The latter was composed mostly of Jewish Communists, refugees from the west who had links with partisans in the countryside. Although Moshkin was arrested and hanged by the Germans in early 1942, some *Judenrat* cooperation with the resistance continued even under his successor, Selig Yaffe. However, there were limits to what such leaders could accomplish. In July 1942 the Germans began a massive *Aktion* that lasted three days: the *Judenrat* was wiped out, its leaders killed, and some twenty-five thousand Jews were taken away. Afterward, the ghetto became a work camp, and the Nazis found a much more compliant Jewish leader.[22]

Investigations of various ghettos enable us to see the rationale behind the "work to live" strategy, in which *Judenrat* leaders undertook to rescue inmates by demonstrating their economic utility. In particular circumstances, this strategy appeared to work. Yitzhak Arad has shown how Jews in Vilna capitalized on conflicts within the German administration over Jewish workers. After the intervention of the Wehrmacht in the latter part of 1941, the German authorities in Lithuania decided to suspend the massacres that began with the attack on the Soviet Union. As a result, the Jews of Vilna were permitted to labor for the Third Reich. As head of the local *Judenrat*, Jacob Gens worked feverishly to make Vilna Jewry productive: "Both in the maintenance of industry, and in our work in individual units, we must prove that, contrary to the accepted assumption that we are not fit for any kind of work, we have been very useful, and under present wartime conditions, there is no viable substitute for us."[23] To the last, Efraim Barash in Białystok believed that the Wehrmacht's order to manufacture boots guaranteed the survival of the Jews. While this stratagem seems utterly fanciful from our vantage point, it is important to envisage quite a different situation in which it was not. A growing body of literature suggests that such economic considerations were vitally important to the Germans, particularly as the war progressed. Under some circumstances, then, Jews who took this desperate gamble reasoned correctly. Nearly seventy thousand Jews of Lodz survived until August 1944, toiling for the Reich. They were finally massacred with the Red Army only a few days' march from the city.[24]

Although the issues posed by Hilberg and Arendt have tended to set the agenda for the study of east European Jews under Nazi terror, there is another approach for which there is plentiful data and which occasionally appears in treatments of the Holocaust. I refer here to the web of meanings and activities that hundreds of thousands of Jews were forced to create for themselves in the ghettos of Poland and occupied Russia—what one might call the culture of east European ghettos.[25] It may seem paradoxical to mention culture in the same breath as these charnel houses of east European Jewry. Yet culture, of a quite particular sort, undoubtedly existed. Within the ghetto walls, doomed communities spun ideas about themselves and their persecutors, wrestled with the problems of governance, and developed remarkable social, educational, and cultural institutions. Abundant evidence exists—in diaries, ghetto publications, postwar accounts by survivors, and even contemporary reports from the German side. Historians occasionally go beyond general description and venture comments about such institutions as welfare agencies, smuggling and the criminal underworld, medical aid, and conflicts between deportees from the Reich, ghetto newcomers, and "longstanding" residents.[26] With the aid of this material, historians sometimes attempt what the anthropologist Clifford Geertz calls "thick description"—trying, as he says, "to bring us into touch with the lives of strangers."[27]

Occasionally too, exploring the circumstances of ghetto life helps us address the issue of alleged Jewish passivity discussed above. Crucial to any evaluation of the reactions of Jews, for example, is an appreciation of what the ghetto inmates understood by the murderous events that occurred all around them. Of killings there was no doubt, of course, but determining how these were perceived is a complex matter. As the ghettos were usually cut off from the outside, the Jewish inmates received relatively little information. As a result, rumors proliferated—some false and some not. Waves of optimism could break over the desperate population. Ringelblum records on 18 May 1942 that word "spread like lightning" that Göring had been assassinated. "On this meager foundation," he goes on, "the Ghetto built complete castles in the air—about an armistice, peace being declared. People drank toasts to the new days coming, and, for a short time, breathed freely. There were even some people who wanted to cross to the Other Side, for who was there to stop them?"[28] Gruesome evidence abounded, but the search for meaning sent people in plenty of false directions. Killings did not necessarily mean mass murder, it was sometimes thought, and even mass murder did not necessarily mean the kind of universal slaughter to which the Nazis were committed in principle. How much was to be believed? As everywhere, individuals varied in what they were prepared to accept. Summing up, Yisrael Gutman insists that even when massive killing operations were under way, the Jews did not have a full appreciation of the Final Solution. "The heads of these *Judenräte*, together with the majority of the Jews in the ghettos, understood and explained the exterminations as the incarnation of unrestrained hatred and extreme disregard for human lives. They saw the extermination campaign more as an unwillingness to distribute food and other vital necessities to a population which the Germans considered to be inferior and inefficient."[29]

To understand these reactions, it is important to grasp the physical framework—in effect, a dying population, overcome by starvation, exhaustion, and disease. The Polish underground courier Jan Karski provided a horrifying description in 1944, recording his impressions of the Jews after a visit to the Warsaw ghetto two years before: "These were still living people, if you could call them such. For apart from their skin, eyes, and voice there was nothing human left in these palpitating figures. Everywhere there was hunger, misery, the atrocious stench of decomposing bodies, the pitiful moans of dying children, the desperate cries and gasps of a people struggling for life against impossible odds. . . . The entire population of the ghetto seemed to be living in the street. There was hardly a square yard of empty space. As we picked our way across the mud and rubble, the shadows of what had once been men or women flitted by us in pursuit of someone or something, their eyes blazing with some insane hunger or greed."[30] To these impressions one can add remarkable evidence collected with clinical exactitude. Doctors in Warsaw, for example, working in the Health Department of the *Judenrat,* organized an elaborate research project in 1942 on the effects of starvation on children and adults. They did not want for subjects. Drawing on their records, smuggled out before the final liquidation of the ghetto, it is possible to examine the effects of the catastrophe with scientific precision.[31]

Despite such horrors, the sources also suggest that life, of a sort, went on. Once conditions stabilized, the ghettos constituted minirepublics of Jews, largely cut off from the outside world and freed to develop their own, Jewish institutions. In their urban prisons, the Jews created theaters and concert halls, schools and hospitals, synagogues and newspapers. Some historians, notably Lucy Dawidowicz and Yehuda Bauer, see these as instruments deliberately intended to foil the Germans' goal of degrading the Jews.[32] There is certainly evidence for this point of view. Describing his fellow Jews in the Warsaw ghetto a few months after it was sealed, Chaim Kaplan noted an uncharacteristic but not unheard of outburst of frivolity: "In the daytime, when the sun is shining, the ghetto groans. But at night everyone is dancing even though his stomach is empty.

Quiet, discreet evening music accompanies the dancing. It is almost a *mitzvah* [a divine commandment] to dance. The more one dances, the more it is a sign of his belief in the 'eternity of Israel.' Every dance is a protest against our oppressors." [33] There is no doubt that the Jews invested tremendous energy in what Dawidowicz calls "the alternative community." Yitzhak Arad mentions the public library established in the Vilna ghetto, with forty-five thousand volumes. In December 1942, residents celebrated the borrowing of the one hundred thousandth book with a festival at the local theater. [34] Vilna was also remarkable for its ghetto theater, producing plays, concerts, choruses, and other entertainments—all faithfully recorded in the records of the ghetto cultural department. Each Sunday in March of 1943, we learn, there were six or seven performances, with two thousand people in attendance. [35] Chroniclers in the ghetto of Lodz noted in November 1943 how Jews responded to the forcible closing of the House of Culture: "the ghetto dweller, hardened by countless misfortunes, always seeks new ways to sate his hunger for something of cultural value. The need for music is especially intense, and small centers for the cultivation of music have sprung up over time. . . . Sometimes it is professional musicians, sometimes amateurs who perform for an intimate group of invited guests. Chamber music is played, and there is singing. Likewise, small, family-like circles form in order to provide spiritual nourishment on a modest level. Poets and prose writers read from their own works. The classics and more recent works of world literature are recited." [36]

Can one speak of the mood of these ghettos? No one has attempted adequately to analyze the flood of different emotions that various sources communicate to us—hope, demoralization, despair, bitterness at being abandoned, fear, anger, piety, and even a sense of shame. Similarly, no one has tried systematically to collate elements of the sociology of particular ghettos, their widely different relationships to work, the larger urban environment, the Nazi authorities, geographic circumstances, and so forth. When historians are able to generalize about these issues more confidently, the dichotomies of acquiescence and resistance that have so dominated discussions of ghetto life will likely fade rapidly from historical discussion. And in the process, our assessments will have matured.

CENTRAL AND WEST EUROPEAN JEWRY

Research on the Jewish leadership in other countries has similarly undermined some of the sweeping generalizations of Jewish passivity. In particular, investigations of German Jewry suggest a far more persistent and resourceful response to persecution—albeit with the most meager of resources—than traditional stereotypes would allow. Studies of Jewish emigration from the Reich, for example, are hardly consistent with the idea of a community burying its head in the sand. One out of ten of the approximately 525,000 people in Germany identifying in some way with the Jewish religion left the country immediately after the Nazis took power, and close to 150,000 emigrated before Kristallnacht, in November 1938. This was roughly one-fourth of the total population deemed "non-Aryan" by the Nazis. Thereafter, under increasingly heavy pressure, another 150,000 left.[37] Undoubtedly more would have done so if they had been permitted access to countries in western Europe and America, and to Palestine. And virtually no one, not even the most experienced Zionist leaders, those who one might think would be especially prescient on the need for mass evacuation from Europe, looked to a complete termination of the Jewish presence in Germany in the immediate future.[38] From the standpoint of emigration, then, the notion of German Jews blindly deluding themselves under Hitler seems hardly tenable.

In a recent study of the cultured German-Jewish elite—the *Bildungsbürgertum*—George Mosse suggests that there was a particular humanitarian ethos shared by German Jewry, defined by an Enlightenment commitment to culture, self-cultivation, and tolerance.[39] Reflecting on his own German-Jewish past, Mosse sees the Jewish identity in Germany as intertwined with such principles. It has often been suggested that such ideals incapacitated German Jews, not only isolating them in German society but also rendering them incapable of assessing the dangers that faced them under the Nazis. Sidney Bolkosky, for example, identifies among German Jews a "refusal to confront real life, a tendency to block out or repress reality."[40] Yet however isolated German Jews may have found themselves in German society, it is doubtful whether these cultural ideals rendered them incapable of attending to their own interests. True, many Jews seem to have believed in 1933 that the Hitler phenomenon would pass and that conditions for Jews in Germany would eventually improve. But Jews were hardly alone in this evaluation. Rather, it was the conventional wisdom, not only among most conservatives and anti-Nazi elements in Germany itself but by experienced observers in the capitals of Europe as well.[41]

For some writers, the remarkable envigoration of Jewish cultural life in the first years of the Nazi regime contrasts with the atrophy of political sense among Jewish leaders. However, a closer look at the umbrella organization for German Jews from mid-1939 that was the counterpart of east European *Judenräte*—the Reichsvereinigung, or National Union of Jews in Germany—suggests a more complicated picture. For as long as they could, German-Jewish leaders strove to further emigration and to minister to the needs of their community. It is hard to gainsay their sense of duty. As Rabbi Leo Baeck, the National Union's president, put it, "I shall be the last to leave. . . . As long as a *minyan* exists in Berlin, here is my place. . . . Not until the last Jew is saved."[42] Dov Kulka's research on the Reichsvereinigung, based on the discovery of voluminous material from its archives in East Berlin, suggests action on a clandestine level as well as that permitted by the Gestapo.[43] The SS constantly badgered and bullied the Jewish leaders, drastically narrowing their field of operation. It is only in retrospect that the Reichsvereinigung's "real function," as Lucy Dawidowicz says, appears as "the final liquidation of German Jewry."[44] Until 1941, one must remember, the Nazis' declared goal for the Jews was mass emigration—a project to which the Jewish leaders devoted serious attention. The Reichsvereinigung can hardly be blamed for taking Nazi spokesmen seriously on this point, and the sources suggest that this was one of the organization's main efforts, along with providing emergency aid to Jews who remained in Germany. When deportations actually began in the autumn of 1941, there is no evidence that the Berlin leadership worked together with the Gestapo in preparing deportation lists, as some historians have implied. Local branches of the organization certainly did so, however, and detailed study of individual communities is likely to indicate the particular circumstances in which this transpired. From his analysis of the situation in the Rhenish town of Worms, Henry Huttenbach notes that the orders came from Berlin and that noncompliance "would in no way have disrupted the deportation process." By the end of 1941 the SS had complete lists of all the local Jews and complete power to do with them what they wished.[45]

Sensitive to how careful one must be in evaluating the sources that describe the activity of the Jewish councils, Livia Rothkirchen refers to the "endless web of deception" enveloping the documents historians use. For obvious reasons neither Jews nor Germans said what they meant in their correspondence with each other. In the case of Slovakia, which she has studied closely, the "Jewish Center" performed a "dual role," both helping the implementation of the Final Solution on the one hand and attempting to safeguard Jewish interests on the other.[46] This pattern is common throughout western Europe, as several historians have observed. Bela Vago has an analogous evaluation of the Rumanian "Jewish Center," accused as "collaborators of the collaborators" for having worked under the authority of Marshal Antonescu. The Rumanian case differs from the German and Slovakian in that the veteran Jewish leadership remained entirely outside the new body. The head of this organization, indeed, was a Jewish convert to Catholicism who was chosen by the Germans. Of "collaboration," in this case, there was no doubt. Notable also, however, were the contacts of the Jewish Center with the traditional Jewish leaders to relieve the effects of persecution—especially for the desperate Jews deported to Transnistria. The leading figure in Rumanian Jewish life, Wilhelm Filderman, intervened energetically with authorities in Bucharest and seems to have used the channels of the Jewish Center in part for this purpose.[47]

Studying the French equivalent, the Union générale des Israélites de France (UGIF), Richard Cohen is similarly cautious in rendering judgment.[48] As with most of the councils outside Poland and occupied Russia, the UGIF never operated in a ghetto situation and was never directly responsible for preparing deportation lists. It did, however, coordinate a range of social services for the Jewish community, kept track of the whereabouts of many Jews, and as such it helped facilitate their rounding up when the Final Solution began in the west, in the summer of 1942. Some writers have charged the UGIF with flagrant negligence, or even worse. Not long ago a French journalist wrote a book in this vein entitled *Jews in Collaboration*.[49] But in editing the remarkable wartime diary of Raymond Raoul Lambert, arguably the most important Jewish official in contact with the Vichy government and the Germans, Cohen has brought to light a Jew who is certainly neither obedient nor ingenuous in his dealings with the oppressors.[50] He may indeed have been wrong to work with the French or German authorities, trying through official channels to ease the lot of indigent Jews or attempting to snatch individual Jews from the camps or deportation trains, but he certainly had good reason for believing that he was right. Lambert, who was murdered in Auschwitz in 1943, was a complex personality, a highly assimilated Frenchman and French patriot. The evidence suggests that, like many heads of the Jewish councils, he became involved in clandestine efforts to ease the lot of Jews and even in resistance activity—at the same time that he was working through official channels. Like many other Jewish leaders, facing tremendous strain and moral pressure, he seems to have fallen victim to the self-serving illusion of his own indispensability for his Jewish charges. In retrospect his actions are best understood in the light of a long history of assimilation, a tradition of paternalistic Jewish community leadership, the profound demoralization of French Jewry, and the extraordinarily difficult objective situation he faced.

In the Netherlands, where deportations devastated the Jewish population of 140,000, carrying away 80 percent of their number, the role of the official Jewish leadership had particular importance. Led by the respected diamond merchant Abraham Asscher and Prof. David Cohen, the Joodse Raad, as it was known, was bitterly opposed by a rival Jewish group that objected to working with the Germans. The council published Nazi ordinances with respect to the Jews in its newspaper, distributed the yellow badges Jews were forced to wear, and benefited from a "privileged" status for themselves and their families. Asscher and Cohen scrupulously avoided resistance, assisted in the implementation of deportations, and eventually handed over the names of seven thousand council members for dispatch to death camps in Poland. Joseph Michman ponders carefully the kind of judgment historians should make in such cases. To put the matter into perspective, he accentuates the extensive help the Germans received from the authorities in the Netherlands—"at all levels, from registration of the Jews to their removal to transit camps in trains guarded by Dutch policemen." More than 90 percent of the Dutch population did not participate in the resistance, and managed to adopt a reasonably decent posture and avoid being killed by remaining in the background. Unfortunately, such non-involvement was simply not possible for the Jews. It makes sense for the historian to examine carefully the assumptions under which men like Asscher and Cohen worked. In very few cases can one find a pattern of deception or a deliberate attempt to betray their co-religionists. Seen in this light, the Jewish administration and its leaders appear more naïve than criminal, more seduced than enticed into collaboration, and far down the chain of responsibility.[51]

"Was there any possibility of a different policy?" This is the question Michman puts about the Dutch Jewish council—a question that could easily be asked about any of the councils we have examined.[52] In my view, the question seems less and less appropriate, and historians appear to be turning from what might have been done to understanding what the Jews actually did do. It is probably true that, in general, the Jewish elite were less disposed than many to believe the worst. Lucjan Dobroszycki points to their "confidence in the strength of international conventions, in the power of law, and in the supremacy of civilization." And he goes on: "they believed that no matter what might happen, there was no place for barbarity in the middle of the twentieth century and in the middle of Europe."[53] This was hardly a Jewish particularity, however. Moreover, it is doubtful whether the Jewish leadership could have made much of a difference. Given the overwhelming nature of Nazi power, and given the disposition of collaborating governments to assist in the Final Solution, the Jews had virtually no chance.

THE CAMPS

Historians have said remarkably little about the world of Nazi camps, whose horrifying landscape has been mainly described in survivors' memoirs and by literary critics who have built upon these accounts.[54] Of the memoirs we shall have relatively little to say here. Hundreds exist. Some are among the most important literary documents of our time; others seem defeated in the struggle with words. Almost all of them seem to despair, in one way or another, of the task to which they are nevertheless committed—to communicate across an abyss of experience, to portray a universe that is unspeakable, yet of which they feel a necessity to speak. Secondary works, while often intended as a basis for philosophical reflection or commemoration, nevertheless provide the grist for historical discussion. About these compilations, historians have something to say.

From the Nazis' administrative accounts, we are able to place the hundreds of concentration camps within the framework of the Third Reich and to differentiate the special role of the handful of death camps—those that were mainly or exclusively devoted to murder. It is important to see these grotesque creations as part of a vast system, holding more than 600,000 inmates of every nationality by 1943 and 1944. This growth coincided with the radicalization of the regime and notably the increasing importance of the SS, under Heinrich Himmler. At the end of 1938 the system held about 30,000 prisoners, with a large turnover as inmates were released after a period of intimidation. With the outbreak of war, the concentration camp network vastly expanded. Thereafter, the rates of violence, maltreatment, and mortality soared. It is not certain how many ultimately passed through the camps. Olga Wormser-Migot estimates between 2 million and 3 million, excluding Jewish deportees, and thinks that one-quarter of these died behind the barbed wire. But the matter has not been thoroughly researched, and we cannot be sure about global figures.[55]

According to most authorities, the entire camp structure underwent significant changes in 1942, as the German war effort bogged down and the demand for labor increased. Gradually, the camps were seen as pools of forced labor in addition to being part of the terror apparatus of the regime. During this period the camps came under the authority of the Main Office for Economy and Administration of the SS (Wirtschafts- und Verwaltungs hauptamt, or WVHA), and several industrial giants of the German economy made arrangements with the SS to exploit the prisoners' labor.[56] At the same time, however, killing became a distinct function of the system. On orders from Berlin, several camps took over part of the murderous operations that were proceeding with such destructive force in former Soviet territories. In the autumn of 1941, the first experiments with the deadly Zyklon B gas were undertaken at Auschwitz, using Soviet prisoners of war. Shortly after, gassings occurred at Chelmno, near Lodz in western Poland. Systematic killings on a similar model followed at Belzec, Sobibor, and Treblinka in 1942. That spring, with Operation Reinhard, murder operations targeted the *Generalgouvernement* of Poland. In the summer, deportations from western Europe reached Auschwitz, which became the principal killing center in 1943. According to Hilberg, up to 3 million Jews died in camps of various kinds, most of whom perished in the principal death camps in Poland. In addition, however, several hundred thousand were worked to death or otherwise died of maltreatment in dozens of satellite camps in Germany or eastern Europe, or in major centers such as Mauthausen, in Austria.[57]

Along with the accounts of survivors, a few memoirs from the Nazi side, written after the war, offer portraits of the victims—highly dubious as representations of reality, but deeply revealing of the motives and blind spots of the perpetrators themselves.[58] Such accounts also provide clues as to the working of the camps and the tortures their victims endured. A recurring theme of relevance to Jewish behavior is the strenuous effort made to deceive the Jews—up to the last moment. Rudolf Höss, commandant of Auschwitz, a man who swelled with pride at the systems he created, recalled how the Jews were herded to their lethal "showers"; hints of murder were everywhere, but efforts to deceive continued, so that everything "should take place in an atmosphere of the greatest possible calm."[59] In his conversations with the journalist Gita Sereny in 1971, Treblinka commandant Franz Stangl told similarly of the camouflage at that death factory. He even built a fake railway station where the tracks reached the camp, complete with clock ("with painted numerals and hands which never moved, but no one was thought likely to notice that"), and signs that pointed in various directions—to Warsaw, Bialystok, and other destinations. There were relatively few Germans present. According to Stangl, Treblinka had only twenty SS and a detachment of eighty Ukrainian guards.[60] Despite his concern with efficiency, Höss gave evidence that Auschwitz could hardly manage under the staggering tasks assigned to it. During the massacre of Hungarian Jewry, he said, as many as nine thousand people were being killed daily (likely a considerable underestimation); reading between the lines, one learns of traffic jams on entry into the camp; crematoria that could not consume enough bodies; and warehouses bulging with unsorted effects of the dead. Far from being a model of efficient management, the camp seethed with corruption. Temptations and bribery were everywhere. "Jewish gold," wrote Höss with grotesque opacity, not to mention his anti-semitism, "was a catastrophe for the camp."[61]

Several writers have tried to say something about the bizarre society of inmates—referring necessarily to those who were spared the first "selections," and survived, for a time, in grueling conditions of forced labor. Following the patterns they established everywhere, the Nazis preferred whenever possible to have others bear the burden of control and management: they empowered camp elders, clerks, block leaders, and so forth to supervise the inmates and assume primary responsibility for the routines of daily life. Kapos, as they were called, directed the laborers and were themselves controlled by a small group of SS who remained in the background. The general impression is of a highly stratified system, in which the Nazis encouraged division and widespread corruption, broadly referred to in camp jargon as "organization." Jews remained at the bottom of this system—ruled by other categories of prisoners (usually non-Jewish Germans or criminals) and encouraged to prey upon their fellows to scrape together the means and conditions of subsistence.[62]

Historians are specialists in context. Their best work often involves a creative leap of the imagination by which they enter a culture entirely different from their own, divined by the materials they read. With the world of camps, however, what David Rousset called *l'univers concentrationnaire,* historians have special difficulties.[63] More than one has balked at a systematic investigation of this universe in general studies of the Holocaust, and historians have added little to the first-hand accounts of survivors. Part of the difficulty may be that administrative records were destroyed in the dying days of the Third Reich. Or it may simply be that the leap requires more imaginative energy than historians usually muster. For this task the terrain is so unfamiliar, the frame of reference so horrifying and bizarre, and the cultural landmarks so unintelligible that customary historical methods may simply fail. Perhaps as a result, many of the accounts that we have of this world come from students of literature or psychology. These writers roam more freely through a nightmarish world separated from ordinary experience, and they have, in a number of cases, provided remarkable insights.

One of the influential treatments came from the German-born psychoanalyst Bruno Bettelheim in 1943. Applying some of the basic canons of his discipline, Bettelheim drew on his experiences as an internee in Dachau and Buchenwald in 1938, in an article that has been republished, revised, and extensively discussed.[64] Bettelheim's theory is sometimes unfairly taken as the psychological counterpart of the arguments by Hilberg and Arendt—seen as disparaging Jews for their passivity.[65] According to the author, a crucial requisite for survival in the camps was the maintenance of individual autonomy and sense of self. Within the camps, the Nazis set out deliberately to dehumanize their victims, to break down their autonomy and turn them into "docile masses from which no individual or group act of resistance could arise." When they succeeded, the result was the often-observed phenomenon known by camp jargon as *Muselmänner,* taken from an alleged Muslim belief in fatalism—"people who were so deprived of affect, self esteem, and every form of stimulation, so totally exhausted, both physically and emotionally, that they had given the environment total power over them." More than one survivor has claimed that the *Muselmänner* formed, as Primo Levi says, "the backbone of the camp," the great majority of the prisoners.[66] As Bettelheim saw it, the Nazi camps stripped these inmates of their individuality, shattered their self-respect, and "made it impossible to see themselves as fully adult persons any more." "The main goal of the Nazi effort," he concluded, "seemed to be to produce in their subjects childlike attitudes and dependency on the will of the leaders."[67]

One could struggle against this system, and some managed, against all odds, to preserve an element of their own autonomy. Bettelheim described his own effort to resist the disintegration of his own personality by provoking an SS officer. But it would be wrong to see his analysis as a slight on the victims themselves. As he quite properly reminds us, survival depended overwhelmingly on being liberated from the outside and on extraordinary good luck. Relatively speaking, there was very little that prisoners could do to affect their fate. Although his mode of analysis may suggest otherwise, Bettelheim is fully aware of how mundane factors could determine the fate of individuals—an indoor work assignment, for example, or a friendship with someone in a privileged position, or the possession of a valued skill. Beyond this, Bettelheim saw no special Jewish vocation for surrender, and he refused to join with Arendt in a wholesale condemnation of Jewish organizations. The focus of his work was the awesome power of the Nazis' totalitarian structures and their crippling effects on the human personality.[68]

Specialists continue to debate these matters, and the issue is by no means settled. Drawing upon the insights of both psychology and history, George Kren and Leon Rappoport suggested that one factor may have been particularly disabling for Jews in Nazi camps— what they call "the fallacy of innocence." According to this notion, the Jews' utter innocence worked against them by weakening their ability to assess their plight. "If individuals or groups cast in the role of victim are aware of being innocent—that is, that there is no rational basis for their status as victims—there follows an almost inevitable and fallacious conclusion. They can only assume that their oppression proceeds from a mistaken judgment or a momentary lapse of rationality by their oppressor. In this case, the cause of their predicament must lie in the oppressor. It then follows that if this cause or fault in the oppressor can be understood ('Why do you mistake me for something I am not?') it can be corrected, or at least moderated."[69] Various writers believe that this frame of mind had a considerable effect on Jews. Elie Cohen, for example, contrasted the Jews' situation with that of criminals in the camps: "This feeling of being innocent and yet having to suffer all this misery aroused self-pity and weakened the energy that was necessary for survival."[70] A Polish sociologist, herself a prisoner in Auschwitz, made a similar observation contrasting those who were sent to the camp for resisting the Nazis and those who were sent there "accidentally"—that is, Jews, hostages, forced laborers, and so forth. "Those who were sent there by chance found it more difficult to accept their lot; most of them were psychically unprepared for the horror of the camp."[71]

Historical context becomes extremely important in assessing the Jews' encounter with this hellish environment. As with the *Judenräte,* historians must take care not to lose sight of how a highly coercive environment conditioned the victims' outlook. In the case of Bettelheim, critics have contended that his psychological models derive from his own experiences of camp life in the late 1930s and may not apply to the even more brutal and regimented regimes introduced a few years later. And more than one other interpretation of Jewish responses seems to have been shaken by a close investigation of the particular conditions described. For example, in an essay entitled "The Ignored Lesson of Anne Frank," Bettelheim suggested that the Frank family responded in an understandable, though highly dangerous fashion to Nazi inhumanity. Their outlook, he contended, depended on "primitive and infantile thought processes": engaging in what he once called "massive denial," the family attempted to maintain normalcy and disregarded the terrible threat they faced. What they should have done, he suggested, was "to hide out singly, each with a different family." Instead, they clung together. Bettelheim's alternative, however, seems to imply a much higher degree of prescience and resourcefulness than is reasonable to expect for a bourgeois Jewish émigré family in occupied Amsterdam. Neither the Franks' prior experience, nor the availability of safe havens, nor their meager resources seem to have made Bettelheim's preferred strategy a reasonable option at the time. Culture and circumstance, therefore, may explain the situation much better than a psychoanalytic model.[72]

A similar line of criticism has led Terrence Des Pres to reject the applicability of Bettelheim's psychoanalytic methods in circumstances of extreme necessity.[73] In Des Pres's view, much of the behavior of prisoners in the camps can be better understood by contemplating the physical impact of the hideous conditions they faced. Other scholars have challenged the focus on survival in much of the writing on the camps, including that of both Des Pres and Bettelheim. This focus, they say, derives from the principal sources used in such work—the testimony of the entirely unrepresentative few who did manage to survive. The rest, as a rule, have left no record of their own and will forever remain silent. To the extent that it is possible, however, historians must tell their story as well.

7. JEWISH RESISTANCE

THE VERY TERM *Jewish resistance* suggests a point of view. We normally think of it as a blow struck on behalf of Jews. But to many Jews in Vilna in 1943, for example, the escape of a group of Jewish fighters from the ghetto to join partisans in the nearby Narotch Forest was not heroic opposition to the Nazis, it was rather a cruel, adventuristic betrayal. What happened next was typical of resistance action and German response. Having obtained a few weapons, the escapees clashed with the Nazis outside the city, and a few Jews were captured. In retaliation for the breakout, the local Gestapo seized the entire family of each fugitive or all who lived with him; they also seized the leaders of all Jewish work parties in the vicinity, together with their families. All were shot. Thereafter, the Germans divided all work parties leaving the ghetto into groups of ten; if one person escaped, the entire group would be killed. Denouncing the first group of escapees, the ghetto newspaper called them traitors—"endangering the existence of our entire ghetto and the lives of their loved ones. . . . They are responsible for the spilt blood." Jacob Gens, the head of the Vilna *Judenrat*, argued that idealism and selflessness required that the Jews remain where they were—behind the ghetto walls. As he reminded his listeners, the local SS chief could easily have liquidated the entire ghetto. At stake, therefore, were the lives of twenty thousand Jews.[1]

In the Lithuanian city of Kovno the *Judenrat* feverishly consulted the elderly rabbi Abraham Duber Shapiro in 1941 when the Germans ordered all the Jewish inhabitants assembled for a "selection." After agonizing discussion, the council followed Shapiro's advice: "If a Jewish community (may God help it) has been condemned to physical destruction, and there are means of rescuing part of it, the leaders of the community should have the courage and assume the responsibility to act and rescue what is possible." The results were catastrophic, but fit expectations: of 26,400 Jews, 9,000 were taken away and shot. But the rest were spared—for a time. Later, the same council worked together with the Jewish underground. Council members assisted escapees by forging documents and providing food and clothing for those about to join the partisans. Ghetto workshops, with the approval of the *Judenrat* head, supplied and armed Jewish partisans in the forests, and the ghetto police provided cover for underground fighters. But in the spring of 1943, the Gestapo struck, arresting the entire council and murdering the leadership of the Jewish police. The ghetto was gradually worn down, its inhabitants deported to camps and killed. Remnants of the Kovno Jewry survived as slave laborers until the summer of 1944, when their ghetto was finally liquidated.[2]

For Michael Dov Ber Weissmandel, the Slovakian rabbi involved in desperate negotiations with the Nazis in the summer of 1942, resistance as conventionally understood would have seemed a cruel joke. His goal was to stop the murders by bribing high-ranking Germans with whom he was in contact. To him, money from abroad was the only justifiable response to mass murder. "We cannot understand how you can eat and drink," he wrote in an anguished letter to Jewish representatives in Geneva, "how you can rest in your beds, how you can stroll in the streets—and I am sure you are doing all those things—while this responsibility rests upon you. . . . We demand deeds! Not great deeds and not acts of sacrifice. Just money—and thousands and hundreds of thousands depend on that money."[3]

DILEMMAS AND OBJECTIVES OF JEWISH RESISTANCE

What we see here are responses to the dizzying conditions imposed on European Jewry by the Germans. Their tactic of "collective responsibility," as the term suggests, held entire communities or their leaders hostage, to suffer for acts of resistance. In most cases, as a result, resistance was guaranteed to punish Jews, rather than assist them. Fearful of massive German retribution, resisters everywhere waited until what they felt was the last moment—the final extinction of hope—for only then could they justify the reprisals that followed. But how was this point to be determined?

Jewish communities agonized over their prospects and were divided sharply over what tactics to follow. Since the Germans were themselves inconsistent, with the pace or character of persecution often depending on local commanders, Jewish leaders could usually find reason for a variety of actions. Time was a critical factor. Some groups of Jews were massacred immediately on contact with the Nazis, while others were spared. And even within regions conditions varied. As Yisrael Gutman has observed, while Jews were dying of starvation in places like Warsaw and Lodz in 1940 and 1941, there were other places, like Czestochowa and Zaglembie, where conditions were "relatively tolerable for a prolonged period."[4] Was there a reason for this? Could Jews influence their fate? If they remained alive long enough, would they be rescued? The calculations were impossibly complex, and the impulse for resistance invariably provoked controversy and disagreement. Understandably, some never gave up hope, and therefore opposed resistance to the bitter end. In a New Year's message in 1942, council chairman Chaim Rumkowski told the Jews of Lodz that they would survive, that all would be well, "if we eradicate the evil in ourselves"—by which he meant any slackening in the ghetto's work for the Third Reich.[5] Even when hopeful signs vanished, there was always the possibility that the Nazis might change their minds. Weissmandel, the Slovakian-Jewish negotiator, may actually have succeeded in one effort at suspending Slovakian deportations in the summer of 1942, while everywhere else Jews were being herded on trains to death camps; he was likely wrong in expecting to save many hundreds of thousands more by further discussions, and he received little encouragement from anyone. But there were at least scraps of evidence to justify his frantic efforts. He therefore poured his considerable energy into a futile scheme to bribe the leadership of the Third Reich. It took some time for underground leaders in various places to dare pronounce the opposite view—that all the Jews were doomed and that there was no hope at all. Up to that point, even those disposed to resistance usually acted cautiously.

Historians evaluating Jewish resistance invariably become tangled in the stormy contemporary debates by Jews over what course to take. Historians may not, in the end, be able to dispense with their own points of view, and according to one notion they should not attempt to do so. But it is well to be aware of such moral or ideological points of departure. There is no doubt that this issue touches a sensitive nerve in the Jewish consciousness, an unspoken assumption of which has been that Jewish resistance somehow validates Jewish self-worth. More so than with most issues associated with the Holocaust, research has often been heavily preoccupied with righting a historical balance—establishing the importance of Jewish heroism in the face of overwhelming force. In Israel, the principal center for both research and commemoration of the Holocaust is Yad Vashem, known in English as the Martyrs' and Heroes' Remembrance Authority.[6]

While such preoccupations continue, it may be possible now to study resistance with greater historical detachment. Certainly a starting point is to note that historians are not always agreed on what they understand by the term *resistance*. Those who adopt the most restrictive definition take the view sometimes advanced by Jewish partisans—that resistance necessarily means armed struggle. While not explicit in his text, it seems clear that Raul Hilberg understands resistance as a violent uprising by Jews against their oppressors. And as we have seen, Hilberg considers that the Jews' "reaction pattern . . . is characterized by almost complete lack of resistance." Its relative insignificance, in his view, can be demonstrated in terms of German casualties: "It is doubtful that the Germans and their collaborators lost more than a few hundred men, dead and wounded, in the course of the destruction process. The number of men who dropped out because of disease, nervous breakdowns, or court martial proceedings was probably greater. The Jewish resistance effort could not seriously impede or retard the progress of destructive operations. The Germans brushed that resistance aside as a minor obstacle, and in the totality of the destruction process it was of no consequence."[7] At the other end of the scale, Yehuda Bauer argues for an inclusive approach, one that declares "keeping body and soul together" under circumstances of unimaginable privation and misery as one way of resisting the Nazis. This case was, essentially, the one made by most Jewish leaders and the *Judenräte* of eastern Europe. Nonviolent resistance made most sense in 1940 and 1941, before the Final Solution, when what Jews faced seemed akin to persecution they had known so often in their past. The Jews' goal, for which they occasionally received religious sanction, was to carry on a struggle by "life-affirming means." Notably, the Jews avoided and evaded Nazi regulations. As Bauer points out, the rules the Germans set for ghettos were often so brutal and so stringent that if Jews had obeyed them they would probably have perished in a short period. Jewish food allocations for Warsaw in 1941, he notes, amounted to 336 calories daily—far below starvation levels.[8] Later, when the Jews came to realize the nature of the Nazis' plans, resistance took other forms. But both are part of a broad pattern of collective Jewish response. Resistance during the Holocaust, Bauer says, is "any *group* action consciously taken in opposition to known or surmised laws, actions, or intentions directed against the Jews by the Germans and their supporters" (emphasis in original).[9]

In the view taken here, resistance is organized activity consciously intended to damage the persecutors of Jews or seriously impair their objectives. Implicitly, this definition involves a political perspective that extends beyond the struggle of particular groups for survival. How that political aim is expressed varies widely, most obviously due to the widely differing means at hand. What matters, from this standpoint, is less what was accomplished than the intent of striking a blow against the Nazi machine. This is, it seems to me, the common thread to be found in studies of Jewish resistance activities, whatever their differences of emphasis and method. The key element, I believe, is to understand how the resisters saw their actions—an exercise that sometimes requires a considerable leap of the imagination. In the Warsaw ghetto, for example, the underground group known as Oneg Shabbat, or OS, busied itself collecting materials on the life of the ghetto and the suffering of its inhabitants. In his ghetto diary for June 1942, Emmanuel Ringelblum described what he felt was a great achievement for the group: some information on the fate of Polish Jewry that they had smuggled outside the walls reached London and was broadcast over the BBC. Ringelblum deemed the achievement of Oneg Shabbat a stunning victory for Jewish resistance: "The O.S. group has fulfilled a great historical mission. It has alarmed the world to our fate, and perhaps saved hundreds of thousands of Polish Jews from extermination. . . . I do not know who of our group will survive, who will be deemed worthy to work through our collected material. But one thing is clear to all of us. Our toils and tribulations, our devotion and constant terror, have not been in vain. We have struck the enemy a hard blow." [10] In one sense, Ringelblum was wrong, and his desperate appeal makes especially painful reading today. The Polish Jews were not saved. In London, the government was not moved. There were no massive retaliatory attacks. And no blow was struck against the Germans. Yet however unrealized, one can hardly deny the resistance goals of Ringelblum and his group and one can hardly challenge their authenticity in pursuing them. My conclusion is that the best yardstick for identifying Jewish resistance is that which the Jews at the time were prepared to accept. Since that was often itself an object of bitter dispute it is best to present the widest possible view.

Historians face a serious challenge in assessing Jewish involvement in the general current of resistance activity in every country. At what point is the resistance of Jews "Jewish resistance"? As we know, many thousands of Jews fought in underground groups across Europe—from Tito's partisans to irregular units attached to the Red Army, to Communist cells in France. Quite often such people fought as Yugoslavs, Soviets, or Frenchmen; their involvement, in these cases, had little or nothing to do with Jewish commitments. But in other cases their struggle was directly related to a Jewish cause. In December 1941 the Soviets formed a Lithuanian infantry division within the Red Army, made up of Lithuanian refugees who had fled eastward during the Nazi invasion. Certainly the Soviets' intention was not to form a Jewish force. But Jews constituted about half of its complement in the initial recruitment stage— about five thousand men—and much of the division was stamped with a Jewish identity. Among these soldiers, Yiddish was the daily language, Jewish religious traditions were respected, and Jewish identity was maintained. Political officers attached to the unit attuned their propaganda, and hence part of their political message about the war, to the Nazi slaughter of European Jews. [11]

Clearly motivations varied with individuals. Most often these were mixed, however, having reference both to a Jewish and a general imperative in the struggle against Nazism. Among Communists or others of the far Left, it was common to declare the Jewish cause to be at one with the rest of the free world. The Soviets encouraged this as a propaganda theme, constituting a Jewish Anti-Fascist Committee in April 1942, with a Yiddish-language newspaper *Eynikayt* (Unity) that carried accounts of Nazi atrocities.[12] Associated with the Soviet-Jewish novelist Ilya Ehrenburg, this effort signaled a remarkable (and, as it turned out, short-lived) Soviet approval of the use of Jewish identity as part of the mobilization against Nazism. The committee made an explicit appeal to the West on behalf of the Jews, who were encouraged to look to Moscow as the principal champion of their cause. All along the line, as a result, Communist organs beamed to Jewish readers some sense of the Nazi Holocaust.[13] Reporting the uprising of the Warsaw ghetto in France, for example, the Jewish Communist journal *Notre Voix* denounced the destruction of "the greatest European center for Jewish life." "Their sacrifice is not in vain. Every French Jew should by now awaken to the fact that only by adopting hard-line attitudes, in this life-and-death struggle with the Hitlerites, can safety be insured for the Jewish people."[14]

To others, the Holocaust fortified the prewar arguments on behalf of a Jewish national home. As the war went on, and as information about the massacre of European Jewry accumulated, Zionist sentiment penetrated Jewish consciousness where it had not existed before and became another means for expressing Jewish motivations in resistance movements. Writing in 1942, the Hungarian Jewish leader Otto Komoly despaired of solving the "Jewish Question" in the Diaspora: "Nowadays there is no serious-minded Jew who would not acknowledge the veracity of the Zionist rationale—that Jews would be unable to assimilate and would remain aliens wherever they lived as long as they were unable, unlike all other peoples, to have a country of their own."[15] Despite official disapproval, there is evidence of a strong Zionist affinity within the Lithuanian division and intense suspicion of this tendency among its political officers.[16] Support for a Jewish national home in Palestine, it seems, together with a heightened national consciousness among Jews, was one of the by-products of the resistance experience of many Jews.

One last remark before looking at some regional manifestations:

in any evaluation of Jewish resistance, one must beware of applying to the Jewish victims of Nazism criteria and scales of judgment that one would not apply to other groups in similar circumstances. Observers sometimes set arbitrary standards for Jewish populations, assume that the incidence of physical resistance among them should have been high, and then seek esoteric explanations as to why this was not so. The case of Soviet prisoners of war highlights how unfair this approach can be. According to Christian Streit, some 3.3 million out of a total of 5.7 million Soviet prisoners perished while in German custody, most of them executed, starved, or worked to death; yet we have no knowledge of any important uprising until the very end of the war among these victims—men of military age and training, about whose fate there was little doubt.[17] Similarly, the caution that Jews expressed about armed resistance should be seen in the context of a European-wide disinclination to incur massive German reprisals for violent operations. We know, from our vantage point, that the Jews were doomed by the Final Solution, and in this sense their fate was unique in Nazi-occupied Europe. But this was not generally evident to the Jews themselves. And even when it was, their response must surely be assessed with an eye to other civilian populations of Europe. Such people virtually never threw themselves against Nazi troops and police in the sort of desperate gesture that many assume now the Jews should have undertaken. It makes no sense to expect communities of Jews, without military traditions or experience, containing people of all ages and backgrounds, to have behaved, for example, like warlike Chetniks in the mountains of Yugoslavia or hardened Communists in Lyon. Commenting on this point, the historian of the French resistance Henri Michel observed how, from the very outset, the Jews lacked basic requisites for resistance found elsewhere: they had no supportive environment of sympathetic populations; they lacked the trained personnel and equipment that partisans drew upon everywhere; and they had no link with the Allies or with governments in exile. The Jews' calamity was indeed unique, but their circumstances hardly favored the kind of physical uprising many feel is missing from the historical record.[18]

GHETTOS, FORESTS, AND CAMPS
IN EASTERN EUROPE

Reflecting on resistance in wartime Yugoslavia, Milovan Djilas speaks of a fundamental psychological requisite that was usually missing from Jewish resistance groups—the "prospect of victory." According to Djilas, who monitored carefully what was necessary to keep Tito's partisans in the field, "victory must be worth the trouble and sacrifice. An insane form of human relations, war is nevertheless a highly motivated and extremely rational act." [19] In eastern Europe this expectation of victory was almost always missing, and the Jews fought, as the apt title of a recent work puts it, "the war of the doomed." But how did a small number reach this point? It takes time, as we know, to abandon all hope.

In Poland and occupied parts of the Soviet Union most Jews were killed before violent opposition of any sort was possible. Survivors of the initial shocks of ghettoization or mass shooting seem to have been overwhelmed. Cut off from the outside, exhausted by prolonged hunger, the Jews seldom had time to build resistance networks or the perspective to see through Nazi deceptions. Historians have traced the beginnings of underground organization to the latter part of 1942, when most communities were already decimated by the massive deportations to death camps. A study of ghetto underground organizations indicates that practical planning began only after the first deportations—by which point a handful of rebels were finally convinced that the inhabitants had no chance for survival.[20] Organization continued into 1943, a year that saw outbreaks in the ghettos of Warsaw and Bialystok, and violent incidents in Czestochowa, Brody, Tarnów, Sandomierz, and elsewhere. In general, the groups that banded together were pitifully small and barely armed at all.

For Warsaw, which saw the most important of several ghetto rebellions, Yisrael Gutman estimates the original insurgents as numbering under a thousand in a ghetto population of about forty thousand. The uprising began in the spring of 1943, following the disappearance of some 80 percent of the original ghetto population, most of whom had been sent to Treblinka to be murdered the previous summer. From the outset, therefore, the Jewish rebels were a small minority within their own community, a fragment of the remnant still alive after massive deportations. The mainstraim Jewish Fighting Organization, or ZOB, with under five hundred fighters, was armed with gasoline bombs, hand grenades, pistols, one or two submachine guns, and about ten rifles. Its Revisionist counterpart apparently had some minor heavier armament. Jewish historians have pored painstakingly over the question of these weapons to the point of counting every pistol and calculating every bit of ammunition the rebels managed to procure. Their conclusion is that the Polish Home Army helped starve the weapon-hungry Jewish fighters, leaving them even more vulnerable than would otherwise be the case.[21] For reasons discussed in chapter 5, anti-Jewish feeling and a different strategic conception of the fight against Nazism ensured that the Warsaw Jews would end their struggle virtually alone.

Against them, the German commander SS-Brigadeführer (Major General) Jürgen Stroop daily mustered over two thousand well-armed men, equipped with armored vehicles, artillery, flame throwers, heavy caliber machine guns, and even aircraft.[22] Once the fighting began, many hundreds of Jews were drawn into the struggle. Eventually, the Germans set fire to the ghetto to drive out its inhabitants, reduced whole blocks to rubble by shelling, and pumped poison gas into sewers and bunkers where the Jews sought shelter. Sporadic resistance continued for more than a month, ending in the total destruction of the ghetto and the deportation of its remaining population. As for German losses, Stroop admitted sixteen dead and eighty-five wounded; Gutman does not dismiss these figures out of hand, but while discounting the highly exaggerated Jewish claims he concludes that the German list was probably incomplete. The significance of the uprising was clearly symbolic, however. This was, after all, the first significant urban revolt against a Nazi occupation in Europe. As Gutman puts it, "the principal impact . . . lay not in the casualties it caused but in the fact that the Germans were forced to invest a substantial number of men and weapons merely to hold their own in what turned out to be a long struggle under the most disadvantageous conditions—from the viewpoint of both political propaganda and the effect of the fighting upon the non-Jewish population of Poland." The greatest impact was undoubtedly on the Jews themselves. News of the Warsaw ghetto rebellion spread among other imprisoned groups of Jews, and inspired pride and emulation. It had a clear if unmeasurable impact on those who were groping toward resistance elsewhere.[23]

Ironically, and underscoring the hopelessness of the revolt, the uprising of the ghetto may have quickened the pace of the Final Solution. According to Gutman the Germans thereafter applied much more armed force than ever before in initiating deportations and took greater care with security matters. They accelerated the liquidation of camps and ghettos in the eastern part of the *Generalgouvernement,* able to demonstrate to recalcitrant officials still eager to exploit Jewish labor the mortal danger posed by the Jews.[24]

Historians are now extending our knowledge of armed resistance in eastern Europe, drawing upon Jewish documentation as well as the Nazis' own appreciation of the insurgents. Increasingly, their work seems less burdened with ideology and more devoted to the reconstruction of a very complex and diverse historical terrain. By any scale, we can now point to considerable resistance activity. Yehuda Bauer identifies armed resistance to the Nazis and their henchmen in twenty-four ghettos of western and central Poland, the heaviest Jewish population concentration, and even more in eastern parts of the country. Full-scale ghetto revolts seldom occurred, to be sure, but armed clashes between Germans and scattered groups of Jews were not uncommon. In several cases organizers deliberately attempted to create confusion and the impression of a full-scale rebellion, giving cover to mass flight to the forests.[25] Thousands of Jews on the run managed to establish so-called family camps in the wooded countryside of Belorussia and Volhynia, where Jewish refugees scratched out a bare existence.[26] Jews also formed their own partisan units—numbering as many as 15,000 in western Belorussia, for example, according to one rough estimate.[27] Krakowski has found more than thirty Jewish partisan groups established in the *Generalgouvernement* of Poland between 1942 and 1943, and notes hundreds of Jews participating in non-Jewish formations as well. He further estimates that more than 50,000 Jews escaped to the forests, most of whom were killed in German manhunts.[28] Studying Lithuanian territory occupied by the Germans in 1941, Dov Levin estimates that resistance fighters numbered at least 10,000 men and women, including some 8,000 Lithuanian partisans and other units fighting with the Red Army and more than 2,000 in ghettos and labor camps. As he notes, these figures represent 4 percent of the 250,000 Jews living in Lithuania on the eve of the Nazi invasion and approximately 16 percent of the Jews who were still alive at the beginning of 1942.[29] By most comparative measurements, this was an extraordinarily high proportion of the victimized communities.

Historians provide insights as well on the organizational framework of Jewish resistance, particularly the ghetto underground. Those unfamiliar with Jewish life in eastern Europe before the Holocaust may see in the politics of Jewish resistance evidence of incorrigible factiousness and division. In Warsaw, for example, the Jewish resistance was built upon the preexisting political groups and splinters of groups within the ghetto, each one of which formed platoon-sized fighting units. It was remarkably difficult for these groups to work together, and only in July 1942 did representatives of Zionist youth movements finally manage to form a united combat organization—the ZOB. And even then some groups remained outside—the right-wing Zionist Revisionists and the various religious factions including the orthodox Agudat Yisrael. In fairness, it should be pointed out that Jewish resistance hardly had a European monopoly on partisan squabbling, as students of underground politics everywhere in Europe can attest. Yet what is striking about the Jewish case may be east European Jewry's zest for political organization, a striking feature of the urban landscape of Poland in the 1930s.[30] Jewish cultural and educational activities also spawned a dense network of organizations, characteristic of Jewish communal life. The organizations that became the vehicles for resistance were not traditional Jewish community agencies, however. Research indicates that most of the long-established leaders of Polish Jewry left their places of authority with the arrival of the Nazis. Some were killed, others simply abandoned their posts, fled eastward, or otherwise disappeared.

According to Gutman, it was Jewish youth movements that filled the vacuum created by the departed leaders. One must understand the European framework of these movements—often militant, activist adjuncts of established political formations, with members somewhat older than present-day North American equivalents. Among Jews, these associations were mainly Zionist and Bundist, ideologically sophisticated, and committed to camaraderie and communal action. Both of these streams had a utopian vision—Jewish autonomy within a socialist society in Poland for the Bundists, and a Jewish nation in Palestine for the Zionists. Both had a historical view that placed their struggle in the context of Jewish victimization and self-assertion. Less inured to traditional patterns of political behavior than their adult counterparts, youth leaders seem to have grasped the Jews' predicament more quickly than established Jewish spokesmen. Young people were generally more adventurous and more hardy than their elders, and had fewer familial responsibilities as well. Almost invariably, they were more prone to draw the revolutionary conclusions implied in resistance. During the occupation they emerged from the cocoon of prewar organizational life to immerse themselves in the struggles of their communities. In one ghetto after another they became the spearheads of opposition to the more conservative *Judenräte* and the core of resistance formations.[31]

Plainly, resisters were a tiny minority. Once formed, resistance groups had frequently to face the strong opposition of the Jewish communities in which they lived. The *Judenräte* often did everything possible to undermine resistance networks. The Jewish police tracked them down, and they were denounced in the official Jewish press. Up to the last moment most ghetto inmates rejected resistance when the suggestion was made. According to Trunk, at least one *Judenrat,* in the town of Shavli, even voted on the matter. The majority rejected the suggestion of their chairman, Mendel Leibowicz, that the Jews take up arms and prepare to set fire to their ghetto if the end was near. Most were unwilling to face the bitter conclusion and also to sacrifice women and children.[32] In one of the most dramatic instances, the Jewish public in the Vilna ghetto demanded that the underground surrender its leader, Yitzhak Witenberg, to the Nazis in 1943, fearing the liquidation of the entire ghetto if they did not.[33] "The truth is that the Jewish public in most of the ghettos neither understood nor accepted the path and assessment of the fighters," says Yisrael Gutman. "As always, it was the select few of the oppressed who decided to go underground and fight."[34]

Every historian of Jewish resistance has had to consider relations with non-Jewish opponents of the Nazis in eastern Europe—an issue that has been touched upon in chapter 5. While hostility toward the Jews was widespread, and in some places intense, it is also clear that circumstances varied, with a corresponding impact on the Jewish resisters. Only scraps of evidence have been published about this theme, and our knowledge has not gone far beyond the collection of anecdotes. One can certainly conclude, however, that the outlook of Polish Jews, the great majority in the region, was stamped with a deep sense of isolation. Generally spurned by the Polish resistance or local partisans, the Jews came increasingly to recognize the helplessness of their position. "After the war Poland will be resurrected," one of them told Jan Karski, a courier from the Polish Home Army. "Your cities will be rebuilt and your wounds will slowly heal. From this ocean of tears, pain, rage, and humiliation your country will emerge again but the Polish Jews will no longer exist. We will be dead. Hitler will lose his war against the human, the just, and the good, but he will win his war against the Polish Jews. No—it will not be a victory; the Jewish people will be murdered." [35] Throughout Poland, Jewish resistance gradually assumed the character of an armed protest—a last, suicidal gesture of anger and vengeance of a doomed community. Without hope, the Jewish rebels were in an utterly different position from non-Jews, many of whom fought precisely with the postwar future in mind.

For Lithuanian Jews, on the other hand, as Levin's book suggests, the Soviet-sponsored military and political network broke through the isolation caused by the hostility of the local population. [36] Unlike much of Poland, the Lithuanian situation was not entirely hopeless. In such places as Kovno, Svencian, and Shavli, the options for Jewish fighters included a desperate flight to nearby forests. While the great majority were slaughtered, some survived. [37] In territory taken from the Soviet Union in 1941 the experience of Jewish resisters seems to have varied. Material is scarce, and researchers are hampered by the lack of access to Soviet archives. According to Hersch Smolar, head of the Jewish underground in the Belorussian capital of Minsk, there was much support for the Jews among the Belorussian population. The ghetto underground there seems to have established important links with partisans in the rest of the city and in the surrounding countryside as well. [38] Throughout the Ukraine, on the other hand, pro-German feeling and anti-Jewish hostility seem to have been extensive from the very beginning, contributing to the isolation of Jews even when the local partisans turned against the Nazi occupation.[39]

Conditions in the concentration and death camps, where a handful of revolts occurred, provide the most extreme illustration of this isolation.[40] In the camps the Jews were enervated by exhaustion, starvation, and disease and crushed by the most complete totalitarian structure to have been devised by man. Help from the outside was nonexistent, and the Jews were utterly alone. "Collective responsibility" was unrestrained: punishment for any infraction of the rules was immediate and lethal. In such circumstances, resistance was a direct, even mortal threat to every Jewish inmate. Opposition, therefore, seemed impossible. Even so, sabotage and individual attempts to escape were not uncommon. And in a few cases there were even substantial, violent clashes. Almost always the rebels had no chance, accounting for the frequent hesitation and delay of inmate strategists. Timing was crucial. A quite sophisticated resistance network existed in the Płaszów concentration camp, for example, but in the end its members failed to revolt. An uprising of the inmates of Treblinka led to a breakout of several score prisoners, only twelve of whom survived; a few months later hundreds burst out of Sobibor, but most of them were immediately killed. In October 1944, when the death factory of Auschwitz was soon to be dismantled, there was a revolt of its Jewish *Sonderkommando*—men employed in grisly tasks by the Nazis before they were murdered themselves. The inmates succeeded in destroying one of the crematoria and killing a few guards. Almost all the rebels fell in the fighting or were captured soon after.[41] Elsewhere, in smaller camps, collective uprisings also occurred, but here too the inmates were wiped out in almost every case.[42]

Important uprisings occurred in three of the six death camps— Treblinka, Sobibor, and Auschwitz. Bauer notes three other camp rebellions—at Kruszyna, Krychow, and Minsk Mazowiecki—observing that "these were the only rebellions that ever did take place in any Nazi camps, except for that of Soviet prisoners of war at Ebensee at the end of the war."[43] We also know that there were several hundred escapes from these camps—many aided by collective action that, in camp conditions, was possibly the only way for resistance to express itself.

SLOVAKIA AND HUNGARY:
RESCUE AS RESISTANCE

Central Europe saw quite a different current of resistance activity associated with the rescue of Jews—smuggling refugees to sanctuary on the periphery of the Nazi empire, often sending them on to Palestine. Most of this activity was conducted secretly, at great risk to the organizers, and with the additional objective of passing detailed information about the Jewish catastrophe to the outside world. Of political motivation in the widest sense, moreover, there is no doubt. "When we see this terrible tragedy before us," wrote an organizer in Bratislava to contacts in Geneva, "we see the continuation of our rescue work as God's sacred wish. The life of every single refugee is sacred to us and we know that you are bound to them with all your heart strings. Let us, then, carry on this work with our united strengths." [44]

Gisi Fleischmann, the author of those lines, was the Slovakian leader of WIZO, the Women's International Zionist Organization, and the head of the emigration department of the so-called Jewish Center, the Slovakian equivalent of the *Judenräte* established everywhere by the Germans. In this case the Jewish Center operated under Slovakian government auspices, in conditions of systematic persecution that also included, for a time, deportations to death camps in the east. In a pattern that occurred elsewhere, activist members of the Jewish agency established to administer persecution used the cover provided by that body to form a network of self-help. During the course of the deportations, as the official Jewish leadership floundered in despair, a committee known as the Working Group came into being to negotiate with Dieter Wisliceny, Adolf Eichmann's representative in Bratislava. These negotiations will be considered in the next chapter. But along with these discussions, the Working Group became involved in other activities, notably underground rescue and intelligence efforts.

The Working Group sent out lines of contact in every direction. Rabbi Weissmandel, the ultra-Orthodox rabbi who relentlessly pursued negotiations with Wisliceny, carried on a sustained secret correspondence with Jewish organizations in Geneva, Istanbul, and Budapest. A courageous and energetic woman, Gisi Fleischmann was in touch with the American Joint Distribution Committee, of which she was the Slovakian representative, sending a stream of coded letters to its deputies in Switzerland. She spent a great deal of effort building an intelligence network with links in Poland and relayed to the west whatever was discovered about the fate of deported Jews.[45] Fleischmann helped establish an underground railway to Budapest, working with the Hungarian Jewish Relief and Rescue Committee. As well, the Slovakian leaders worked closely with the Zionist youth organization Hechalutz, smuggling Jews across the frontier into Hungary. They even sent envoys to the Nazi death camps of Lublin and Majdanek to ascertain the fate of Jewish deportees. Evidence suggests that members of the Jewish Center who were also part of the Working Group had a "dual role," as Livia Rothkirchen puts it.[46] Officially, they were part of the apparatus of the pro-Nazi Tiso regime, doing the bidding of Slovakian authorities; at the same time, using the instruments provided by their office, and fully conscious of the peril Jews faced, they worked to subvert the machinery of destruction. Such work involved enormous risks. Fleischmann herself was arrested twice and was finally murdered in Auschwitz in the autumn of 1944. Weissmandel was similarly arrested, released, and then deported, but he managed to jump from the train and eventually escaped to Switzerland.

After learning details about the killings at Auschwitz-Birkenau from two Jewish escapees, Weissmandel seems to have been the first to propose an Allied bombing of the railway approaches to the camp as a way of disrupting the killings. In mid-May 1944 he sent two coded telegrams from Bratislava to Swiss Orthodox leaders for transmission to the United States. At the same time he was involved in complex and ultimately futile negotiations originating in Hungary for the cessation of the Final Solution. Bitterly disappointed at the lack of support he felt he received, he fulminated against world Jewry for not providing the funds to support his efforts to bribe high-ranking Nazis. Between the negotiator on the spot, knowing the worst of the Nazis' atrocities, and Jews in the free world, snared in the bureaucracies of their own organizations as well as the indifference of Allied governments, there was a profound gulf of misunderstanding. Beyond this, a clash of cultures possibly impeded communication. Weissmandel was an extremely pious Jew whose language and worldview were steeped in rabbinic traditions; some of his Jewish interlocutors were freethinking Zionists or worldly professionals, suspicious of Orthodoxy, and inclined to dispute his evaluation of Nazi policies and his efficacy in opposing them. Present-day assessments of these negotiations may still be affected by such differences of outlook.[47]

The Hungarian counterpart to the Working Group operated more openly, given the buffer that the government in Budapest placed between the Jews of that country and anti-Jewish extremists. At the beginning of 1943 a handful of Jewish activists established a Relief and Rescue Committee, which operated within the framework of the government-sponsored Jewish Council and was empowered to assist Jewish refugees entering the country from Slovakia and Poland. Known by its Hebrew name—the Vaada (for Vaadat Ezra ve'Hatzalah)—this committee played an important and extremely controversial role, to be considered later, in negotiations with the SS in 1944 for the ransom of Hungarian and other threatened Jews. Its leaders included Otto Komoly, Rezsö Kasztner, and Samuel Springmann—prominent figures in the world of Hungarian Zionism. Sharply divided internally, and quarreling also with its counterpart in Istanbul, the Vaada seems to have functioned usefully, smuggling Jewish escapees into the country, maintaining them when they arrived, and arranging their subsequent escape elsewhere, even to Palestine. Several hundred of these refugees formed an underground network in Budapest, led by a Polish-Jewish partisan Boris Teicholz.[48] In all, as many as fifteen thousand Jewish refugees may have entered Hungary during the war, although the numbers cannot be determined with any certainty.[49] Much of this refugee work was clandestine—organized by one of its officials, Joel Brand, who doubtless drew upon his underground experience after the First World War in the German Communist party. Pursuing these rescue efforts, the Vaada worked closely with Fleischmann and Weissmandel in Bratislava. The committee also conducted negotiations with the Hungarian government that was trying to untangle itself from the Nazi embrace and maintained shadowy ties with Admiral Canaris's dissident intelligence unit of the Wehrmacht, known as the Abwehr. As the Hungarian deportations began in 1944, the Vaada extended its underground activities, manufacturing counterfeit identity documents, smuggling refugees to safety in Rumania, and relaying news to Jewish representatives in Switzerland and Turkey.[50]

With the Nazi invasion of Hungary in March 1944, the Vaada shifted direction and became deeply involved with the German authorities. Having escaped the Final Solution for so long, Hungarian Jewish leaders, including the Zionist rescue activists, believed that their luck might hold. As Braham suggests, the members of the Vaada made the quite logical deduction at the time that their best chance was to deal with the Germans. They began complex, eventually tortuous negotiations, which ended in failure. Massive deportations to Auschwitz began in the spring, and anti-Jewish terror spread throughout the country. About this time some dissident leaders of the Jewish Council attempted to arm Jewish labor servicemen in conjunction with an anti-Nazi uprising; this attempt misfired, however, and was crushed by the Germans and the Hungarian fascists. Resistance in Hungary now passed to a relatively small group of young Zionists, who became ever more scornful of the established Jewish leaders in Budapest. Here too, according to Braham, the structures of the Jewish establishment helped provide cover, for a time, for resisters. Youthful Hehalutz activists used the headquarters of the Jewish Council in Budapest, until they finally broke with the established leaders. These resisters, likely a very small number, maintained an underground existence, acquired weapons, and established links with anti-Nazi forces in the Hungarian capital.[51]

WESTERN EUROPE: JEWISH AFFIRMATION

Throughout western Europe, Jews blended far more easily than elsewhere into the national struggles against Nazism. Despite the rise of antisemitism in the 1930s, assimilation in these countries was very extensive, and Jewish patriotism was strong. Jews flocked to the colors in 1939. In France, as many as forty thousand foreign Jews joined the armed forces when war broke out, most assembled into special foreigners' units.[52] Jewish soldiers fought in the various armies that engaged the Wehrmacht and were prominently involved in resistance movements that arose in countries occupied by the Germans. The resistance, however, seldom accented Jewish concerns in the manner, for example, of the Soviet-sponsored Jewish Anti-Fascist Committee. Generally speaking, resistance in the west did not address Jews separately and did not attune its strategies to the particular Jewish predicament. Anti-Jewish currents among resisters were rare—unlike the situation with the Polish Home Army, for example—but occasional hostile voices were also heard. In addition, resistance propagandists were aware of popular anti-Jewish feeling under Nazi occupation and sometimes trimmed their messages to the people accordingly. Thus while condemning the Vichy government's betrayal of "the national conscience" in its persecution of Jews in October 1942, the underground French newspaper *Combat* appealed to widespread hostility to recent Jewish immigrants from eastern Europe; *Combat* called for a special law restricting the rights of foreigners and urged a "naturalization that rewards their assimilation instead of initiating it."[53] Such expressions were infrequent, however, and Jewish veterans of the resistance often strenuously deny the existence of any such sentiment among their comrades. Certainly many thousands of Jews participated in the general resistance without ever having to face the dilemmas of their coreligionists in eastern Europe, where antisemitism was deeply rooted and widespread.

Historians usually distinguish between this participation in the broad current of resistance and resistance that affirmed some Jewish specificity.[54] The latter has assumed an important place in the Jewish history of the various countries under Nazi occupation and is now the object of considerable historical investigation, most of it concerning France. Arguing for the importance of a Jewish consciousness in the formation of resistance sentiment, Renée Poznanski notes how Jews found themselves facing fundamental choices long before their non-Jewish contemporaries. She argues that these measures had the effect upon Jewish existence in France that the forcible labor drafts of February 1943 had for the French population as a whole: they galvanized resistance, sending a wave of new recruits into newly founded clandestine organiations.[55] However, this kind of Jewish affirmation was generally much less widespread and intense than in the German *Lebensraum* in the east. For one thing, Jews were not generally separated physically from non-Jews as in Nazi-occupied Poland and the Soviet Union. For another, Jews in Nazi-occupied Belgium, Holland, France, and Denmark could not build upon an extensive Jewish cultural foundation firmly set in the Jewish community at large. For these reasons, resistance groups never constituted a countercommunity that had broad, mass appeal among Jews. Also, there were no Einsatzgruppen massacres of Jews in France, Holland, Belgium, or the Netherlands and no process of mass starvation as elsewhere. Until the massive deportations to the east in the summer of 1942, and sometimes even later, when the police began extensive roundups of natives as well as foreign Jews, few had any idea that their very survival was at stake. Jewish resistance, therefore, generally lacked the suicidal desperation that we have noted elsewhere and was far more attuned to underground relief and rescue activity. In this sense it operated on the margins of what is commonly called "resistance," pursuing armed opposition only occasionally and in the last year of the occupation.

With the great majority of its Jewish population coming from eastern Europe in recent decades, Belgium had a particularly strong concentration of left-wing Zionist and Bundist supporters as well as Communist activists. Jewish Communists took the initiative to establish a clandestine Jewish Defense Committee in 1942, operating under the aegis of the national underground organization, the Comité national du front de l'indépendence. Eventually the Defense Committee won broad support among Jewish activists and coordinated illegal resistance activity among Belgian Jews. Its most important achievement was the rescue of three or four thousand Jewish children, many of whom were hidden with the assistance of the Catholic church. Determined to oppose the Germans and unwilling to have its activity "degenerate into simple social work," the Defense Committee worked closely with a wide variety of underground organizations.[56] Armed opposition was a controversial option, however, broadly opposed by a Jewish underground that feared the cycle of reprisals this would bring, and the resulting further isolation of Belgian Jews. The more militant among the resisters sharply opposed the *Judenrat* equivalent, the Association des Juifs de Belgique (AJB), and engaged in a futile campaign imploring Jews not to heed its call to assemble for deportation. A few armed Jewsh resisters attacked the AJB headquarters in Brussels in 1942, and a year later conducted the only assault anywhere on a deportation convoy.[57]

Concentrating on Paris, Jacques Adler emphasizes the role of the Jewish Left, especially the Communists. He contends that immigrant Jews were less entranced by the liberal heritage of France and less subject to illusions about French beneficence than were well-

established French Jews—the "Juifs français de vieille souche." [58]
Psychologically better prepared for their ordeal, they strove to unify
Jewish responses. As in the general sphere of resistance, the Jewish
Communists were the first in the field, mounted the most extensive
attacks on the Nazi-Vichy system, and suffered the most for their
efforts. In the Jewish and non-Jewish sphere, they were known as
the "parti des fusillés," the party that paid the heaviest price before
the firing squads. Their Paris-based organization, known as Solidarité, linked the internments of Jews and other anti-Jewish moves
in the Occupied Zone with Vichy policy in the south. After the attack on the Soviet Union in June 1941, the Jewish Communists
moved into active resistance, while at the same time championing a
collective Jewish response to persecution. Specifically Jewish units
were formed; Jewish internments became a focal point for agitation
and self-help; and wider Jewish political activity was encouraged in
the shape of the Communist-sponsored Union des Juifs pour la résistance et l'entraide (UJRE). From mid-1942, according to Adler,
there was an even greater accent on specifically Jewish issues and an
affirmation of a Jewish national consciousness.

Yet despite this heroic struggle, we can question how much the
Jewish Communists offered persecuted Jews as a whole in France or
Belgium. The starting point of the movement was Jewish identification with the cause of the Soviet Union, engaged in its titanic struggle
with the Hitlerian Reich. For the Communists, Russia was the principal champion of oppressed peoples, and its interests ultimately determined resistance strategy. Therefore, Jewish Communists made
few direct assaults on the Nazis' anti-Jewish machinery: they blew
up no deportation trains; assassinated no SS Jewish affairs specialists; and left it to others, for example, to liberate the camp of
Drancy, the Paris antechamber to Auschwitz. The French party's immigrant organization, the Main d'oeuvre immigré (MOI), refused
to consider Solidarité or the UJRE as specifically Jewish bodies, dis-
owning the line taken by immigrant activists and leaving them even
more vulnerable to the Gestapo than would otherwise have been the
case. Other Jewish resistance groups drew upon secular Jewish ide-
ologies—mainly Bundism and Zionism—to form networks less
powerful than those of the Communists, but more strictly attuned
to Jewish needs in the latter part of the occupation period. Their
desperate and dangerous efforts span the full range of underground

activity, from independent fighting units, such as the French Armée juive, which later became the Organisation juive de combat, to rescue operations like those of the underground railway to Spain organized by youthful Zionist pioneering groups in the Netherlands.[59] Finally, we should note how such work involved extraordinary risks—comparable to armed resistance elsewhere. Historians have not contested the evaluation of Olga Wormser-Migot: three out of four Jewish resisters were deported, and one of these deportees out of three returned after the war.[60]

As seen in this chapter, Jewish resistance spans the full range of activity noted by historians of resistance in general. With the Jews, as with everyone else, armed conflict was on the peak of a great pyramid of resistance activity, most of which was designed in other ways to impede German objectives and contribute to the victory over Nazism.[61] For most Jews, however, overwhelming German force prevented even minor achievements, and a final victory was impossible. Even the most clear-sighted resistance leaders had no answers for most Jews caught in the maelstrom of 1940–44—in the east or west. For the young, for those without family responsibilities, armed combat provided a means for Jewish affirmation in the last, terrible moments before the inevitable German onslaught or in the final months of Nazi presence; for others, the rescue of Jewish children, the manufacture of false identity papers, and the secret passage of the frontiers into Spain, Switzerland, Rumania, or Hungary were realistic possibilities. But these were exceptions—and relatively very few. For most Jews, very little could be done without the assistance of the surrounding population, the willingness of local authorities and police to look aside, and extraordinary good luck. And as we have seen, every one of these was in short supply.

8. BYSTANDERS

WRITING ON BYSTANDERS to the Holocaust conveys a persistent and depressing theme—disbelief in reports of mass murder, widespread indifference, and unwillingness to break established patterns to help the Jews. We now have a growing shelf of books and a burgeoning file of articles on this topic, tracing how news of mass murders spread from Nazi-occupied Europe and charting the reactions of the Anglo-American allies, neutrals, churches, the Jews themselves, and others. Of course, research has uncovered particular variations on this theme—mechanisms by which various agencies and governments absorbed the information and adopted policies to deal with it. But there are few breaks in the pattern previously mentioned. The drift of scholarly opinion is summed up by the titles of two of the most recent additions to the list of scholarly volumes—*The Abandonment of the Jews,* by David Wyman, dealing with American reactions, and *The Jews Were Expendable,* by Monty Penkower, discussing diplomatic responses of the Western world.[1]

In assessing this work, we should note that many of these analyses center explicitly on what did *not* happen—an awkward approach for the historian. Information on the Holocaust was not digested, Jews were not admitted, Jewish communities failed to unite, Allied governments spurned rescue suggestions, and access to Auschwitz was not bombed. It is, essentially, a negative report—the history of inaction, indifference, and insensitivity. It should be obvious that there is a pitfall here: in any such assessment, there is great danger that the historian will apply to subjects the standards, value systems, and vantage point of the present, rather than those of the period being discussed. We believe that people should have acted otherwise, and we set out to show how they did not. Occasionally the thrust of such work is an extended lament that the people being written about did not live up to our standards. This temptation is the historians' form of hubris: to yield fully to it is to denounce the characters we describe for not being like ourselves.

Put more simply, there is a strong tendency in historical writing on bystanders to the Holocaust to condemn, rather than to explain. And while opinions differ on the degree to which historians should exercise some form of judgment, I suggest that we shall go much further in the attempt to comprehend the behavior and activity (or inactivity) of bystanders by making a painstaking effort to enter into their minds and sensibilities. Holocaust survivors have, it seems to me, frequently warned about problems of comprehension that are relevant to this point. "It was like another planet," they say, "it simply cannot be imagined." There is a truth here, but before examining its implications in detail we should appreciate an obvious implication. If the Holocaust was indeed unprecedented, as has been argued in this book, then it is also true that people had no experience upon which to base their understanding at the time, and no reliable guides for action. To a degree, everyone was in the dark. Historians have quite properly combed the seamy underside of Allied and Jewish policy, searching through records sometimes deliberately hidden from view. But they should take care in using such material, to give contemporaries a fair hearing.

WHAT WAS KNOWN?

Behind every aspect of the history of bystanders to the Holocaust lies the question of what facts were available about the fate of European Jewry, and how these were understood. More than with many subjects, the historical record plays tricks on the historian of European Jewry during the Second World War, making it extremely difficult to grasp what was known at any given moment. The problem is especially complex because the character of mass murder was seldom adequately grasped. "Almost everyone who lived through the period of the Holocaust, observing it from either near or far will readily testify that information concerning the Nazi murder of the Jews, when it first came out, seemed absolutely unbelievable—impossible." This is the view of historian Jacob Katz, in a thoughtful essay written several years ago. But Katz goes on to identify a paradox that underlies much interpretation of this question: "Yet once it became evident that the unbelievable had indeed occurred, it began to seem altogether necessary and inevitable."² Discordant voices continue to cry out on this issue. To some, the news of the killings in Europe was everywhere; to others, the truth remained hidden until the end of the war.

In a discussion of these matters some years ago, Yehuda Bauer made a crucial distinction between what he called information and knowledge. Increasingly, historians have shown how much general information was available in the West about Nazi persecution, and how, by early 1942, reports regularly reached England, for example, about widespread massacres of Jews in Poland and the Soviet Union. Such accounts appeared first in the Jewish press—the *Jewish Chronicle* and the *Zionist Review*—but were also carried by the Jewish Telegraphic Agency to publications in New York. Reports appeared almost immediately in the non-Jewish press and by the summer of 1942 were published with increasing frequency. But the presence of such information does not mean that it was *known*, in the usually understood sense. As Bauer notes, "knowing usually came in a number of stages: first, the information had to be disseminated; then, it had to be believed; then, it had to be internalized, that is, some connection had to be established between the new reality and a possible course of action; finally, there came action, if and when action came."³

As most students of this subject have observed, there were great obstacles to knowing that blocked the path of information at every step of the way. Barriers were still in place in 1945, when the camps in central Europe were liberated and when Allied soldiers stumbled on sites they had never expected to find. "You can't understand it, even when you've seen it," wrote one journalist about Buchenwald in April 1945.⁴ So thought thousands of horror-struck witnesses, including many Jews, for whom several years of information on the

Nazi Holocaust left them completely unprepared for what they found. Incomprehension, however, did not stop there. Probing the evidence carefully after the war, even the judges at Nuremberg found the facts difficult to accept: "One reads these accounts again and again—and yet there remains the instinct to disbelieve, to question, to doubt," they wrote. "There is less of a mental barrier in accepting the weirdest stories of supernatural phenomena as, for example, water running uphill and trees with roots reaching to the sky, than in taking at face value these narratives which go beyond the frontiers of human cruelty and savagery." [5]

Walter Laqueur's *Terrible Secret,* published in 1980, reviewed the many paths by which information seeped out of Nazi-occupied Europe. The "pivotal role," he claimed, was played by the Polish underground, which had a remarkable intelligence-gathering capacity and good facilities to relay findings to London and elsewhere. True, relations between Jews and the Polish authorities were frequently strained in exile, and were even worse, at times, within occupied Poland. Polish spokesmen consistently portrayed the Jewish catastrophe as part of the larger tragedy of the Polish nation, stressing that all Poles were being victimized, whatever their background. Some Jews blamed the Polish authorities for constricting and obstructing the flow of the news and for submerging information on the Holocaust in a sea of atrocity stories from Poland. While acknowledging the presence of antisemitism among the Polish leadership, Laqueur does not find any pattern of holding back news about the Holocaust. [6] Many of these reports from Jewish sources relied heavily on the Polish underground to carry them to the West. The conduit provided by the Poles carried more information than any other and transmitted decisive news about the killings in the summer of 1942, when massive deportations to death camps were conducted throughout the *Generalgouvernement.*

Along with the facilities of the Polish Home Army, we know of dozens of other ways by which information came to the West. Refugees trickled into Switzerland carrying tales about slaughters in the east; others escaped to Turkey, with similar accounts. German soldiers who had witnessed mass shootings in Russia returned home on leave, and their stories spread. Newspaper correspondents from neutral countries, stationed in Germany, picked up such rumors and reported on the disappearance of the Jews. Thousands of visitors from cobelligerent or neutral countries visited Germany during the war, and some of them undoubtedly heard such accounts as well. Diplomatic officials, particularly those of the Vatican, learned a great deal and relayed vital information across Europe. The papal nuncio in Bratislava, Giuseppe Burzio, may have been the first to report the fate of Jewish deportees. In March 1942, when Operation Reinhard had only just begun, Burzio told authorities at the Holy See that "the deportation of 80,000 persons to Poland at the mercy of the Germans means to condemn a great part of them to certain death."[7] Yehuda Bauer stresses the importance of a long, authoritative account on mass murder relayed by the socialist Jewish Bund in May 1942, referring to deportations and killings throughout Poland, the gassings at Chelmno, and mentioning that "the Germans have already killed 700,000 Polish Jews."[8]

The best known signal on European-wide mass murder came to the West via the representative of the World Jewish Congress in Switzerland, Gerhardt Riegner, in August 1942. Using the offices of the British embassy in Bern, Riegner cabled New York and Washington about an "alarming report" of a plan that "all Jews in countries occupied or controlled by Germany," would be deported, concentrated in the east, and "exterminated at one blow to resolve once and for all the Jewish Question in Europe." Up to this point, news about *particular* massacres circulated—even the Bund report was limited to the assault on Polish Jews. Riegner's telegram prompted some to think of these killings in continental terms—a previously unimaginable scale of destruction. With what is for us chilling verisimilitude, the cable also mentioned "prussic acid," the actual gas used at Auschwitz.[9]

While there has been much discussion of the Riegner telegram, and while the flaccid bureaucratic reaction to it in Britain and the United States tells us much about the official disposition in those countries, it would be wrong to exaggerate the importance of this particular communication, as some have done, in conveying the decisive information about the Nazi Holocaust. In context, Riegner's telegram appears as part of a flurry of messages from Nazi-occupied Europe in mid-1942, each of which depicted part of the story. Some of Riegner's information was incorrect, as Laqueur and others have noted. The plan was not "under consideration," but had already been decided; the Jews were not to be killed "at one blow," and the murder was already under way. Moreover, Riegner himself had transmitted the story "with all possible reservation," and those who read his cable were understandably reluctant to believe it.[10]

In addition, significant gaps remained. Even the best informed had no real sense of the assembly-line organization by which so many hundreds of thousands met their deaths in Polish camps. Even an attentive reading of the reports from Poland yielded only a partial view of the Holocaust and conveyed little sense of its historical uniqueness. And even those who had the deepest anxieties, such as Rabbi Weissmandel or Gisi Fleischmann in Slovakia, for example, continued to nourish unrealistic hopes as late as 1943.[11] Martin Gilbert has argued persuasively that until the escape of four young Jews from Auschwitz in mid-1944, that immense death factory remained successfully hidden from the outside. Up to that point hardly anyone knew the place at which trainloads of Jews arrived from across the Continent and where, at its peak, as many as twelve thousand perished every day.[12]

Yet the drift of the news was unmistakable. Even as the bureaucrats temporized, others worked to sound the alarm. While occasionally inaccurate, or incomplete, or insufficient, the facts that were spread were ghastly enough. The BBC broadcast material from the Bund report on 2 June 1942, and in the weeks that followed several press conferences elaborated details. In one of these, the British minister of information Brendan Bracken appeared with the Polish deputy prime minister Stanisław Mikołajczyk to denounce "the beginning of the wholesale extermination of the Jews." A week before the Riegner telegram arrived at its two destinations the *Montreal Star* carried a headline "'Nazi Slaughterhouse'—Germans Massacre Million Jews in Extermination Drive."[13]

Words, however, can be deceptive. Note that the *Montreal Star*'s lead appeared within quotation marks. In a recent book aptly entitled *Beyond Belief,* Deborah Lipstadt showed how, while the American press was full of news about the Holocaust, it persistently ignored the scope and significance of the events it described.[14] Editors remained skeptical about what their own news columns and the wire services said. Often priding themselves on their incredulity, journalists toned down what reached them from European sources, qualifying the magnitude and ubiquity of mass murder. And even when the information was accepted, it was often buried in the back pages, dulling the impact on the reading public. The American press, worse in this respect than its British counterpart according to Lipstadt, prided itself on its skepticism and was conditioned by its experience with inflated atrocity stories of the First World War. Journalists hesitated to accept second- or third-hand reports, especially when they came via the Soviets or squabbling Europeans. Moreover, few had the imagination to perceive the kind of massacre the reports suggested. Traditionally pragmatic American reporters failed to grasp the significance of the facts they encountered for the same reason that intelligence analysts often fail to digest the bits of information they get from agents in the field. In intelligence, as in much of life, people believe what they are prepared to believe.

In the United States and elsewhere, journalistic attitudes may also have been shaped by an important measure of popular antipathy toward the Jews. Opinion polls taken during the war consistently reported a high degree of anti-Jewish feeling among the American public. Indeed, American antisemitism may never have been so high as during the Second World War. Yehuda Bauer cites a survey of July 1939 in which 31.9 percent of those polled thought that the Jews had excessive power in the business world and that something should be done about this; 10.1 percent also thought that Jews should be deported. In July 1942, 44 percent thought that Jews had too much power and influence. According to Lipstadt, "Jews were consistently seen as a greater menace to the welfare of the United States than were any other national, religious, or racial group." In June 1944, with France about to be liberated, 44 percent of Americans still thought the Jews a threat, while only 6 percent thought this of the Germans, and 9 percent so viewed the Japanese.[15]

In global terms, moreover, Americans were inclined throughout the war to view Imperial Japan as the great criminal power rather than the Third Reich—a point sometimes ignored in works that focus too narrowly on responses to the Holocaust. Films, books, radio, newspapers, and magazines in the United States projected the most vicious racist stereotypes of the Japanese, and attention concentrated upon them as the chief repository of wartime criminality.[16] According to one historian, this impression persisted until December 1944, when in a dramatic incident in the Battle of the Bulge, unarmed American prisoners were shot down by a Waffen SS unit near the Belgian town of Malmédy. Only then, according to Bradley

Smith, did Americans begin to comprehend that "the Nazis deliberately carried out millions of killings in cold blood and that this killing system could directly touch them."[17]

In England, bombed regularly by the Luftwaffe, there was of course a greater inclination to address Nazi criminality. Lipstadt found the British press to have been far more direct and forceful than that of the United States in covering massacres of Jews in the summer of 1942, when the most ominous reports from occupied Europe accumulated.[18] Generally speaking, public figures in the United Kingdom seem to have been much more inclined than their American counterparts to take up the cause of the Jews. In contrast with the response of British government officials, Bernard Wasserstein reports a wave of public sympathy for Jews in the second half of 1942. British Jews called strongly for action, and so too did a number of prominent churchmen, sections of the press, and the Polish authorities in London.[19] Eventually, the government was pressured into sponsoring an inter-Allied declaration denouncing the murder of Jews, formally issued on 17 December in the name of eleven governments and the French National Committee, and released simultaneously in Washington, London, and Moscow.

This declaration referred to "Hitler's oft-repeated intention to exterminate the Jewish people in Europe," a goal that the German authorities "are now carrying into effect." It could hardly have been more clear. Stressing the significance of this statement, Laqueur takes its release as the terminal point for his study of information on the Final Solution. "By December 1942 the Jewish institutions outside Europe had declared days of mourning and the United Nations had confirmed the news about the mass slaughter in a common declaration. The news had been broadcast all over the world and featured in all major newspapers outside Nazi-occupied Europe. The majority of Jews in eastern Europe knew and so did millions of Germans and other residents of Nazi-occupied Europe. Every European government had heard the news, if not necessarily most of its citizens."[20]

And yet, the story from this point is full of occasions when people either forgot or rejected what they once knew, or showed signs of not having fully absorbed what the declaration said so clearly. This is the significance of the statements of incredulity we have noted coming from those who liberated the camps or who pored over the evidence immediately after the war. Jews were affected along with non-Jews. Throughout much of the war Jewish leaders planned on the basis that millions of Jewish refugees would be left in Europe after Hitler's collapse; in the face of so many reports of mass killing, the World Jewish Congress continued to believe that starvation was the major cause of death at German hands; and even Jews in Palestine hoped that some of the reports were sensationalist and imbalanced. Perceptions of the Jewish reality in Europe continued to be affected by what Laqueur calls "the denial of reality, the psychological rejection of information which for one reason or another is not acceptable."[21]

UNWANTED REFUGEES

Misperceptions of the massacre in Europe were accompanied by an almost universal unwillingness to receive Jewish refugees, sluggishness in responding to Jewish appeals for help, and an unwillingness to test various rescue possibilities. In almost every country, historians have seen a continuity between wartime restrictions and policies established in the 1930s. Numerous works document the closing of doors in the 1930s, in one Western country after another.[22] The refugees, of course, sought entry at the worst possible moment: world depression brought restrictionist sentiment everywhere and a fear that newcomers would become a burden on host countries or would take jobs that properly belonged to natives. But almost everywhere as well such sentiment combined with anti-Jewish feeling, making the Jewish exiles from Nazism particularly unwanted. The contrast with the 1920s is often quite striking in this respect. In France, for example, the decade immediately following the First World War saw a remarkably open policy; citizenship became easier to obtain, and the doors were thrown open to strangers who, it was hoped, would close the demographic wound opened by four years of bloody fighting. With economic collapse in the 1930s, however, old antisemitic passions surfaced once again, and Jews were denounced. Particularly in Europe, these prejudices were fed by fears of war. Politicians and officials pronounced themselves suspicious of Jews, who, it was charged, were seeking to embroil western European countries in a conflict with Nazism. Anti-Jewish opinion and appeasement sentiment flowed together in the European Right, providing ample ammunition for restrictionists.

Restriction also marked British policy in Palestine, which many Jews came to see as their last possible refuge. A booming, bustling place in the late 1920s, the tiny Jewish settlement in that country, mandated to Britain by the League of Nations, numbered about 400,000 in the mid-1930s. In 1936 Palestinian Arabs began a violent revolt against British rule, prompting the mandatory power to reconsider its earlier promises to the Jews. Previously, the British had exercised loose controls over the numbers of Jewish immigrants—largely determined by an assessment of the economic capacity of the country to absorb new inhabitants. And up to this point the real problem for Zionists had not been British restrictions, but rather the scarcity of Jews willing to pursue a pioneering life and go to Palestine. Now everything changed. From 1936 the British cut immigration to Palestine substantially on political grounds, just as increasing numbers turned there in desperation. The British finally fixed their program in the White Paper of May 1939, setting a limit of 75,000 on Jewish immigration over the next five years, after which further entries were to depend on Palestinian Arab acquiescence.[23] A shattering blow to the Zionists (stoutly opposed by Winston Churchill, an eloquent champion of Jewish refugees), the White Paper was nevertheless part of a policy of girding for war against the Nazis. As Bernard Wasserstein has shown, the British government was not so much moved by the Palestinian Arab case as by its strategic responsibilities in the Middle East. Britain wanted to end the Arab uprising and ensure the support of neighboring Arab states for the coming contest with Germany.[24]

Restriction intensified everywhere with the outbreak of war, while the Nazis maintained their commitment to Jewish emigration. In Yehuda Bauer's calculation, 71,500 Jews managed to flee the Greater German Reich between September 1939 and the end of 1941.[25] Even after the fall of France, ships continued to carry refugees to the Western Hemisphere from Lisbon, Casablanca, Tangier, Oran, and Marseilles. Spain became an important highway for Jews moving westward. According to Haim Avni's research, the Spanish authorities did not oppose Jewish refugees in principle, and more than 37,000 Jews may have passed through Spanish territory on their way to refuge somewhere else.[26] Those who escaped were the lucky few, however. Many more would have traveled all of these routes if refuge had been available.

Throughout the war, officials spoke of the severe restrictions placed upon refugee traffic by the lack of shipping space. Historians have shown, however, that the scarcity of carriers, while real enough, posed no absolute barrier to the transport of refugees. Ships were found during the war to transport over 400,000 German prisoners of war to camps in the United States. Ships carried Polish refugees from India to the west coast of the United States, Spanish Loyalist refugees to Mexico, and Yugoslav refugees to southern Italy and Egypt. Ships constantly returned to the New World lightly loaded after ferrying troops and munitions to Europe. As David Wyman says, "when the Allies wanted to find ships for nonmilitary projects, they located them." In the end the ships were not found because the directors of war priorities simply did not want to use them for that purpose, and other officials did not want to take the Jews in.[27]

What explains the near-universal opposition to receiving Jews in their hour of need? In every country, restrictionist and anti-immigrant sentiment, stimulated by economic depression, continued into the war period when nationalistic priorities blunted almost all humanitarian appeals. The fear of foreigners, deemed potential spies or saboteurs, played a part. Beyond this, historians have identified factors peculiar to each of the places studied, while acknowledging that anti-Jewish ideology was everywhere at work. The importance of antisemitism varied, however. Where it was particularly strong, as in the Canadian province of Quebec, for example, political leverage against Jewish refugees could be brought to bear.[28] In both Canada and the United States there was a strategically important second-echelon official strongly disposed against Jewish immigration who wielded unusual authority to bar the doors. Each of them, undoubtedly, was prejudiced against Jews.[29] In Britain, concerns over Palestine predisposed officials to suspect the motives of Jewish spokesmen and to oppose suggestions judged contrary to Imperial interests. Both the Colonial Office and the Foreign Office feared the radicalization of the Yishuv throughout the war and considerably exaggerated the Jewish political as well as military threat.[30]

Generally speaking, few historians believe antisemitism to have been decisive in blocking aid to the Jews. Much more significant in the United States, according to David Wyman, was the indifference of Franklin Delano Roosevelt, a lapse the author calls "the worst failure of his presidency." Although well informed about events in Europe, FDR was prepared to run no risks for the Jews, felt that action on their behalf meant trouble politically, and seems to have kept the issue out of his mind. Revered and even idolized by American Jews, the president had only a superficial grasp of Jewish issues and trimmed his policies to winds of political expediency. In his insouciance, indeed, the politically astute FDR reflected the wider indifference of the American public.[31] By contrast, the British prime minister seems to have had a far more imaginative and generous view of the Jewish catastrophe, referring to it in the summer of 1944 as "probably the greatest and most horrible crime ever committed in the whole history of the world."[32] Churchill, however, acted rarely in matters that concerned Jews, and in the final analysis ministerial officials had their way in most decisions that might have made a difference. According to Bernard Wasserstein, Jewish policy does not seem to have been decisively affected by antisemitism. "It was rather that within the context of the total war effort aid to the Jews of Europe was seen as a low priority which must give way to what were believed to be inexorable strategic realities." "Official thinking," he concludes, was constantly bound by imaginative limitations—the inability to grasp the import of the Final Solution, the unwillingness to acknowledge special Jewish needs because of the fears over Palestine, the extreme disinclination to consider rescue proposals, and "the blunting of ordinary human feelings when institutionalized in the straitjacket of bureaucratic procedure."[33]

In all countries the fate of the Jews was submerged in the global contest, the outcome of which appeared strongly in doubt until mid-1943. As Henry Feingold reminded us some time ago, the key decision makers in the war against Hitler rarely thought about Jews at all.[34] Jewish suppliants returned again and again from their interviews with statesmen and government officials with a single answer: the best way to help the Jews was to bring the war to the earliest conclusion. At the Bermuda Conference in April 1943, as Penkower has shown particularly clearly, the British and Americans proved most adept at postponing serious efforts to change matters. By this point, opinion was mobilized on behalf of several schemes for rescue and refuge. Such views were deflected, however; the press was kept at arm's length; and little was achieved.[35] A breakthrough of sorts came only in early 1944, when Roosevelt finally bowed to public pressure and established the War Refugee Board (WRB) to expedite various relief and rescue projects. Relying heavily on the WRB's own evaluation, Wyman surmises that the organization saved approximately 200,000 Jews and may have contributed to the survival of thousands more by warnings to Nazis, the dispatch of food parcels, and stimulating others to rescue attempts. Significant though this was, Wyman's analytical focus is on what might have been, agreeing with the agency's former director, John Pehle: "What we did was little enough. It was late. . . . Late and little, I would say."[36]

JEWISH COMMUNITIES

The theme of "too little, too late" frequently extends to analyses of Jewish communities outside Nazi Europe, providing material for anguished soul-searching and sometimes acrimonious debates over what could have been done to save some of Hitler's victims. For some, the eloquent appeals of Rabbi Weissmandel of Bratislava, pleading to Jewry in the free world for aid, have become a standing accusation against those who did not heed his call: "We cannot understand how you can eat and drink, how you can rest in your beds, how you can stroll in the streets—and I am sure that you are doing all those things—while this responsibility rests upon you. We have been crying out for months and you have done nothing."[37] Rabbi Weissmandel eventually despaired of world Jewry and became increasingly bitter over what he felt was their failure of solidarity. Several writers have taken up his charges.

Accusations against Jewish bystanders often share, it seems to me, two assumptions about the character of Jewish life at the time—that Jews easily grasped the essence of the Holocaust in Europe and that they were capable of "responding" effectively to it. It would be wrong, I believe, to assume that it was easier for Jews than for non-Jews to grasp the essence of the news from Europe. Indications are that it was equally difficult for both groups; much the same story of disbelief and uncertainty in the fact of the evidence can be told about the Jews themselves. In retrospect, the reports that came through Geneva, for example, analyzed by representatives of the

Jewish Agency and the World Jewish Congress, seem remarkably accurate and perceptive. But the Zionist agent in that city, Richard Lichtheim, constantly had difficulty convincing Jews in London, Washington, and Jerusalem. Walter Laqueur devoted a lengthy article to this subject appropriately entitled "Jewish Denial and the Holocaust"; his theme was not some insidious rejection of kinship with European Jews, but rather the much more simple bewilderment and confusion among a disorganized agglomeration of Jews facing unprecedented calamity.[38]

As to the realistic prospects for rescue, these will be considered shortly. But it may be useful to note at this point that hopes were highly inflated in certain Jewish quarters. Many felt, and some still feel, that Jews could impede the tide of death in Europe. "Jews believed then that there existed somewhere in the world, whether in the Oval Office or the Vatican or Downing Street, a spirit of civilization whose moral concern could be mobilized to save Jews," observes Henry Feingold. "The failure to arouse and mobilize that concern is the cause of the current despair regarding the role of the Jewish witness, and which leads to the search for betrayers. It is an assumption that continues to hold sway in Jewish political culture, despite the fact that there is little in recent Jewish experience that might confirm the existence of such a force in human affairs."[39]

Moreover, as opposed to what is sometimes assumed, there was no such thing as "world Jewry," in the sense of a unified, structured community, able to speak with one voice. Divided on national, cultural, religious, and political lines, Jewish leaders were incapable of agreeing among themselves. Zionists, Orthodox, religious moderates, and assimilationists divided most of the Jews between them, but these affinities were subdivided, and allegiances crossed from one group to another. As with historical treatments of various categories of bystanders, the best work on Jewish responses outside Nazi Europe has focused on particular groups, rooting their reactions in an identifiable culture and political outlook.

The Jewish community of Palestine, known as the Yishuv, provides remarkable confirmation of what has just been said. Almost half a million people at the time, this was a highly politicized and overwhelmingly European population—about 80 percent had come from eastern Europe. Most were newcomers and still had relatives in the countries that were being decimated during the Holocaust. If any Jewish community was likely to follow events in Hitler's Europe keenly, therefore, it was the Yishuv. And yet much the same story of reluctance to believe and a slowness to grasp the magnitude of the destruction can be told about Palestinian Jewry as about Jews elsewhere.[40] Reports from Nazi Europe were sometimes treated as unduly sensational or alarmist, and editors refused to believe what they printed in their own news columns. Publicists grasped at straws of hope and were reassured by Nazi ruses. Those who spread the most pessimistic reports were even accused of irresponsibility and divisiveness. "The news had reached Palestine," one labor leader reflected, "the newspapers had published [it] and also the [mandatory] radio service. The community read it and heard it but did not absorb it; and it did not raise its voice to alarm Jewish communities elsewhere."[41]

Palestinian Jewry responded to the war crisis much as Jews did everywhere. About thirty thousand joined the British army, some forming Jewish units that ultimately fought in North Africa and Italy as well as the Middle East.[42] Jewish authorities in Palestine organized public protests and collected money for "rescue" projects, but quarreled among themselves about the disposition of communal funds and the most appropriate action. For the first two years of the war most felt there was little that could be done, and attention remained focused on the Yishuv's domestic problems. These were serious enough, of course, and were made worse by the threat to Palestine from Rommel's Afrika Corps in the North African desert. The turning point for the Yishuv came in November 1942, when a group of former Palestinian Jewish residents returned to the country from Europe, after being exchanged for a group of German nationals held by the Allies. These refugees carried horrifying first-hand accounts of systematic murder that could not be doubted or ignored. For a small community such as the Yishuv, with close links to the Jews then being destroyed, the impact was devastating. Thereafter, public pressure mounted for some sort of reaction. Strategic concerns eased somewhat at the same time, following the German defeat at El Alamein. Disagreement continued, however. Within the Jewish Agency, the representative body of the Yishuv, opinion was split between those who wanted the focus of Jewish efforts to remain the building of the National Home in Palestine and those who wanted to pour the slender resources of the community into emergency aid for their European brethren. Jewish Agency leaders, men like David Ben Gurion, Moshe Shertok, and Eliezer Kaplan, tended to resist the emotional calls from a Palestinian Jewry for various kinds of action. In 1943 the Agency established a United Rescue Committee to probe and organize rescue possibilities. But the Jews continued to argue over priorities.[43] Many would agree with one scholar who judged it "extremely debatable whether the Yishuv mobilized its forces to their full potential during World War II."[44]

Division and a feeling of impotence also marked the reactions of Jewish leaders in the Western democracies. Critics now question such responses sharply, even prompting a private investigatory commission in the United States to look into the matter, headed by former U.S. Supreme Court justice Arthur Goldberg.[45] From that vantage point the established American Jewish leadership is seen as unduly timid and hesitating. Distracted by communal squabbling, American Jewish organizations were dominated by Stephen Wise, an aging Reform rabbi who shared his coreligionists' awe and trust in President Roosevelt. Dynamism and imagination came rather from the fringes of the American Jewish world.[46] Largely agreeing with this analysis, David Wyman paints a largely positive picture of the right-wing Palestinian emissary Peter Bergson and his group of prorefugee activists who burst on the American scene in early 1943 to goad Jews and non-Jews into more decisive action. Bergson's deliberately provocative Emergency Committee to Save the Jewish People of Europe generated shock waves of protest, contributing vitally, in Wyman's view, to the creation of the WRB. Yet while the Emergency Committee proved strong enough to shake the established Jewish leadership and provoke bitter divisions over rescue priorities, it was too weak to move the Roosevelt administration wholeheartedly to saving Jews. So long as American Jewry did not join this campaign, Wyman implies, an American-backed rescue potential could not fully be realized.[47]

Against this view, one may question whether American Jewry, which amounted to only 3.6 percent of an indifferent public, among which antisemitism was widespread, could ever have exercised important political leverage in Washington—united or disunited.[48] The Jews, as many of them realized, faced a near-hopeless situation—accounting for much of the demoralization that analysts now have the luxury to condemn. And as has also been pointed out, Jewish contemporaries had little alternative. The Republican party offered no plausible appeal to rescue advocates, and in any event the prospect of prying loose masses of Jews from Roosevelt's New Deal was virtually nonexistent. Attempting a media campaign, as Wyman's work suggests, was futile. One particularly forlorn exercise may be taken as emblematic of Jewish powerlessness: in December 1942, in New York City, half a million Jewish workers stopped work for ten minutes to protest the Nazis' murder of Jews. Labor leaders had considered striking for an hour, but abandoned the idea lest they be accused of hampering war production. The following day the Jews made up the ten minutes of lost working time.[49] However much it may be disparaged now, the argument that real rescue could only come with an Allied victory was compelling and persuasive. This was the position that Eleanor Roosevelt, presumably one of the staunchest friends of the Jews, maintained throughout. Breaking with this line seemed a sure way of increasing anti-Jewish feeling and injuring the Jews' postwar prospects for a national home.

Similar charges and responses could be mentioned with reference to Jewish communities in other Western countries, although the historian must make important allowances for particular circumstances in various places. Canadian Jews were at least as divided as their American counterparts, but felt far more vulnerable and exposed in their society than did the latter. Following the disappointment of the Bermuda Conference in 1943, when Rabbi Stephen Wise was conducting a vigorous public campaign, Canadian Jewish Congress leaders still hesitated to pressure their government forcefully to admit more refugees.[50] British Jews could never function as an ethnic pressure group—something that was both foreign to the British political culture and beyond the power of the extremely weak communal leadership. On the other hand, a handful of extremely influential Anglo-Jewish figures managed to expand the intake of refugees before the outbreak of war, although they won only minor concessions thereafter.[51] Swiss Jews faced an even more difficult task in persuading their highly cautious government to alter its stand against Jewish refugees. Constituting less than 0.5 percent of the population, nearly half of whom were not Swiss citizens, their national role was bound to be extremely limited.[52]

Readers may detect an undercurrent of masochism in some of these discussions—a disposition among Jews to deal with grief, a sense of loss, and possibly even guilt by casting blanket accusations against certain sections of the Jewish community itself. To many it will also seem that these exercises are profoundly unhistorical—involving little effort to probe the assumptions of the day, and an inadequate appreciation of contemporaries' limited horizons. Clearly more could have been done—by Jews as well as by non-Jews. But more could always have been done, and the best that historians can do, it seems to me, is to try to understand the reasons why it was not done.

THE SOVIET UNION

Writing on bystanders to the Nazi Holocaust has largely ignored the Soviets, whose policies toward Jews, to the extent that these were even formulated, remain locked in Soviet archives, protected from historical investigation. What we do know, however, is grim enough. Jews escaping from Nazi Germany during the prewar period could scarcely consider going to the Soviet Union, torn by forced collectivization of agriculture and the catastrophic famine entailed by Stalin's policies, along with the bloody purges against the designated enemies of the great dictator. During the late 1930s the Soviet Union officially rejected the idea of receiving Jewish refugees from Hitler—the only great power to have taken an open, principled stand against doing so. The Soviets argued that the refugees, predominantly middle class and assumed to be conditioned by capitalism, were unsuited to life in their country. Their homelessness, moreover, derived from fascism and the quarrels among the capitalist states, matters declared not the responsibility of the USSR. During the late 1930s Soviet delegates to the League of Nations opposed refugee-aid projects, and Soviet diplomats flatly rejected all approaches by Western countries hoping to share the burden with them.[53]

Soviet policy toward Jewish refugees during the war is best understood in the context of the Russian effort to bind to the Soviet state newly incorporated subject peoples in territories on her western frontiers and the phenomenal mobilization of this huge society to meet the Nazi challenge. Around a million Jews came under Soviet rule after the Red Army moved into eastern Poland in 1939, partitioning that country with the Germans, and an estimated 300,000 more, almost 10 percent of the Polish-Jewish population, fled German-held territory soon afterward to parts held by the Russians. (Some Jews fled in the other direction, from the Soviet to the German zone.) Additional Jews came under Soviet domination with the annexation of the Baltic states and some former Rumanian territory in mid-1940. Altogether the Russians absorbed approximately 2 million Jews. For the next year and a half, before the Germans attacked eastward, the Soviets worked hard to break up the institutions of Polish and other national allegiance and to subdue any opposition to the Soviet state. Jews were accorded Soviet citizenship, and to some degree their ethnic identity was favored as a means to offset alternative loyalties.[54]

When the Germans struck in 1941, Moscow ordered masses of people evacuated from the path of the Wehrmacht, and hundreds of thousands left in panic and confusion. Polish sources estimated the number of Polish evacuees at between 1 million and 2 million. Yisrael Gutman puts the number of Jews among these exiles at 400,000— yielding a proportion substantially greater than among the prewar non-Jewish Polish population. Other Jews from the Baltic region and from elsewhere in the Soviet Union were either evacuated or fled eastward on their own. According to another scholar, between 1 million and 1.5 million Jews escaped the invaded Soviet territory, including Soviet Jews as well.[55] Despite Soviet claims that Moscow struggled to save the Jews from the special dangers they faced from the Germans, there is no hint that such concerns preoccupied the Soviet leadership at the time. Jews doubtless figured importantly among the evacuees because their proportion among Polish exiles in Russia was previously high, because of loyalties to Moscow kindled in the preceding months, and because most of them knew of the mortal threat they faced under the Nazis. The German attack seems to have so stunned the Soviets that concerted policy of any kind was virtually impossible. Jews fleeing eastward were blocked by troops at certain points but their passage was facilitated at others. To the extent that there was any planning behind the evacuations, the authorities seem to have been concerned to pull back from the war zone those elements of the population most able to rebuild the shattered Soviet economy. Only in the Crimea were Jews evacuated en masse, and it is possible that these were simply caught up in the sweeping removals of ethnic Germans whom the Russians did not want to see behind German lines.[56]

Many Jews did not survive the rigors of exile in the Soviet Union following their deportation, evacuation, or flight to the interior. Conditions were terrible, although it is unlikely they were any worse for Jews than for other evacuees moved about the vast expanses of the Soviet state. So far as one can tell, Moscow remained suspicious of many of the Jewish refugees from Poland, particularly those who had not accepted Soviet citizenship when it had been offered. Tens of thousands of Jews ended up in labor camps of northern Russia and Siberia, where mortality was extremely high.[57] Soviet policy toward Polish Jews, as Yisrael Gutman has shown, was largely a function of Stalin's wider geopolitical concerns, particularly his relations with a future Polish state. When Moscow reached agreement with the Polish authorities in 1941, the Russians permitted Jews to join the Polish army under General Władysław Anders recruited in the Soviet Union; however, the Soviets also encouraged Jews as well as Ukrainians and Belorussians to join the Red Army instead, thereby undermining, as a precedent for the future, Polish claims to rule territory in which there were non-Polish nationalities.[58]

There was never any question of Soviet participation in rescue efforts directed at Nazi-held territory, despite the Russians' proximity to the German killing centers. Given their resolute refusal to assist the Polish Home Army at the time, when the non-Communist Poles were in desperate straits, no one seems to have believed that the Soviets would bomb access to the camp of Auschwitz or otherwise intervene to stay the hands of the Nazi executioners.[59] The Soviet military machine rolled through former Polish territory in 1944, when the Nazis were killing up to twelve thousand Jews a day in Auschwitz, but there is no indication that concerns about the Holocaust affected tactical decisions. It was the Red Army that liberated the death camps in Poland, of course, and soldiers of a Soviet Ukrainian division who first entered Auschwitz in January 1945. In stark contrast to the blaze of publicity that accompanied the grisly discoveries in the west, the Soviets then imposed their habitual secrecy. For weeks after the inmates were freed, contemporaries heard nothing. Not long after Auschwitz was captured, the British enquired politely what the Soviets had found. Foreign Minister Andrei Vyshinski sent a stock reply and alluded to an elaborate report on the

camp, then in preparation. When this report was finally released, in
May, the broadcast version did not even mention the word *Jew*.[60] It
seems reasonable to conclude with the historian Dov Levin about
Soviet policy that "the humanitarian component and the desire to
save Jews were insignificant."[61]

NEUTRALS

Throughout the war neutral governments were in a unique position to lend aid to Jews—either by receiving refugees, passing crucial information to the West, or intervening diplomatically to rescue
individuals. Broadly speaking, the research on neutral countries has
discovered few instances of magnanimity. In each of these countries
political leaders learned how unrelenting the Germans were on Jewish matters and feared offending the Nazis on issues they judged pe-
ripheral to their own national interests. With the outbreak of war,
moreover, all felt themselves highly vulnerable economically—to
the point in some cases of being at the mercy of the Axis states.
Moreover, European governments that remained outside the conflict worried constantly—and usually with good reason—that they
might be drawn into the fighting. Up to the end of 1942 Nazi Germany appeared invincible and likely to consolidate its domination
of the continent. Then came the battles of Stalingrad and El Alamein, and the American landings in North Africa. More reverses
followed in 1943—the spectacular German defeat in the great tank
battle of Kursk, the collapse of Mussolini, the Anglo-American in-
vasions of Sicily and the Italian peninsula, and the powerful air of-
fensive against the Reich itself. Opponents of Nazism everywhere
took heart. Manifestly weakened, the Germans became notably less
effective at bullying neutral governments. In consequence, the policy of the neutrals began to shift. Some refugees were admitted, and
protection was occasionally extended to threatened Jews under
Nazi control. This is the broad context within which historians
have examined the policies of Switzerland, Sweden, Spain, Portugal,
and Turkey during the Holocaust.

As we have already noted, Spain and Portugal received tens of
thousands of refugees, many of them Jews, despite the superficial

affinities of their regimes with the Third Reich. Haim Avni emphasizes the extreme caution that marked Spanish policy: Jews who eluded German or French patrols along the Franco-Spanish frontier and who managed the harrowing trip across the Pyrenees could enter Spain; but the Spaniards made it clear that they would have to pass through the country, as Foreign Minister Jordana y Sousa once put it, "as light passes through a glass, leaving no trace." [62] Refugees suffered terribly from poor conditions in Spanish transit camps, from corrupt officials, and from extortionate shipping companies. But the flow was never interrupted for long, and as many as forty thousand Jews may have been saved as a result. The port of Lisbon, the goal of most refugees entering Spain and hoping to sail for the New World, became the refugee capital of Europe and the nerve center of various relief agencies trying to help Jews escape. [63]

The Swiss have acknowledged their own sharply restrictive policy toward refugees, following a thorough parliamentary report in 1957 by Carl Ludwig. [64] In essence Swiss policy rested on a perception of extreme vulnerability—popularized by an image of the Swiss Confederation as "a lifeboat in a great sea disaster, with only very limited space and even more limited provisions." [65] Antisemitism and exaggerated fears of foreigners certainly played some role on the lifeboat as well, however, and may indeed explain the unusual collusion between German authorities in Berlin and the head of the Swiss police, Heinrich Rothmund, in establishing special markings for Jews' passports in 1938. Rothmund continued to wield authority over refugee matters during the war, claiming afterward that such caution was absolutely necessary in view of the dangers the Confederation faced. Barring the door whenever the flow of refugees increased, as for example in the summer and autumn of 1942, the Swiss eased their restrictions somewhat toward the latter part of the war. During 1944, with the end in sight, masses of new refugees were accepted, including some Jews who had miraculously escaped the Nazis' dragnet to that point. The Swiss saved nearly twenty-two thousand Jews during the war, but also turned back many thousands. No one can say how many were expelled from Switzerland or dissuaded by the reality of expulsions from even trying to reach refuge there. [66]

Was the fear that the Germans would swamp the neutrals' lifeboats exaggerated? However much they may have wished, the Nazis do not seem to have been in a position to apply the ultimate pressure during the period 1943–45, when the Final Solution was consuming its victims everywhere, and when neutrals were proving uncooperative participants in the Nazis' New Order of Europe. The Swiss never faced direct Nazi pressure to refuse refugees or to send back specific fugitives who did find refuge in the Confederation. It was much the same with the Swedes. Providing badly needed raw materials to the Reich without the latter having to pay the costs of occupation, Stockholm was able to defy the Führer in the autumn of 1943 by receiving thousands of Jewish refugees from Denmark. The Spaniards and Turks, even though more disposed to the Germans than democratic neutrals, felt obligations toward Jews of their respective nationalities when they were threatened by deportation from Nazi-occupied states.[67] From our vantage point it is easy to go even further and call the Nazi threats a bluff; in places such as Bern, Stockholm, Istanbul, Madrid, and Lisbon, however, this seemed to most a dangerous gamble until very late in the game.[68]

There were plenty of Jews to be saved at the very end, however, as we shall see in the next chapter. By that point, every neutral was willing to do more, and sometimes much more. Particular circumstances lent themselves to unusual diplomatic activity and extensive rescue. One of these occurred in Budapest in the autumn and winter of 1944–45, when many thousands of Jews were suddenly faced with deportation from a former ally of the Reich, just as the tide of war was turning decisively against the Nazis and the Soviet armies were approaching the Hungarian capital. The Swiss, Spanish, Portuguese, and the Vatican embassies saved large numbers of endangered Hungarian Jews, but the most energetic efforts of all were coordinated from the Swedish embassy, energized by Raoul Wallenberg, a businessman turned diplomat from Stockholm. Financed by the American Jewish Joint Distribution Committee via the War Refugee Board, and with the support of his own government, Wallenberg used bribery, bluff, and deception to pluck many thousands of Jews from certain death. There is scarcely a better example of how an intrepid, strategically placed individual could capitalize on the standing of a neutral power to effect large-scale rescue.[69]

THE CATHOLIC CHURCH

It is not always appreciated that the Vatican too was neutral, having committed itself from the very beginning of the war to the policy of conciliation that marked church diplomacy in the interwar period. To the Vatican, neutrality meant remaining apart from the two power blocs and, most important, maintaining an environment in which the church could operate as freely and openly as possible. Particularly since the presentation of Rolf Hochhuth's angry play, *Der Stellvertreter* (*The Deputy*) in 1962, this posture has been subjected to withering criticism. The Vatican has responded with the publication of a voluminous collection of documents on the role of the Holy See during the war, generating one of the most extensive historical discussions of the many ethical questions associated with the history of the Holocaust.[70]

Historians generally see the policy of Pius XII as consistent with a longstanding tradition of Vatican diplomacy. During political storms of the depression years, this tradition was interpreted by Eugenio Pacelli, cardinal secretary of state under Pius XI, and later to become the wartime pope. Pacelli exemplified a profound commitment to the spiritual and pastoral mission of the Holy See; he saw his role as avoiding association with power blocs and forging diplomatic links with conservative or even fascist regimes. As fascism extended its influence in Europe during the 1930s the Vatican remained aloof, occasionally challenging fascist ideology when it touched on important matters of Catholic doctrine or the legal position of the church, but unwilling to interfere with what it considered to be purely secular concerns. Beyond this, the Vatican found most aspects of right-wing regimes congenial, appreciating their patronage of the church, their challenge to Marxism, and their frequent championing of a conservative social vision.[71]

The Vatican quarreled with both Hitler and Mussolini on race, but hardly out of concern for the welfare of Jews. Throughout this period the church seldom opposed anti-Jewish persecutions and rarely denounced governments for discriminatory practices; when it did so, it usually admonished governments to act with "justice and charity," disapproving only of violent excesses or the most extravagant forms of oppression. Much more important for church policy was the clash between the pseudobiological bases of racism and the fundamental principles of Catholicism and church authority. The tendency of fascist movements, especially Nazism, to use race as a foundation of their regimes directly challenged the church's claims in the fields of baptism, marriage, and, more broadly, the definition of who was and who was not a Catholic. The Holy See sometimes muted its opposition, usually preferring conciliation and diplomacy even on fundamental questions such as these. Nevertheless, conflict could break through the surface. One notable occasion was March 1937, when the papal encyclical *Mit brennender Sorge* (*With Burning Concern*) condemned the false and heretical teachings of Nazism.[72] The Holy See openly protested Mussolini's turn toward racism the following year. Yet at the same time the Vatican strove to avoid an open breach—as it was to continue to do throughout the war. As always the goal was political neutrality and the safeguarding of the institutional interests of the church in a perilous political world.

Church policy toward Jews during the war can be seen in this historical perspective. For the first few years persecution seems to have caused few ripples at the Vatican and awakened no more interest or sympathy than in the 1930s. Church diplomats continued to speak in favor of "justice and charity," but were largely unconcerned about the persecution of Jews by the Nazi or collaborationist governments. A striking illustration comes from the autumn of 1941, when the French ambassador to the Holy See, Léon Bérard, sent an extensive report to Vichy on the Vatican's views. According to this diplomat the Holy See was not interested in the French antisemitic laws and worried only that they might undermine church jurisdiction or involve occasional breaches of "justice and charity." So far as the French were concerned, the Vatican essentially gave them a green light to legislate as they chose against Jews.[73]

When mass killings began, the Vatican was extremely well informed through its own diplomatic channels and through a variety of other contacts. Church officials may have been the first to pass on to the Holy See sinister reports about the significance of deportation convoys in 1942, and they continued to receive the most detailed information about mass murder in the east.[74] Despite numerous appeals, however, the pope refused to issue explicit denunciations of the murder of Jews or call upon the Nazis directly to stop the killing. Pius determinedly maintained his posture of neutrality and declined to associate himself with Allied declarations against Nazi war crimes. The most the pope would do was to encourage humanitarian aid by subordinates within the church, issue vague appeals against the oppression of unnamed racial and religious groups, and try to ease the lot of Catholics of Jewish origin, caught up in the Nazis' net of persecution. And with distinguished exceptions, the corps of Vatican diplomats did no better.[75]

As Léon Papeleux makes clear, the Vatican's posture shifted during the course of the war, as did that of other neutrals: the Holy See gradually became more forthcoming in its *démarches* on behalf of Jews and more overt in its assistance to the persecuted. But the pope remained reluctant to speak out almost until the very end. In the autumn of 1943, with Rome under German occupation, the Nazis began roundups of Jews virtually on the doorstep of the papal palace. On a knife's edge, the pope seems to have balanced carefully, fearing at any moment that the SS might descend on the Vatican itself. In his signals to Berlin, the German ambassador to the Holy See Ernst von Weizsäcker portrayed a pro-German pope, alluding to his reluctance to protest the assault on the Jews. Was Weizsäcker delicately trying to subvert the intentions of the SS by suggesting the high price the Reich might have to pay for the persecutions? Was he trying to protect the pope from direct Nazi moves against him? Or was he accurately reporting the perspectives of the Holy See? Interpretations of this episode vary widely—from those who see Pius playing a delicate, complicated game with Nazi occupiers, expressing himself cryptically, to those who read the incident as a further indication of church reluctance to take any risks on behalf of Jews.[76]

Our understanding of church policy now extends considerably beyond Hochhuth's accusations and related charges of pro-German and antisemitic pressures at the Vatican. It is true that Pacelli had served many years as papal nuncio in Germany and feared mightily during the war that the defeat of the Nazis would lead to the triumph of Bolshevism in Europe. But Vatican documents do not indicate a guarded pro-Nazism or a supreme priority of opposition to the Soviet Union. Nor do they reveal a particular indifference to the fate of Jews, let alone hostility toward them. Rather, the Vatican's communications, along with other evidence, suggest a resolute commitment to its traditional policy of reserve and conciliation.

The goal was to limit the global conflict where possible and above all to protect the influence and standing of the church as an independent voice. Continually apprehensive of schisms within the church, Pius strove to maintain the allegiance of Catholics in Germany, in Poland, and elsewhere. Fearful too of threats from the outside, the pope dared not confront the Nazis or the Italian Fascists directly. Notably, the papacy maintained its reserve not against Jewish appeals but in the face of others as well. The Holy See turned a deaf ear to anguished calls from Polish bishops to denounce the Nazis' atrocities in Poland; issued no explicit call to stop the so-called euthanasia campaign in the Reich; deeply offended many by receiving the Croatian dictator Ante Pavelić, whose men butchered an estimated 700,000 Orthodox Serbs; and refused to denounce Italian aggression against Greece. Beyond this, there is a widespread sense that, however misguided politically, Pius himself felt increasingly isolated, threatened, and verging on despair. With an exaggerated faith in the efficacy of his mediative diplomacy, Pius clung to the wreckage of his prewar policy—"a kind of anxiously preserved virginity in the midst of torn souls and bodies," as one sympathetic observer puts it.[77]

Individual churchmen, of course, reacted otherwise, and there is a long list of Catholic clergy who saw their Christian duty as requiring intervention on behalf of persecuted Jews. Often the deportation convoys galvanized priests to action. In some cases, as with the intervention of the apostolic delegate Giuseppe Burzio in Catholic Slovakia, such appeals may well have made a difference. In Bucharest Nuncio Andreia Cassulo pleaded with the Rumanian government for humane treatment for the Jews and actually visited Jewish deportees in Transnistria. In Budapest Nuncio Angelo Rotta intervened repeatedly with Admiral Horthy on behalf of Hungarian Jews and may have helped secure papal intervention in the summer of 1944. Angelo Roncalli, the apostolic delegate in Turkey and the future Pope John XXIII, was among the most sensitive to the Jewish tragedy and most vigorous in rescue efforts despite his reflection, at the time, of traditional Catholic attitudes toward Jews.[78] Elsewhere, on the other hand, church leaders replicated the posture of the Vatican itself—or even deferred with greater or lesser sympathy to those directing the machinery of destruction. Outstanding in this respect was the timid and profascist Cesare Orsenigo, the nuncio in

Berlin, who appeared wedded to the views of the German government. The pope did not dictate policy on such matters to his subordinates and allowed them to go their own way. His timidity in this respect may be one of the most important charges against him.[79]

In retrospect, some historians have come to appreciate the tactical caution of the Holy See. Günther Lewy, for example, suggests that a "flaming protest" by the pope against the perpetrators of genocide would almost certainly have failed to move the German public and would likely have made matters worse—especially for the half-Jews or *Mischlinge,* as well as for practicing Catholics in Germany.[80] Others claim that much of the present condemnation of Vatican policy springs from mistaken assumptions about church doctrine. It may be quite correct to say, as does Father John Morley, that the Vatican "betrayed the ideals it set for itself."[81] But sincere churchmen at the time could certainly judge those ideals otherwise. As Leonidas Hill reminds us, "the theology of the Church lays far less emphasis on saving lives than on saving souls through the consolations of religion."[82] Seeing the institutional church as a supreme value in its own right, those in charge of its fortunes tended unhesitatingly to put these ahead of the victims of Nazism.

9. THE END OF THE HOLOCAUST

THE LAST PHASE of the Holocaust contains an important puzzle for the historian. On the one hand there is every sign that the Nazis pressed forward zealously with their objective to eliminate the Jews. In May 1944 the deportations of Hungarian Jewry to Auschwitz began, carrying over 400,000 Jews northward to their deaths. Jews streamed to the camp from other places as well—from Lodz, where a remnant had continued to work, grimly hoping to avoid the murderous end of so many ghettos; from Theresienstadt, where Jews had been kept in an antechamber to Auschwitz—photographed and visited to prove to the world Germany's benign intentions; and from other camps, where according to SS calculations it no longer paid to keep the Jews alive. In France regular deportation convoys left Paris for Poland for two months after the Allies went ashore in Normandy, with SS officers working frenetically to accomplish as much as they could before the liberating armies arrived. On the other hand, even as 10,000 Jews a day were being murdered in the most destructive stage of the Final Solution, some who had been involved in the killings sent signals to the West about possible negotiations to end the process of mass murder. The evidence suggests, moreover, that the offers to suspend the Final Solution and ransom the remaining Jews of Europe were not wild proposals of a few Nazi underlings. There are indications that they were part of a much wider scheme that may have originated with

Himmler himself. There remains considerable dispute about this paradoxical situation—not least of all because interpretations might reflect importantly on Nazi policy.

Historians have often departed from their customary descriptive and analytical text to ask whether more could have been done, particularly at the end of the war, to rescue Jews. Put this way, as it often is, the answer must invariably be yes. More could always have been done, and as we saw in the last chapter historians have had no trouble documenting the unwillingness of the Allies to alter wartime priorities to save Jewish lives. The last phase of the Final Solution casts this refusal into particularly sharp relief, however, because concrete rescue proposals were aired in London and Washington, and because possibilities of intervention which had not existed before suddenly presented themselves.

RANSOM NEGOTIATIONS

Nazi suggestions about ransoming Jews first reached the West in the last days of 1942, when a representative of the World Jewish Congress in Geneva received word that the Rumanian authorities, with the approval of Berlin, might permit the emigration of a large number of Jews interned in horrible circumstances in Rumanian-controlled Transnistria, after payment of a large sum of money. About the same time Dieter Wisliceny, formerly Eichmann's representative in Bratislava, discussed with Slovakian Jewish leaders the possibility of the Germans' ending deportations from part of Europe in exchange for 2 million dollars and agreement on additional negotiations. This was the so-called Europa Plan, which ran into the sand after a few months, but which was supposed to be resumed, according to Jewish sources, at a more propitious moment. In the following year, which was disastrous for German arms, the pace of negotiations quickened. In mid-1944 Wisliceny, then part of Eichmann's team in Budapest, began tortuous negotiations with Hungarian Jewish leaders. Eichmann himself took charge of the discussions and apparently offered to save the lives of a million Jews in exchange for ten thousand trucks and some other material—suggesting that the vehicles would only be used against the Red Army and not the western Allies. This offer was carried out of Hungary by

Joel Brand, who immediately fell into the hands of the British, together with a mysterious comrade named Bandi Grosz, who was probably a German agent. Highly suspicious of this bizarre venture, London and Washington did not pursue it directly. The Americans, however, were prepared to string the Germans along.

Meanwhile, complicated talks continued between the Nazis and Hungarian Jews, notably the thirty-year-old Zionist leader Rezsö Kasztner. Before long these led to contacts between Kurt Becher, an SS emissary of Himmler, and Jewish representatives in Switzerland. Eventually the Americans became directly involved in the person of Roswell McClelland, a War Refugee Board officer on the staff of the American embassy in Bern. Himmler himself undertook negotiations in the last months of the war—meeting on several occasions in late 1944 and early 1945 with a Swiss politician and former pro-Nazi named Jean-Marie Musy, who acted as an intermediary for the Union of Orthodox Rabbis in the United States. In April 1945 the SS chief even talked with a Swedish representative of the World Jewish Congress, Norbert Masur, apparently still hoping to join the West in a crusade against Bolshevism. According to Himmler's personal physician, Felix Kersten, the SS chief declared that he wanted "to bury the hatchet between us and the Jews."[1] Not much came of all these discussions beyond the liberation of a few thousand Jews, although it is possible to link these talks with detailed arrangements, at the very end of the war, providing for the surrender of some Nazi concentration camps to the Allies before the SS had a chance to murder all of the inmates.

Little is known for certain about what motivated the Germans who made these *démarches,* and it is difficult to say how such proposals originated.[2] Although Wisliceny referred to the Europa Plan in postwar testimony, the German records are generally silent on the subject, and much of the story is pieced together from descriptions by the Jews of their meetings with the Nazis, Allied diplomatic correspondence, and postwar records of some of the Germans involved. In his testimony in Jerusalem in 1960, Eichmann cast little light on the matter; he attributed all his own negotiations to Himmler, implying that while instructions for trading with the Jews may have gone against the grain professionally, they had to be followed as any other orders.

Historians diverge in their interpretations of these events. Lucy

Dawidowicz apparently thinks the ransom talks unimportant, barely mentioning them in her full-length treatment of the Holocaust. Hilberg discusses them more fully, but seems mainly interested in the failure of the western Allies to take up the offers, and the allegedly pusillanimous role of Hungarian Jewish leaders who are seen to have preferred negotiation to resistance.[3] In *Auschwitz and the Allies,* Martin Gilbert follows the fervently advanced opinion of Rudolf Vrba, who escaped from Auschwitz in the spring of 1944 and hoped to galvanize Hungarian Jewish leaders to oppose deportations. Vrba insists that the negotiations were another of the Nazis' ingenious deceptions, intended to lull the Jews into inaction. In correspondence with Gilbert, he termed the German offer "a clever ruse . . . to neutralize the potential resistance of a million people."[4]

Yehuda Bauer takes the German offers much more seriously. In his view, high-ranking Nazis seriously considered the possibility of bartering with the Jews of Europe from the end of 1942, when the Germans suffered stunning defeats in North Africa and the Soviet Union, and when it appeared that the Hitlerian empire might contract. Bauer postulates that, having previously determined on the murder of European Jewry, the Nazis may have entertained the possibility of reverting to the earlier policy of emigration—at least for some Jews—as another means of ridding Europe of its Jewish plague. All of this is to be seen, suggests Bauer, in the context of the quest by certain highly placed Germans for a separate peace with Britain and the United States. These probes involved no break with Nazi anti-Jewish ideology. To the contrary, the fantastic idea of using the Jews to open talks with their western enemies may best be understood within the framework of the Nazis' obsessive anti-semitism. Himmler and his followers, according to Bauer, "believed the Nazi theory that the Jews, a demonic force, were running the world; in an attempt to strike a compromise with the West the European Jews in SS hands thus might be key hostages (*Faustpfand*), compelling the Western powers (under their Jewish dominance!) to come to terms with an SS-run Germany."[5]

A recent biography of Himmler's deputy Ernst Kaltenbrunner reminds us of how important, in the final stages of the war, were the bitter rivalries among the highest-ranking Nazi dignitaries, leading sometimes to bizarre, eleventh-hour proposals to reorient the Reich. SS police boss Kaltenbrunner opposed Himmler's negotiating efforts with Becher, possibly for ideological reasons, but certainly also out of anger for having been bypassed in these sensitive discussions. In order to sabotage these efforts, Kaltenbrunner disclosed aspects of the negotiations to Hitler, who promptly threatened with death any German who allowed Jews to escape. By this point, however, the Führer's grip on reality may have been insufficient to prevent the Byzantine intrigues of his satraps. Strange as it may seem, the ideologically unimaginative police chief may have drifted into his own schemes to ransom Jews in the last months of the war. Unlike the Reichsführer SS, however, the conservative Kaltenbrunner was unwilling to break fully with Hitler on the issue and never carried these talks to their treasonous conclusion. As Peter Black sees it, such efforts were not desperate attempts to provide postwar alibis or other means of escaping justice, as some have claimed; rather they were last-ditch efforts to save the battered Reich. "Himmler and Kaltenbrunner believed that the only inevitable collapse was that of the Grand Alliance and sought to use their miserable hostages to gain time until events turned to their advantage."[6]

Did the Nazis really expect results from these discussions? It is impossible to say. No doubt there was something absurd and contradictory about all of these efforts. But Nazi ideology itself was equally ludicrous, and so was practically everything that continued to be done in its name until the final moments of the war. Some of Hitler's lieutenants, apparently, were ready to abandon the genocidal program in favor of other objectives of a dying regime. On the other hand, the Führer drew opposite conclusions from the desperate situation, forbidding any negotiation on Jews or any other matter, and in his last moments fulminating against "International Jewry," now held responsible for the German catastrophe.[7]

The role of the Allies in these curious negotiations has generated relatively little dispute. Quite apart from their engrained skepticism about German intentions and their reluctance to negotiate with the enemy, British officials opposed suggestions that large numbers of Jews might be evacuated from Nazi Europe, fearing that this would put pressure on their immigration restrictions for Palestine. Where, these officials regularly asked themselves, would the liberated Jews go? American State Department officers also looked askance at such proposals, being extremely cautious about any transfer of funds to the enemy camp. The British, always eager to tighten their blockade against the Reich, presented an even stronger obstacle to such transfers. Also, both London and Washington were cognizant of German hopes to split them from their Soviet allies and insisted that they work in tandem with Moscow. For their part, the supremely defensive Soviets refused to countenance discussions of any sort with the enemy, leaving Westerners with no choice but to denounce the various offers. The British prime minister did so with particular gusto, despite his obvious sympathy for the Jews and his recognition of their plight. Having declared since taking office in May 1940 that there could be no negotiation or parley with the enemy, one can hardly read his refusal to do so during the Brand mission as an outstanding lapse or an instance of special callousness toward the Jews.[8] Roosevelt, on the other hand, seems to have been interested in exploring possibilities for saving Jews, and the War Refugee Board certainly countenanced talks with the Nazis in the last months of the Reich. Washington differed from London about pursuing such talks and showed far more energy in prying loose refugees from Axis control near the end of the war.[9]

Debate over the Jewish response to the Nazi offers is much more intense and focuses particularly on the Hungarian leadership. Ever since a spectacular libel trial in Israel in the mid-1950s dealing with accusations against Kasztner for negotiating with the Nazis, and the subsequent murder of Kasztner, there has been acrimonious dispute about the motivation of Jews involved in the negotiations.[10] As we have seen, some insist that the entire business was a Nazi ruse, intended to lull Jews into complying with the Germans and assisting the process of deportation. Rudolf Vrba believes that the message he carried from Auschwitz, together with his fellow escapee Gerhard Wetzler, ought to have galvanized Hungarian Jewish leaders for resistance; instead, they were seduced by the prospect of obtaining favors from the Nazis, including, it must be said, special privileges for their own families. "Passive *and* active potential resistance of a million people would create panic and havoc in Hungary," he estimated. "Panic in Hungary would have been better than panic which came to the victims in front of burning pits in Birkenau. Eichmann knew it; that is why he smoked cigars with the

Kastners, 'negotiated,' exempted the 'real great rabbis,' and meanwhile, without panic among the deportees, planned to 'resettle' hundreds of thousands in orderly fashion."[11]

Others defend the Hungarian Jewish negotiators, seeing them as caught in a near-hopeless situation and trying to hold off the Germans with the few, inadequate tools at their disposal. Hungarian Jewish leaders had been in constant touch with their coreligionists in Slovakia and believed that negotiations there had succeeded in suspending deportations. At the center of much wartime refugee activity, they had also established contacts in the Abwehr, the ramshackle and ideologically fickle intelligence unit of the German army. Having succeeded for several years in clandestine operations smuggling Jews out of the Nazis' clutches, and having links also with the American Jewish Joint Distribution Committee, Jews such as Kasztner and Joel Brand had reason to hope that they might succeed in their fantastic scheme.[12]

Randolph Braham concludes that the Hungarian leaders based their rescue attempt on what was a perfectly logical assumption at the time—that their best chance was to deal directly with the Germans instead of the Hungarians. Even when the prospects for a deal began to crumble, says Braham, Kasztner was drawn by the prospect of saving a remnant of Hungarian Jewry—including, to be sure, some of his own friends and relatives. In essence the Hungarians seem to have faced one of those impossible dilemmas that we have seen before in discussing the behavior of Jewish leaders. What was their alternative? One can only speculate on how Hungarian Jews might have reacted to the strategy Vrba urged from the beginning—sounding an alarm. Bauer believes that this would have made little difference. After all, stories about the destination of the deportation convoys already circulated in Hungary; as elsewhere, Jews in Hungary were reluctant to believe the worst and rejected such information from whatever source. It seems unlikely, as well, that much could have been done to organize resistance. Most of the men between ages twenty and forty-eight were absent, having been taken off to labor battalions. The Jews were effectively isolated in Hungarian society. Much of the population and administration were hostile. Flight was virtually impossible. The Hungarian Jews were trapped.[13]

Jewish negotiators inside the prison of the Third Reich, pleading desperately with Jews in the West to conclude agreements with the Nazis, were understandably impatient and often accused their co-religionists of bad faith. As we have seen, Rabbi Weissmandel in Bratislava fulminated against Jews in the West for their delay and lack of energy in pursuing rescue. Several authors have accepted this perspective on the rescue negotiations, giving rise to additional controversies surrounding the response of Jews abroad. In particular, this has prompted a harsh evaluation of Saly Mayer, the sixty-two-year-old former head of the Swiss Jewish community federation, the Gemeindebund, and the Swiss representative of the American Joint Distribution Committee (JDC), who engaged in key discussions with the Germans in 1944. Mayer played an important role in the talks with the SS that began in Budapest with Eichmann's offer to exchange Jews for trucks and met with Himmler's emissaries to discuss how the Germans would be paid. Critics portray him as a tight-fisted bureaucrat, unwilling to strain every effort to save fellow Jews.[14] Yehuda Bauer, after a thorough examination of the JDC, American, and British documents, concludes that Mayer was playing a hopeless bluff—"impossible diplomacy (*die unmögliche Diplomatie*)," in his own words.[15] Forbidden at the start by the Americans to transfer goods or money to the Germans, and hobbled by his inability to dispose of large amounts of cash from Jewish organizations abroad, the brittle and sometimes abrasive Mayer pursued several complicated lines of negotiation at once—drawing out the discussions, promising much and delivering little, in the hope that lives eventually could be saved. Bauer has some critical words for both Mayer and the Jewish organizations involved—about the former for his excessive secretiveness and pettiness in dealing with Jewish agencies, and about the latter for their lack of unity and tendency to quarrel with one another. Nevertheless, Mayer's achievements seem real, in an area where few organizations or individuals can say as much: several hundred Jews were indeed saved, as "down-payments" on future releases; some Germans were sufficiently convinced by the bluff to continue talking for months, possibly restraining, in a few instances, the most murderous forces in the Reich; and a breach with the Americans was prevented—something that would have had catastrophic results. No one can say for sure that another negotiator would have done better.[16]

As this short survey suggests, uncertainty persists to this day, not only about various German motivations, but also about the negotiations' potential. Could large numbers of Jews really have been saved by such means? As one might expect, those who credit the Germans with serious intentions usually believe that large-scale rescue was at least possible. But the question of how many and under what circumstances Jews could have been rescued depends on other factors as well, some which will be explored below.

OTHER RESCUE OPTIONS

Proposals made in 1944 that the Allies help the Jews by bombing the death camp of Auschwitz have involved considerable analysis by historians.[17] In essence, this discussion concerns a path not taken; the key questions are how the idea arose and why it was not taken up. The first suggestion of this nature probably came in May 1944 from Rabbi Weissmandel in Bratislava who envisioned the imminent deportation of Hungarian Jewry to Auschwitz. In a coded telegram to the Swiss Orthodox community intended for transmission to the United States, Weissmandel urged the bombardment of the railway lines leading to the camp, in order to interrupt the deportations. Similar demands followed, including a plea from Zionist leaders Chaim Weizmann and Moshe Shertok (Sharett) in London, Nahum Goldmann of the World Jewish Congress in Washington, and Yitzhak Gruenbaum, head of the Jewish Agency's rescue committee in Palestine. Although some continued to press for bombing of the access routes to the camp, others urged the destruction of the murder facilities themselves—the gas chambers and the crematoria, now known about in detail following reports that had reached the West. From several quarters at once Jewish representatives rained down requests in London and Washington. How would the Allies respond?

By the summer of 1944 the Allies knew a great deal about the proposed target, including its functioning as a factory for mass murder. Practically, this kind of bombing raid into eastern Europe could only be mounted by the British or Americans after the clearing of the heel of the Italian boot at the end of 1943 and the establishment of air bases at Foggia and Brindisi. Another prerequisite was the Allies' ability to conduct powerful, long-distance operations, facilitated by the introduction of the long-range Mustang fighter about the same time, enabling bombers to fly fully loaded to their targets with adequate escorts. Improvements in precision bombing techniques were also important and had gone very far by the time the Auschwitz proposals were made. When the Auschwitz bombing proposals came before military planners, the Allies enjoyed massive air superiority practically everywhere in Europe and were already heavily in action in the vicinity of the Silesian death camp. The context of this bombardment was the "oil war," a major effort to destroy the Germans' fuel supplies by disrupting synthetic oil production and distribution. Early in April Allied reconnaisance aircraft flew over Auschwitz, when its death-dealing machinery was fully functioning, in order to photograph the oil and rubber production facilities in the Monowitz subcamp—barely four kilometers from the killing installations.[18] Bombs fell throughout the region that summer, and Monowitz itself was hit for the first time on 20 August. Massive raids continued thereafter—notably on Blechhammer and Moravska Ostrava, a few dozen kilometers away, but also on the Auschwitz industrial facilities themselves. Technically, then, there was no doubt that the bombs could be dropped where the Jews wanted.

Why were they not? According to Bernard Wasserstein's close analysis of the British side, the prime minister gave the suggestion a much-needed push. "Get anything out of the Air Force that you can and invoke me if necessary," Churchill told Eden on 7 July. It was officials at the Foreign Office who finally subverted the project, as they had often blocked aid of other kinds to European Jews—"a striking testimony to the ability of the British civil service to overturn ministerial decisions," according to Wasserstein.[19] David Wyman's recent examination of the decision making in Washington reveals a similar disinclination on the part of officials to accept the idea. Here the support of the War Refugee Board ran into a fixed policy of the War Department against the use of military force "for the purpose of rescuing victims of enemy oppression"—a policy worked out months before.[20] In both cases officials dug in their heels despite repeated efforts to change their minds. Planners expressed strong doubts about the supposed efficacy of the proposed raid, hid behind demonstrably specious arguments about technical incapacity, and protected their unwillingness to divert energy from military targets—precisely when this was being done to aid the Polish Home Army's futile and tragic uprising in the city of Warsaw.[21]

To understand their reticence, it makes sense to enter a world of military planning that was far indeed from the issues and facts that have been discussed in this book. As Jews discovered, military planners were even less likely to grasp the significance of the mass murder of European Jews than were political leaders, and the latter tended naturally to defer to the former on tactical issues. Those in charge of such decisions were persistently averse to hearing pleas on behalf of civilians, unless there were weighty political gains to be won or debts to be paid. (Such was the case with Warsaw.) And they were even more ill disposed to crediting civilian ideas of any kind about how military operations were to be conducted. Jews were not the first to demand military strikes to relieve suffering, and they were not the only ones to be disappointed. At various times the Poles and Czechs made such appeals as well, and almost always in vain.[22] As early as 1940, when bombs were raining on London, Churchill rejected a suggestion of retaliatory raids, for example, despite the appeal of the idea to his romantic sensibility. "My dear sir," he told an associate, "this is a military and not a civilian war. . . . I quite appreciate your point. But my motto is 'Business before Pleasure.'"[23] We naturally tend to be champions of the bombing idea, and assume that it ought to have struck the imagination as a relatively inexpensive gesture that might have saved lives, and certainly would have been a moral blow against Nazi genocide. So, in retrospect, we know it would have been. In the summer of 1944, however, even Jews had their doubts. Leon Kubowitsky of the World Jewish Congress, for example, opposed the bombing as likely to kill large numbers of Jews; Zionist leaders Chaim Weizmann and Moshe Shertok did not accord particular importance to the project when they first met with Eden on 30 June to discuss a variety of suggestions, and Shertok felt that it would achieve little practically, in the sense of saving lives.[24] As the evidence shows, no one factor explains the failure to act on Weissmandel's anguished call for help. The failure, as Gilbert notes, was multifarious: ill will in some cases, but also lack of imagination, incomprehension, and dulled sensibilities—more familiar failings than we usually like to admit.

In the last months of the war there was reason to hope that some of the murderous impulses of the Third Reich might be stilled and the systematic killing somehow stopped. To put these aspirations into context one must take account of the rapid advance of the Red Army through eastern Europe, actually reaching the murder facilities of Auschwitz on 27 January 1945. By that time important changes in the implementation of the Final Solution had already occurred. Beginning in 1943, after the completion of Operation Reinhard and the massacre of the Polish Jews, the various other killing centers were closed, and strenuous efforts were made to eliminate all traces of the murders.[25] Priorities, on occasion, seemed also to shift. According to some accounts there was already in motion, by the second half of 1944, a vast movement of Jews, destined for extermination, into armament production and other defense-related projects in a final spasm of mobilization of the Third Reich. At Auschwitz itself there was a suicidal uprising of the *Sonderkommando* on 7 October 1944 that stunned the direction of the camp. Meanwhile, in connection with events in Hungary as well as intensive fighting in France, the Allies issued solemn warnings to the Germans that perpetrators of war crimes would be severely punished. Simultaneously, meetings were occurring in Switzerland, leading to direct contact between Himmler's emissary and an American representative on 5 November. In response to these developments, Himmler apparently forbade the further extermination of Jews and actually ordered the dismantling of the killing facilities at Auschwitz later that month.[26]

While some have seen these moves by the Reichsführer SS as a direct result of the bargaining process, others accord them far less importance, imputing to Himmler the view that, practically speaking, the "Jewish Question" was already solved.[27] We do know that negotiations continued to the very end, with various attempts being made to get the Germans to surrender camps to the liberating armies before further loss of life among their inmates. The government of Sweden participated actively in these discussions, stimulated in part by representatives of the Norwegian underground and Jewish spokesmen in Stockholm. A key figure in some of the last negotiations was Count Folke Bernadotte, nephew of the Swedish king and vice-president of the Swedish Red Cross, who contacted Himmler through his personal physician, Felix Kersten, then living in the Swedish capital. Bernadotte flew to Germany and had several secret meetings with Himmler, Kaltenbrunner, and Ribbentrop.

These discussions were extraordinarily complex, becoming tangled subsequently in sharp recriminations among the various participants. Although his mission was originally concerned only with Scandinavian prisoners, Bernadotte eventually pressed for the release to the Allies of the entire mass of concentration camp inmates in the last weeks of fighting. In the end, while these efforts failed in their larger objective, they may have secured the abandonment of some of the major camps without the final orgy of killing that was widely feared. It is unlikely in any event, given the mounting chaos in Germany, that much more could have been done.[28] To understand the wider import of these moves, however, they should be seen in the perspective of massive killing outside the framework of gassings in the death camps—in the death marches of 1945.

THE DEATH MARCHES AND LIBERATION

According to German historian Martin Broszat, Himmler issued a fateful order in January 1945 to evacuate the camps in eastern Europe about to be engulfed by the Soviets and to force westward all inmates able to move. This massive transfer, beginning in the depth of winter and involving Jews and non-Jews, led to a staggering mortality among the already weakened and brutalized camp population. In Broszat's evaluation, "at least a third of the more than 700,000 inmates recorded in January 1945 lost their lives on the exhausting evacuation marches, in the transport trains which took weeks to reach their destination, and (particularly) in the hopelessly overcrowded reception camps in the months and weeks immediately before the end of the war."[29] About half of these victims, in Yehuda Bauer's estimate, were Jews. From the survivors of this uprooting we have the most horrifying accounts of the accompanying catastrophe. Not only, it is clear, did the evacuees perish from cold, hunger, and disease, they were also periodically massacred by shootings, in what Bauer describes as a deliberate continuation of the Final Solution by other means.[30]

How is one to understand this final chapter in the massacre of European Jewry? Some of the calamity may be explained by the chaos of the last days of the Third Reich—the breakdown of the meager provisioning of camps, the interruption of lines of communication by the destruction of road and rail routes, the severing of chains of command leaving concentration camp authorities on their own, the crushing congestion of camps to which the marchers were directed in Germany and Austria, and the rampant outbreaks of typhus and typhoid fever that accompanied the final collapse. Bauer also places much of the responsibility on local Nazi officials, remarkably faithful to their Nazi ideology: "transport commanders had but the vaguest idea of what to do with the prisoners beyond a general order to kill all the stragglers. It seems to me unlikely that an actual order was given to murder the victims on the way—it is here that the general consensus of the Nazi regime in relation to its real or imagined opponents came into its own."[31] Some SS officers may have wanted to prevent survivors from telling their stories to the liberating armies; some may have felt a continuing imperative to kill all enemies of the Reich, especially those who were incapable of work. Still another factor seems to have been the replacement of trained camp guards by energized, newly recruited SS personnel who behaved in a way reminiscent, says Bauer, of the SA in the 1930s rather than the SS of the death camps—engaging in pogrom-style brutalities (although now on an unprecedented scale) rather than the assembly-line killings of the death camps, which were now impossible.

German policy, it now seems clear, followed two quite different tracks during the last part of the war. Along with negotiations, the momentum of murder was largely maintained and even at times accelerated. Hitler set a tone of vengeful fanaticism, although his writ no longer extended throughout his rapidly shrinking empire. According to various accounts, the Führer ordered the liquidation of all prisoners who could not be evacuated to prevent them from falling into the hands of the Allies. Hitler is supposed to have been enraged that the Allies found prisoners still alive in Buchenwald and ordered that this not happen again; the Jews, he is reported as saying, should not emerge from the war as victors.[32] In at least one camp—Ohrdruf, a subunit of Buchenwald just outside of Gotha—the SS made sure they did not, slaughtering the survivors before they left.[33] So far as one can tell from scattered bits of evidence, however, it would be wrong to exaggerate the degree of direct control from Hitler himself, as he increasingly withdrew from the real world after the 20 July plot against him and was even less disposed than before to follow and control events closely. Ever since mid-1944, moreover, at least some high-ranking German officers issued similar orders on their own against allowing Jews to be liberated by the Allied troops. In the view of some, Eichmann's SS office also resolutely obstructed all efforts at a negotiated surrender of the camps or a suspension of the Final Solution, preventing interventions by the Red Cross, for example, and speeding the forced marches away from the path of the liberating armies.[34]

Liberation was remarkably different in east and west. Of the millions of every background, religion, and nationality who had been sent to the camps, only a few hundred thousand were found there at the end, most of them barely alive. The Soviets came first to Auschwitz and Majdanek and to the camouflaged sites of other death factories in Poland. More secretive and security-conscious than the Westerners, they revealed little, immediately, of what they found. The British and Americans were the first to enter some of the largest German camps—Mauthausen, Buchenwald, Bergen-Belsen, Dora Nordausen—often doing so in the full glare of publicity. But in both east and west, there was abundant, devastating evidence of Nazi depredations that those in charge could not possibly hide. Robert Abzug's recent book on the freeing of the camps shows the "potent mixture of shock, anger, shame, guilt, and fear" among American liberators—an unhealthy brew that would soon become a great source of political trouble.[35] In east and west, moreover, the toll of the Final Solution mounted even after liberation. Tens of thousands continued to perish of starvation, disease, and the effects of maltreatment for weeks after the liberating soldiers arrived. In Bergen-Belsen, for example, a British medical team decided that 25,000 inmates needed immediate hospitalization, and that of these 10,000 might die in the next few weeks. They underestimated: 13,000 died.[36] No one can be sure about the number of Jews alive in central Europe at the end of the war, and in any case mortality was so high among the liberated that such figures are of little significance in themselves. Historians reckon that there may have been a million Jewish survivors in Europe outside the Soviet Union in the spring of 1945. According to Bauer, 250,000 of an original 400,000 Polish and Baltic Jews who obtained refuge in the Soviet Union survived in 1945. In the camps of central Europe, however, there were far fewer—probably no more than between 50,000 and 100,000.[37]

CONCLUSION

The Holocaust took the lives of between 5 million and 6 million people—about two-thirds of the European Jews and one-third of the world's Jewish population. This conclusion comes from the Nazis' own accounts, with historians differing somewhat in computing portions of the record and extrapolating from various statistical reports prepared by German agencies. Six million remains the popularly accepted toll—the figure mentioned by the International Military Tribunal at Nuremberg in its final judgment and referred to by an associate of Eichmann (reporting Eichmann's own words, in August 1944) as the total number of Jews killed. Of these, it is generally assumed, 4 million died in camps and 2 million perished elsewhere—mainly by shooting in the Soviet Union or by starvation and disease in the ghettos of eastern Europe.

Following the war, Jewish researchers reached similar conclusions about Jewish mortality by using indirect means—attempting to ascertain the number of Jews alive in Europe in mid-1945 and subtracting this total from the prewar Jewish population. Once again the results showed between 5 million and 6 million killed. Exact numbers were impossible to obtain, of course, and there were particular difficulties because of border changes, migrations, and the need to estimate population totals where censuses were missing. One of the most difficult problems has been to establish the toll of Soviet Jews, for which scholars have had to move backward from the census of 1959, taking into account incorporated Polish, Baltic, and Rumanian territories. It has also been pointed out that several tens of thousands of murdered Christians, considered Jews by the Nazis, would not be counted by such indirect methods.[38]

Precise totals continue to elude us, and the German documentation leaves substantial room for conflicting interpretations. The main problem is that while the Nazis recorded some portions of the Final Solution with great accuracy, they failed at other times even to report other killings, or did so imperfectly or incompletely. Also, some records have been destroyed. In several countries, deportation convoys were carefully enumerated, and the surviving documentation includes the names of each and every deportee, together with the place and date of birth. For France, for example, we have such detailed lists of individuals who made up almost all of the seventy-six convoys that left the country, totaling almost seventy-six thousand people. Of these, we know that only twenty-five hundred, approximately 3 percent, survived.[39] In other places, on the other hand, the death of tens of thousands of people went undocumented, either through negligence, incompetence, or indifference. For example, while German occupation officials carefully computed statistics on Jewish mortality in Warsaw and Lodz, they often neglected to do so for the smaller ghettos. Hilberg notes that descriptions of shootings by the Einsatzgruppen are uneven—very detailed for 1941, for example, and much less so for 1942 and 1943. Global figures were assembled by the SS statistician Richard Korherr, but his analysis extends only to early 1943 and is itself obscured by language that camouflaged murder and by the omission of portions of the killing program.[40]

The Holocaust researcher and international jurist Jacob Robinson presented a judicious summary of the Jewish losses in an *Encylopaedia Judaica* article published in 1971, concluding that the total was 5.8 million. As the notes that sprinkle his table of estimates make clear, however, there are dozens of pitfalls and qualifications, any one of which could shift the figures upward or downward somewhat.[41] Of all the major authorities writing in recent decades, Raul Hilberg's assessment is the most conservative, concluding now—as he did in the first edition of his book more than twenty-five years ago—that the total number of deaths is 5.1 million.[42] We are therefore more or less where we were forty years ago, with an estimate of between 5 million and 6 million.

While our sense of the overall magnitude of destruction has changed little over the past four decades, historians have been able to impart to those who read their work a much more finely grained understanding of the nature of the Jewish catastrophe than in the past. Hilberg has recently reminded audiences of the lonely task that research on the Holocaust was when he first began in 1948. Professional writers and academic historians were virtually ignoring the subject, Philip Friedman lamented at the time, and few if any scholars were known to be working on it.[43] For about a decade and a half after the end of the Second World War there was scant popular interest in the matter, very little was published in English, and the destruction process itself was ghettoized, so to speak, remaining outside the stream of general history or even the history of the Hitler era.[44]

Since the beginning of the 1960s, however—the turning point is generally seen to have been the Eichmann trial in Jerusalem—there has been a wave of interest and a wealth of serious scholarship. The work of historians has proceeded on a broad front. At Nuremberg, partly conditioned by the tactics of the American prosecutors, Nazi policy was commonly presented as a conspiracy—one aspect of which was the plan, conceived from a very early point in time, to murder all the Jews. As we have seen, this general perspective persists in the form of "intentionalist" historiography, which has now added substantially to the ramshackle structure of evidence hurriedly assembled in 1945. But just as the general interpretative drift by historians of the Third Reich has been to qualify the notion of an unwavering Hitlerian aim or an absolute control by the Führer, so much of the research on Nazi policy toward the Jews has moved in a similar direction.

By the same token, subjects avoided in the postwar decade and a half, perhaps seen as professionally inappropriate, are now systematically investigated. One example is the study of the victims. In 1957 Philip Friedman, himself a survivor of the Holocaust and a pioneer in its investigation, called for a Judeocentric view of the subject as opposed to one that saw everything from the standpoint of the Nazis—a view of the Jews "not only as the victim of a tragedy, but also as the bearer of a communal existence."[45] The controversy over Hannah Arendt's portrayal of Jewish reactions in *Eichmann in Jerusalem*, quite apart from the historical issues raised, helped clear the air, encouraging serious research and discussion of such sensitive topics as the *Judenräte* in eastern Europe. There have been plenty of hesitations, nevertheless. Jacob Robinson's 1972 *Encyclopaedia Judaica* article began its consideration of Jewish behavior during the Holocaust with an entire section entitled "Who Is Competent to Judge This Behavior?" The trend has been unmistakably in the direction of open research and discussion, however, as dozens of books and articles now attest.

Not everyone is happy, of course. To some, the academic tone adopted by some who have written on the Holocaust is itself a violation. They fear that the use of professional historical discourse will turn the Holocaust into a subject like any other, robbing it of its historic uniqueness. While opposing "mystification around the Holocaust," Yehuda Bauer has also warned of "the growing tendency of immersing tears and suffering in oceans of footnotes, of coming up with a remote quasi-scientific approach which would be as inhuman as that of those who committed the crime or of those who stood by and watched it indifferently." [46] Others fear vulgarization—a tendency to exploit the Holocaust for political or aesthetic reasons or to make a trivial point. Clearly, however, it is the historians' task to guard against distortions as well as to discover truth. Can those who write history be trusted with the Holocaust? In a book published in 1981, oddly disdainful of much of recent historiography, Lucy Dawidowicz complained that "historians do not always turn out to be reliable guides to the recovery of the past." Her work was an extended protest against the mistreatment of the Holocaust by historians, their purported neglect of the subject, and their apparent unwillingness to attribute responsibility where it belongs.[47] The historians, she seems to conclude, cannot be trusted.

My own belief is that we have little choice but to do so. For better or for worse, we shall have to rely increasingly upon historians to transmit what is known about the massacre of European Jewry. No one else is likely to do so in a way that commands credibility and standing in our culture. But as historians convey their accounts, no one should expect them to do so with one voice, or with a single perspective. Historians will continue to see the Holocaust as they see every other issue they study, from a variety of interpretative viewpoints. They will also make mistakes—choose inappropriate references, neglect certain vantage points, make clumsy generalizations, or fail to find words to describe what they know. Critics will have to demand that they do better. Holocaust history is likely to be in as sound a state as the general historical culture of our society. On the basis of much of the work examined in this book, I believe there are grounds for optimism. Unfortunately, the same cannot be said about the dreadful events that Holocaust historians describe.

NOTES

I. INTRODUCTION

1. Geoff Eley, "Holocaust History," *London Review of Books*, 3–17 March 1982, 6. See also the excellent discussion in Ian Kershaw, *The Nazi Dictatorship: Problems and Perspectives of Interpretation* (London, 1985), ch. 5.

2. Nora Levin, *The Holocaust: The Destruction of European Jewry, 1939–1945* (New York, 1973), xi–xii.

3. Elie Wiesel, "Does the Holocaust Lie Beyond the Reach of Art?" *New York Times*, 17 April 1983. Cf. idem, "Trivializing the Holocaust: Semi-Fact and Semi-Fiction," ibid., 16 April 1978.

4. Yehuda Bauer, *The Holocaust in Historical Perspective* (Seattle, 1978), 3. Reviewing Robert Jay Lifton's *The Nazi Doctors*, the renowned analyst Bruno Bettelheim suggested that "there are acts so vile that our task is to reject and prevent them, not to try to understand them empathetically as Dr. Lifton did." "Their Specialty Was Murder," *New York Times Book Review*, 5 October 1986, 62.

5. See Gerd Korman, "The Holocaust in American Historical Writing," *Societas* 2 (1972), 251–70.

6. Paul R. Mendes-Flohr and Jehuda Reinharz, eds., *The Jew in the Modern World: A Documentary History* (New York, 1980), 482.

7. Léon Poliakov, *Bréviare de haine: La IIIe Reich et les Juifs* (Paris, 1951); Gerald Reitlinger, *The Final Solution: The Attempt to Exterminate the Jews of Europe, 1939–1945* (London, 1953).

8. See Harold Rosenberg, "The Trial of Adolf Eichmann," *Commentary* 32 (1961), 369–81; Léon Poliakov, "The Proceedings," *American Jewish Year Book* 63 (1962), 54; Jacob Robinson, And the Crooked Shall Be Made Straight (New York, 1965).

9. Quoted in Hannah Arendt, *Eichmann in Jerusalem: A Report on the Banality of Evil* (New York, 1965), 10.

10. Vera Laska, *Nazism, Resistance and Holocaust in World War II: A Bibliography* (Metuchen, N.J., 1985), xvii.

11. Herbert Butterfield, *History and Human Relations* (London, 1951), 14–15.

12. "[Lawrence] Langer Discusses Teaching about the Holocaust," *Facing History and Ourselves News*, Fall 1985, 8.

13. Dan Magurshak, "The 'Incomprehensibility' of the Holocaust: Tightening Up Some Loose Usage," *Judaism* 29 (1980), 233–42.

14. "Researching the Holocaust," *Jerusalem Post International Edition,* 28 June 1986.

15. See Bauer, *Holocaust in Historical Perspective,* 4.

16. A. B. Yehoshua, *Between Right and Right,* trans. Arnold Schwartz (Garden City, N.Y., 1981), 5–6.

2. THE HOLOCAUST IN PERSPECTIVE

1. Isaac Deutscher, *The Non-Jewish Jew and Other Essays,* ed. Tamara Deutscher (London, 1968), 163–64.

2. Joseph Schechtman, *Fighter and Prophet: The Vladimir Jabotinsky Story, The Last Years* (New York, 1961), 352.

3. See Jehuda Reinharz, *Fatherland or Promised Land: The Dilemma of the German Jew, 1893–1914* (Ann Arbor, Mich. 1975), esp. ch. 1.

4. Vicki Caron and Paula Hyman, "The Failed Alliance: Jewish-Catholic Relations in Alsace-Lorraine, 1871–1914," *Leo Baeck Institute Year Book,* 26 (1981), 16–17.

5. See Pawel Korzec, *Juifs en Pologne* (Paris, 1980), 55; Arieh Tartakower and Kurt R. Grossmann, *The Jewish Refugee* (New York, 1944), 19.

6. See Peter Pulzer, "Why Was There a Jewish Question in Imperial Germany?" *Leo Baeck Institute Year Book* 25 (1980), 133–46.

7. Richard Levy, *The Downfall of the Antisemitic Political Parties in Imperial Germany* (New Haven, 1975).

8. Peter Pulzer, *The Rise of Political Anti-Semitism in Imperial Germany and Austria* (New York, 1964), 219. Cf. Werner Jochmann, "Struktur und Funktion des deutschen Antisemitismus," in Werner E. Mosse and Arnold Paucker, eds., *Juden im Wilhelminischen Deutschland, 1890–1914* (Tübingen, 1976), 389–477.

9. Shulamit Vokov, "Antisemitism as a Cultural Code: Reflections on the History and Historiography of Antisemitism in Imperial Germany," *Leo Baeck Institute Year Book* 23 (1978), 25–46. For an attempt to differentiate among various strands of antisemitism see Michael R. Marrus, "The Theory and Practice of Anti-Semitism," *Commentary,* August 1982, 38–42.

10. Uriel Tal, *Christians and Jews in Germany: Religion, Politics, and Ideology in the Second Reich, 1870–1914,* trans. Noah Jacobs (Ithaca, N.Y., 1975).

11. On this point see especially George L. Mosse, *The Crisis of German Ideology: Intellectual Origins of the Third Reich* (New York, 1964), ch. 17; and idem, *Nazism: A Historical and Comparative Analysis of National Socialism* (Oxford, 1978), 59–60.

12. Sarah Ann Gordon, *Hitler, Germans, and the "Jewish Question"* (Princeton, N.J., 1984), 53–54.

13. See Eva Reichman, "Diskussionen über die Judenfrage, 1930–1932," in Werner Mosse, ed., *Enscheidungsjahre 1932: Zur Judenfrage in der Endphase der Weimarer Republik* (Tübingen, 1965), 503–34; idem, *Hostages of Civilization: The Social Sources of National Socialist Anti-Semitism* (Boston, 1951); Martin Needler, "Hitler's Anti-Semitism: A Political Appraisal," *Public Opinion Quarterly* 24 (1960), 665–69; Donald Niewyk, *The Jews in Weimar Germany* (Baton Rouge, La., 1980); Mosse, *Crisis of German Ideology.*

14. Peter Merkl, *Political Violence under the Swastika: 581 Early Nazis* (Princeton, N.J., 1975), 498–527; and Gordon, *Hitler, Germans, and the "Jewish Question,"* ch. 2. Gordon further observes: "The majority, or nearly 60 per cent of all anti-Semites, were moderates, that is, confirmed but nonaggressive bigots" (p. 56).

15. Martin Broszat, "Zur Struktur der NS-Massenbewegung," *Viertlejahrsheft für Zeitgeschichte* 31 (1983), 62.

16. Henry Ashby Turner, Jr., *Big Business and the Rise of Hitler* (New York, 1985), 337.

17. Jeremy Noakes, *The Nazi Party in Lower Saxony, 1921–1933* (Oxford, 1971), 206–10; Geoffrey Pridham, *Hitler's Rise to Power: The Nazi Movement in Bavaria, 1923–1933* (New York, 1974), 237–44. "In most parts of Germany . . . even where the NSDAP did proportionately well at the polls, there was little history of outright hostility towards the Jews going beyond latent prejudice, and anti-Semitism was not usually a particularly striking feature of Nazi propaganda." Ian Kershaw "Ideology, Propaganda, and the Rise of the Nazi Party," in Peter D. Stachura, ed., *The Nazi Machtergriefung* (London, 1983), 168.

18. William Sheridan Allen, *The Nazi Seizure of Power: The Experience of a Single German Town, 1930–1935* (Chicago, 1965), 77.

19. Richard F. Hamilton, *Who Voted for Hitler?* (Princeton, N.J., 1982), 606. It is important to remember, in this context, that the Nazis were by no means the only antisemitic party in Weimar Germany, and this plank did not always distinguish them from political competitors on the Right. See, for example, Thomas Childers, *The Nazi Voter: The Social Foundations of Fascism in Germany, 1919–1933* (Chapel Hill, N.C., 1983), 188 and passim.

20. Speech at Kulmbach, 5 February 1928, quoted in Alan Bullock, *Hitler: A Study in Tyranny* (Harmondsworth, England, 1962), 36.

21. Adolf Hitler, *Mein Kampf,* trans. Ralph Manheim (Boston, 1943), 23.

22. Ibid., 22.

23. *Hitler's Secret Book,* trans. Salvator Attanasio (New York, 1961), 215.

24. Ibid., 13, 138.

25. Ibid., 41–42.

26. Eberhard Jäckel, *Hitler's Weltanschauung: A Blueprint for Power,* trans. Herbert Arnold (Middletown, Conn., 1972), 98–99.

27. Ibid., 106.

28. Otto Dov Kulka, "Major Trends and Tendencies in German Historiography on National Socialism and the 'Jewish Question' (1924–1984)," *Leo Baeck Institute Year Book* 30 (1985), 234; Ernst Nolte, *Three Faces of Fascism: Action Française, Italian Fascism, National Socialism*, trans. Leila Vennewitz (New York, 1966).

29. Rudolph Binion, *Hitler among the Germans* (New York, 1976).

30. On the trauma of the war years see Peter Loewenberg, "The Psychohistorical Origins of the Nazi Youth Cohort," *American Historical Review* 76 (1971), 1457–1502.

31. Robert G. L. Waite, *The Psychopathic God: Adolf Hitler* (New York, 1978), 448; idem, "Adolf Hitler's Anti-Semitism: A Study in History and Psychoanalysis," in B. B. Wolman, ed., *The Psychoanalytic Interpretation of History* (New York, 1970), 192–229. See also Norbert Bromberg and Verna Volz Small, *Hitler's Psychopathology* (New York, 1983), which defines Hitler's "narcissistic-borderline personality."

32. Alan Bullock, "The Schicklgruber Story," *New York Review of Books*, 26 May 1977, 13. For other assessments of this literature see Peter Loewenberg, "Psychohistorical Perspectives on Modern German History," *Journal of Modern History* 47 (1975), 229–79; Geoffrey Cocks, "The Hitler Controversy," *Political Psychology* 1 (1979), 67–81; John P. Fox, "Adolf Hitler: The Continuing Debate," *International Affairs* 55 (1979), 252–64.

33. Fred Weinstein, *The Dynamics of Nazism: Leadership, Ideology, and the Holocaust* (New York, 1980), 101–2.

34. Hans Mommsen, "Die Realisierung des Utopischen: Die 'Endlösung der Judenfrage' in 'Dritten Reich,'" *Geschichte und Gesellschaft* 9 (1983), 399.

35. Milton Himmelfarb in *Commentary*, March 1984, 37–43.

36. Geoff Eley, "Holocaust History," *London Review of Books*, 3–17 March 1982, 6.

37. See Emil Fackenheim, "Concerning Authentic and Unauthentic Responses to the Holocaust," *Holocaust and Genocide Studies* 1 (1986), 101–20; and idem, "The Nazi Holocaust as a Persisting Trauma for the Non-Jewish Mind," *Journal of the History of Ideas* 36 (1975), 369–76. In fairness, one should note that Fackenheim criticizes the category of "uniqueness." See idem, "Concerning Authentic and Unauthentic Responses," 104.

38. George M. Kren and Leon Rappoport, *The Holocaust and the Crisis of Human Behavior* (New York, 1980), 3.

39. Louis P. Lochner, *What about Germany?* (New York, 1942), 2.

40. Kevork B. Bardakjian, *Hitler and the Armenian Genocide* (Cambridge, Mass., 1986).

41. Gérard Chaliand and Yves Ternon, *Le Génocide des Arméniens* (Brussels, 1980), 84,

42. Yehuda Bauer, "The Place of the Holocaust in Contemporary His-

tory," *Journal of Contemporary Jewry* 1 (1984), 204; Leo Kuper, *Genocide* (Harmondsworth, England, 1981), 22.

43. Justin McCarthy, *Muslims and Minorities: The Population of Ottoman Anatolia and the End of the Empire* (New York, 1983), 123; Chaliand and Ternon, *Génocide des Arméniens,* 81.

44. Eugen Weber, "Jews, Antisemitism, and the Origins of the Holocaust," *Historical Reflections* 5 (1978), 1–17. See also Vahakn N. Dadrian, "The Role of Turkish Physicians in the World War I Genocide of Ottoman Armenians," *Holocaust and Genocide Studies* 1 (1986), 169–92.

45. Bernard Lewis, *Semites and Anti-Semites: An Inquiry into Conflict and Prejudice* (New York, 1986), 21.

46. Bauer, "Holocaust in Contemporary History," 202.

47. Robert Conquest, *The Harvest of Sorrow: Soviet Collectivization and the Terror Famine* (New York, 1986), ch. 16.

48. See Kuper, *Genocide,* ch. 1.

49. Gil Elliot, *Twentieth Century Book of the Dead* (London, 1972), 83 and *passim;* X. Lannes, "Les Conséquences démographiques de la seconde guerre mondiale en Europe," *Revue d'histoire de la deuxième guerre mondiale* 5 (1955), 1–14.

50. The minutes may be found in Raul Hilberg, ed., *Documents of Destruction: Germany and Jewry, 1933–1945* (Chicago, 1971), 89–99; and in Lucy S. Dawidowicz, ed., *A Holocaust Reader* (New York, 1976), 73–82.

51. *Deutscher Wochendienst,* 2 April 1944, quoted in Raul Hilberg, *The Destruction of the European Jews,* rev. ed. (New York, 1985), III, 1021.

52. Dawidowicz, *Holocaust Reader,* 133.

53. J. P. Stern, *Hitler: The Führer and the People* (Berkeley, Calif., 1975), 69; Martin Van Creveld, "Hitler as Warlord: Some Points Reconsidered," *European Studies Review* 4 (1974), 57–79; Milton Shulman, *Defeat in the West,* rev. ed. (London, 1986).

54. Karl A. Schleunes, *The Twisted Road to Auschwitz: Nazi Policy toward the Jews, 1933–1939* (Urbana, Ill., 1970); Uwe Dietrich Adam, *Judenpolitik im Dritten Reich* (Düsseldorf, 1972); Wolfgang Scheffler, *Judenverfolgung im Dritten Reich, 1933–1945* (Berlin, 1960); Helmut Genschel, *Die Verdrängung der Juden aus der Wirtschaft im Dritten Reich* (Göttingen, 1966); Werner Angress, "German Jews, 1933–1939," in Henry Friedlander and Sybil Milton, eds., *The Holocaust: Ideology, Bureaucracy, and Genocide* (Millwood, N.Y., 1978), 69–84.

55. Christopher R. Browning, *The Final Solution and the German Foreign Office: A Study of Referat D III of Abteilung Deutschland, 1940–1943* (New York, 1978), 83; Adam, *Judenpolitik im Dritten Reich,* chs. 6–7.

56. *The Goebbels Diaries, 1942–1943,* ed. and trans. Louis P. Lochner (Garden City, N.Y., 1948), 148.

57. Ibid., 300.
58. Martin Gilbert, *The Holocaust: A History of the Jews of Europe during the Second World War* (London, 1986), 683. In charge of deportations from the Greek islands was Lieutenant General Alexander Löhr, hanged as a war criminal in 1947, one of whose staff officers was the future secretary general of the United Nations, Kurt Waldheim. See John Hondros, *Occupation and Resistance: The Greek Agony, 1941–1944* (New York, 1983), 93.

3. THE FINAL SOLUTION

1. Emil Schumberg circular, 25 January 1939, *Documents on German Foreign Policy*, Series D, V, 926–33.
2. Office of the United States Counsel for Prosecution of Axis Criminality, *Nazi Conspiracy and Aggression* (Washington, D.C., 1946–48), VI, 97–101.
3. Memorandum of Luther, 21 August 1942, citing a letter of Heydrich to Ribbentrop, 24 June 1940, *Trials of War Criminals before the Nuremberg Military Tribunals* (Washington, D.C., 1947–49), XIII, 245; memorandum of Rademacher, 3 July 1940, ibid., 154–55; Christopher Browning, *The Final Solution and the German Foreign Office: A Study of Referat DIII of Abteilung Deutschland* (New York, 1978), 44 and 232, n. 32.
4. International Military Tribunal, *Trial of the Major War Criminals* (Washington, D.C., 1947–49), XXXVI, 266–67. The text of this document may also be found in Lucy S. Dawidowicz, *A Holocaust Reader* (New York, 1976), 72–73.
5. Quoted in Christopher Browning, *Fateful Months: Essays on the Final Solution* (New York, 1985), 26.
6. Raul Hilberg, *Documents of Destruction: Germany and Jewry, 1933–1945* (Chicago, 1971), 90.
7. David Irving, *Hitler's War* (New York, 1977), xiv, 330–32, 392–93, 503–5, 575–76, 601–2, 851, and *passim*.
8. See Charles Sydnor, Jr., "The Selling of Adolf Hitler: David Irving's *Hitler's War*," *Central European History* 12 (1979), 169–99; Alan Bullock, "The Schicklgruber Story," *New York Review of Books*, 26 May 1977, 10–15.
9. Raul Hilberg, *The Destruction of the European Jews*, rev. ed. (New York, 1985), III, 996.
10. Lucy Dawidowicz, *The War against the Jews, 1933–1945* (New York, 1975), 111.
11. Ibid., 158. For a more recent analysis in the same vein see Simon Taylor, *Prelude to Genocide: Nazi Ideology and the Struggle for Power* (London, 1985).
12. Tim Mason, "Intention and Explanation: A Current Controversy about the Interpretation of National Socialism," in Gerhard Hirschfeld and

Lothar Kettenacker, eds., *Der Führerstaat: Mythos und Realität* (Stuttgart, 1981), 21–40; Christopher R. Browning, "La Décision concernant la solution finale," in *Colloque de l'Ecole des Hautes Etudes en sciences sociales, L'Allemagne et le génocide juif* (Paris, 1985), 190–91.

13. On American legal strategy see Bradley Smith, *The Road to Nuremberg* (New York, 1981); idem, *Reaching Judgment at Nuremberg* (New York, 1977).

14. Gerald Fleming, *Hitler and the Final Solution* (Berkeley, Calif., 1984), 2. Fleming notes "a single, unbroken, and fatal continuum" of Hitler's anti-Jewish ideas and observes a "straight path" from killings established under the so-called euthanasia program and the gassing of Jews in Sobibor (pp. 13, 24).

15. Studying the Führer's military conferences, for example, Felix Gilbert was struck by the "strange attraction that talking about deaths and sacrifices seemed to have had for Hitler." Felix Gilbert, ed., *Hitler Directs His War: The Secret Record of His Military Conferences* (New York, 1982), xxvi.

16. Ian Kershaw notes that, in hindsight, "it is easy to attribute a concrete and specific meaning to the barbarous, but vague and fairly commonplace, generalities about 'getting rid' [*Entfernung*] or even 'extermination' [*Vernichtung*] of Jews, which were part and parcel of Hitler's language (and that of others on the *völkisch* Right) from the early 1920s onwards." *The Nazi Dictatorship: Problems and Perspectives of Interpretation* (London, 1985), 91.

17. Gerhard Weinberg, *The Foreign Policy of Hitler's Germany: Starting World War II, 1937–1939* (Chicago, 1980), 369–464.

18. N. H. Baynes, ed., *The Speeches of Adolf Hitler* (London, 1942), I, 735–41.

19. Uwe Dietrich Adam, *Judenpolitik im Dritten Reich* (Düsseldorf, 1972), 235–36; Shlomo Aronson, "Die Dreifache Falle: Hitlers Judenpolitik, die Allierten und die Juden," *Vierteljahrshefte für Zeitgeschichte* 32 (1984), 49; Telford Taylor, *Munich: The Price of Peace* (New York, 1980), 946.

20. Eberhard Jäckel, *Hitler's Weltanschauung: A Blueprint for Power*, trans. Herbert Arnold (Middletown, Conn., 1972), 60–61, 64–65.

21. Ernst Nolte, *The Three Faces of Fascism: Action Française, Italian Fascism, National Socialism*, trans. Leila Vennewitz (New York, 1966). Nolte's views have taken a bizarre turn, part of an ultraconservative current in Germany. He argues against the "demonisation of the Third Reich," and considers that the annihilation of the Jews (which he now terms "the so-called annihilation of the Jews") was somehow "a reaction born out of the anxiety of the annihilating occurrences of the Russian Revolution." See Ernst Nolte, "Between Myth and Revisionism? The Third Reich in the Perspective of the 1980s," in H. W. Koch, ed., *Aspects of the Third Reich* (London, 1985), 36–37. Disturbingly, these views have found favor among certain historians. See, for example, the review of Koch's book by Klaus Hildebrand in *Historische Zeitschrift* 242 (1986), 465–66. For a sharp cri-

tique of what is termed "the apologetic tendencies in German writing of contemporary history," see Jürgen Habermas, "Eine Schadensabwicklung," *Die Zeit,* 18 July 1986. Two excellent outsiders' views of the wider controversy are Charles Maier, "Immoral Equivalence," *New Republic,* 1 December 1986, 36–41; and Gordon Craig, "The War of the German Historians," *New York Review of Books,* 15 January 1987, 16–19.

22. Nolte, *Three Faces of Fascism,* 400, 405, and *passim.* For a critique of methodology of this work see Kershaw, *Nazi Dictatorship,* 27: "Nolte's self-proclaimed 'phenomenological method' seems to amount in practice to little more than taking the self-depiction of a phenomenon seriously—in this case the writings of fascist leaders."

23. Andreas Hillgruber, "Die Endlösung und das deutsche Ostimperium als Kernstuck des rassenideologischen Programs des Nationalsozialismus," *Vierteljahrshefte für Zeitgeschichte* 20 (1972), 133–53; and idem, "Die ideologisch-dogmatische Grundlage der Nationalsozialistischen Politik der Ausrottung der Juden in den besetzten Gebeiten der Sowjetunion und ihre Durchführung, 1941–1944," *German Studies Review* 2 (1979), 263–96.

24. Eberhard Jäckel, *Hitler in History* (Hanover, N.H., 1984), 46.

25. Helmut Krausnick and Martin Broszat, *Anatomy of the SS State,* trans. Dorothy Long and Marian Jackson (London, 1968), 77. Cf. Helmut Krausnick, "Kommissarbefehl und 'Gerichtsbarketierlass Barbarossa' in neuer Sicht," *Vierteljahrshefte für Zeitgeschichte* 25 (1977), 682–738.

26. Helmut Krausnick and Hans-Heinrich Wilhelm, *Die Truppe des Weltanschauungskrieges: Die Einsatzgruppen der Sicherheitspolizei und des SD, 1938–1942* (Stuttgart, 1981), 150–72 and *passim.* A new contribution to our understanding of this campaign, by Yehoshua Büchler, "Kommandostab Reichsführer-SS: Himmler's Personal Murder Brigades in 1941," *Holocaust and Genocide Studies* 1 (1986), 11–25, suggests that, together with the Einsatzgruppen, mass murders were committed by these special units, as well as by other SS police and army formations. See also Jürgen Forster, "The Wehrmacht and the War of Extermination Against the Soviet Union," *Yad Vashem Studies* 14 (1981), 413–47; and idem, *Das Deutsche Reich und der Zweite Weltkrieg:* vol. VI, *Der Angriff auf der Sowjetunion* (Stuttgart, 1983), 413–47, 1030–78. See also Norman Rich, *Hitler's War Aims:* vol. I, *Ideology, the Nazi State, and the Course of Expansion* (New York, 1973), ch. 18, and vol. II, *The Establishment of the New Order* (New York, 1974), ch. 1; and Gerhard Hirschfeld, ed., *The Policies of Genocide: Jews and Soviet Prisoners of War in Nazi Germany* (London, 1986).

27. Alfred Streim, *Die Behandlung sowjetischer Kriegsgefangenen im "Fall Barbarossa"* (Heidelberg and Karlsruhe, 1981), 74–93. Christian Streit, *Keine Kameraden: Die Wehrmacht und die sowjetischen Kriegsgefangenen, 1941–1942* (Stuttgart, 1978), 127 and *passim.* Referring to the systematic killing of some 3.3 million Soviet prisoners of war, Streit

suggests that Hitler had no direct influence on their fate and probably did not know in detail about it.

28. Martin Broszat, "Hitler und die Genesis der 'Endlösung': Aus Anlass der Thesen von David Irving," *Vierteljahrshefte für Zeitgeschichte* 25 (1977), 739–75, and later published as "Hitler and the Genesis of the 'Final Solution': An Assessment of David Irving's Thesis," *Yad Vashem Studies* 13 (1979), 73–125. See also idem, "Soziale Motivation und Führer-Bindung des Nationalsozialismus," *Vierteljahrshefte für Zeitgeschichte* 18 (1970), 405–8.

29. Broszat, "Hitler and the Genesis of the 'Final Solution,'" 85–102.

30. Hans Mommsen, "Die Realisierung des Utopischen": Die 'Endlösung der Judenfrage' im 'Dritten Reich,'" *Geschichte und Gesellschaft* 9 (1983), 397; idem, "National Socialism: Continuity and Change," in Walter Laqueur, ed., *Fascism: A Reader's Guide* (Harmondsworth, England, 1979), 180. For a critique of Mommsen see Saul Friedländer, "From Anti-Semitism to Extermination: A Historiographical Study of Nazi Policies toward the Jews and an Essay in Interpretation," *Yad Vashem Studies* 16 (1984), 30–32.

31. Kershaw, *Nazi Dictatorship*, 104.

32. Karl A. Schleunes, *The Twisted Road to Auschwitz: Nazi Policy toward the Jews, 1933–1939* (Urbana, Ill., 1970), 257. See Uwe Dietrich Adam, "An Overall Plan for Anti-Jewish Legislation in the Third Reich?" *Yad Vashem Studies* 11 (1976), 33–58.

33. Adam, *Judenpolitik im Dritten Reich*, 303–12, 355–61.

34. Christopher Browning, *Fateful Months: Essays on the Final Solution* (New York, 1985), ch. 1, *passim*. For other recent assessments see Eberhard Jäckel and Jürgen Rowher, eds., *Der Mord an den Juden im Zweiten Weltkrieg: Entschlussbildung und Verwirklichung* (Stuttgart, 1985).

35. Christopher Browning, "Zur Genesis der Endlösung: Eine Antwort an Martin Broszat," *Vierteljahrshefte für Zeitgeschichte* 29 (1980), 97–109. Cf. Wolfgang Scheffler, "Zur Entstehungsgeschichte der 'Endlösung,'" *Aus Politik und Zeitgeschichte: Beilage zur Wochenzeitung "Das Parlament,"* B43/82 (30 October 1982), 3–10.

36. Klaus Hildebrand, *The Third Reich*, trans. P. S. Falla (London, 1984), 149.

37. Jäckel, *Hitler in History*, 57.

38. Adam, *Judenpolitik im Dritten Reich*, 303–16; Sebastian Haffner, *The Meaning of Hitler*, trans. Ewald Osers (London, 1979), 142–45.

39. Franz Halder, *Kriegstagebuch*, ed. Hans-Adolf Jacobsen (Stuttgart, 1962), III, 123, cited in Michael Geyer, "German Strategy in the Age of Machine Warfare, 1914–1945," in Peter Paret, ed., *The Makers of Modern Strategy: From Machiavelli to the Nuclear Age* (Princeton, N.J., 1986), 591; Milton Shulman, *Defeat in the West*, rev. ed. (London, 1986), 77–78; John Erickson, *Stalin's War with Germany*: vol. I, *The Road to Sta-*

lingrad (London, 1975), 195, 231–32; Russel H. S. Stolfi, "Barbarossa Revisited: A Critical Appraisal of the Opening Stages of the Russo-German Campaign," *Journal of Modern History* 54 (1982), 27–46.

40. See Martin Van Creveld, "War Lord Hitler: Some Points Reconsidered," *European Studies Review* 4 (1974), 69.

41. Karl Dietrich Bracher, *The German Dictatorship: The Origins, Structure and Effects of National Socialism*, trans. Jean Steinberg (New York, 1970), 231.

42. Kershaw, *Nazi Dictatorship*, 102.

43. Browning, "Zum Genesis der Endlösung," 105. Cf. Walter Wuttke-Groneberg, *Volk und Gesundheit: Heilen und Vernichten in Nationalsozialismus* (Tübingen, 1982); Streit, *Keine Kameraden, passim*.

44. Martin Broszat, "Soziale Motivation und Führer-Bindung des Nationalsocialismus," *Vierteljahrshefte für Zeitgeschichte* 18 (1970), 399–401; idem, *The Hitler State: The Foundation and Development of the Internal Structure of the Third Reich*, trans. John W. Hiden (London, 1981), 323; idem, "Genesis of the Final Solution," 109.

45. Streit, *Keine Kameraden*, 300; idem, "The German Army and the Politics of Genocide," in Hirschfeld, *Policies of Genocide*, 1–14; Robert Koehl, *The Black Corps: The Structure and Power Struggles of the Nazi SS* (Madison, Wis., 1983), 245; Omer Barov, *The Eastern Front, 1941–45: German Troops and the Barbarisation of Warfare* (Oxford, 1985), ch. 4.

46. See, for example, the case of Treblinka commandant Franz Stangl, reported in Gitta Sereny, *Into That Darkness* (London, 1974). But cf. the critique of Sereny's presentation by Lucy S. Dawidowicz, *The Jewish Presence: Essays on Identity and History* (New York, 1978), ch. 16.

47. Mommsen, "Realisierung des Utopischen," 382–83.

48. Hilberg, *Destruction of the European Jews*, I, ix.

49. Ibid., I, 53; III, 1011.

50. Ibid., I, 9, 28, 55; III, 998. Cf. Fred E. Katz, "Implementation of the Holocaust: The Behavior of Nazi Officials," *Comparative Studies in Society and History* 24 (1982), 510–29.

51. Hilberg, *Destruction of the European Jews*, II, 401–2, and n. 30.

52. See Uwe Dietrich Adam, "Persecution of the Jews: Bureaucracy and Authority in the Totalitarian State," *Leo Baeck Institute Year Book* 23 (1978), 139–48, a pertinent study of the issuing and the implementation of a single anti-Jewish measure.

53. Browning, *German Foreign Office and the Final Solution*, 28.

54. Ibid., 184.

55. Browning, *Fateful Months*, 67; Ernst Klee, *"Euthanasie" im NS-Staat: Die "Vernichtung lebensunwerten Lebens"* (Frankfurt am Main, 1983), 106–8, 112–15, 370.

56. George L. Mosse, *Toward the Final Solution: A History of European Racism* (London, 1978), 226.

57. For some links with foreign policy see Shlomo Aronson, "Die drei-

fache Falle: Hitlers Judenpolitik, die Allierten, und die Juden," *Vierteljahrshefte für Zeitgeschichte* 32 (1984), 29–65.

58. Robert Jay Lifton, *The Nazi Doctors: Medical Killing and the Psychology of Genocide* (New York, 1986), 17 and *passim.* "National Socialism," said Hitler's deputy Rudolf Hess at a rally in 1934, "is nothing but applied biology" (p. 31). See also Wuttke-Groneberg, *Volk und Gesundheit.*

59. Klee, *Euthanasie,* 340–42; Lothar Gruchmann, "Euthanasie und Justiz im Dritten Reich," *Vierteljahrshefte für Zeitgeschichte* 20 (1972), 244. Lifton says that these figures are too low and that the killing may have involved twice these amounts.

60. Klee, *Euthanasie,* 370–72; Mosse, *Toward the Final Solution,* 215–19; Fleming, *Hitler and the Final Solution,* 23–25; Sereny, *Into That Darkness,* 79–82 and *passim;* Lifton, *Nazi Doctors,* pts. 2 and 3, *passim.*

61. See Rich, *Hitler's War Aims,* vol. II, ch. 4.

62. See Robert L. Koehl, *RKFVD: German Resettlement and Population Policy, 1939–1945: A History of the Reich Commission for the Strengthening of Germandon* (Cambridge, Mass., 1957).

63. Ibid., 232. See also Larry V. Thompson, "Lebensborn and the Eugenics Policy of the Reichsführer SS," *Central European History* 4 (1971), 57–71.

64. See Michael R. Marrus, *The Unwanted: European Refugees in the Twentieth Century* (New York, 1985), ch. 4.

65. See Helmut Heiber, "Die Generalplan Ost," *Vierteljahrshefte für Zeitgeschichte* 6 (1958), 281–325. See also Ihor Kamenetsky, *Secret Nazi Plans for Eastern Europe: A Study of Lebensraum Policies* (New York, 1961), *passim.*

66. See Bohdan Wytwycky, *The Other Holocaust: Many Circles of Hell* (Washington, D.C., 1980).

67. Yehuda Bauer, "The Holocaust in Contemporary History," *Studies in Contemporary Jewry* 1 (1984), 205–6.

68. Kurt Pätzold, "Von der Vertreibung zum Genozid: Zu den Ursachen, Triebkräften und Bedingungen der antijüdischen Politik des faschistischen deutschen Imperialismus," in Dietrich Eichholz and Kurt Gossweiler, eds., *Faschismusforschung: Positionen, Probleme, Polemik* (Berlin, 1980), 207.

69. Marrus, *Unwanted,* 224–27; Christopher Browning, "Nazi Resettlement Policy and the Search for a Solution to the Jewish Question, 1939–1941," *German Studies Review* 9 (1986), 497–519; idem, "Nazi Ghettoization Policy: Attritionists vs. Productionists," paper presented at the German Studies Association Conference, Albuquerque, N.M., September 1986.

4. GERMANY'S ALLIES, VANQUISHED STATES, AND COLLABORATIONIST GOVERNMENTS

1. Raul Hilberg, *The Destruction of the European Jews,* rev. ed. (New York, 1984), III, 1220. These figures are rounded to the nearest 100,000.

2. See Yehuda Bauer, "The Death-Marches, January–May, 1945," *Modern Judaism* 3 (1983), 2–4.

3. Helen Fein, *Accounting for Genocide: National Responses and Jewish Victimization during the Holocaust* (New York, 1979), xvi.

4. For other lines of criticism see Aharon Weiss, "Quantitative Measurement of Features of the Holocaust: Notes on the Book by Helen Fein," *Yad Vashem Studies* 14 (1981), 319–34.

5. The memorandum may be found in Yehuda Bauer, *A History of the Holocaust* (New York, 1982), 252–54; and Ihor Kamenetsky, *Secret Nazi Plans for Eastern Europe: A Study of Lebensraum Policies* (New York, 1981), 193–96. In it, the Reichsführer SS determined that schooling for the non-German population of the east must be no higher than fourth-grade elementary school. "The sole goal of this school is to be: Simple arithmetic up to 500 at the most; writing of one's name; the doctrine that it is a divine law to obey the Germans and to be honest, industrious, and good. I don't think that reading is necessary."

6. Hilberg, *Destruction of the European Jews,* I, 188.

7. Heydrich's instructions are in Lucy Dawidowicz, ed., *A Holocaust Reader* (New York, 1976), 59–64. On ghettoization see Hilberg, *Destruction of the European Jews,* I, 215–34; Isaiah Trunk, *Judenrat: The Jewish Councils in Eastern Europe under Nazi Occupation* (New York, 1972), chs. 1–2.

8. Christopher R. Browning, "Nazi Ghettoization Policy: 'Attritionists' vs. 'Productionists,'" paper presented at the German Studies Association Conference, Albuquerque, N.M., September 1986.

9. Robert Koehl, *RKFDV: German Resettlement and Population Policy, 1939–1945: A History of the Reich Commission for the Strengthening of Germandom* (Cambridge, Mass., 1957).

10. Norman Rich, *Hitler's War Aims:* vol. II, *The Establishment of the New Order* (New York, 1974), 76.

11. Martin Broszat, *Nationalsozialistische Polenpolitik, 1939–1945* (Stuttgart, 1961), 91, 101–2; Christopher Browning, "Nazi Resettlement Policy and the Search for a Solution to the Jewish Question," *German Studies Review* 9 (1986), 497–519.

12. See, for example, Helmut Heiber, "Die Generalplan Ost," *Vierteljahrshefte für Zeitgeschichte* 6 (1958), 281–325; Kamenetsky, *Secret Nazi Plans for Eastern Europe,* ch. 2; Gerald Reitlinger, *A House Built on Sand: The Conflicts of German Policy in Russia* (New York, 1960); Alexander Dallin, *German Rule in Russia, 1941–1945: A Study of Occupation Policies* (London, 1957).

13. Philip Friedman, "The Lublin Reservation and the Madagascar Plan: Two Aspects of Nazi Jewish Policy during the Second World War," in Joshua A. Fishman, ed., *Studies on Modern Jewish Social History* (New York, 1972), 354–80.

14. Lucy Dawidowicz, *The War against the Jews, 1939–1945* (New York, 1975), 118.

15. Christopher R. Browning, *The Final Solution and the German Foreign Office: A Study of Referat DIII of Abteilung Deutschland, 1940–1943* (New York, 1978), 35–43. For close examinations of the Lublin Plan see Seev Goschen, "Eichmann und die Nisko-Aktion im Oktober 1939: Eine Fallstudie zur NS-Judenpolitik in der letzten Etappe vor der 'Endlösung,'" *Vierteljahrshefte für Zeitgeschichte* 29 (1981), 74–96; and Jonny Moser, "Nisko: The First Experiment in Deportation," *Simon Weisenthal Annual* 2 (1985), 1–30.

16. Yitzhak Arad, "'Operation Reinhard': Extermination Camps of Belzec, Sobibor and Treblinka," *Yad Vashem Studies* 16 (1984), 236.

17. See Helmut Krausnick and Hans-Heinrich Wilhelm, *Die Truppe des Weltanschauungskrieges: Die Einsatzgruppen der Sicherheitspolizei und des SD, 1938–1942* (Stuttgart, 1981); Jürgen Forster, "The Wehrmacht and the War of Extermination against the Soviet Union," *Yad Vashem Studies* 14 (1981), 7–34; and idem, in Horst Boog et al., *Das Deutsche Reich und der Zweite Weltkrieg*: vol. IV, *Der Angriff auf die Sowjetunion* (Stuttgart, 1983), 413–47, 1030–78; Yehoshua Büchler, "Kommandostab Reichsführer-SS: Himmler's Personal Murder Brigades in 1941," *Holocaust and Genocide Studies* 1 (1986), 11–25; Omer Bartov, *The Eastern Front, 1941–45: German Troops and the Barbarisation of Warfare* (Oxford, 1985); Christian Streit, "The German Army and the Politics of Genocide," in Gerhard Hirschfeld, ed., *The Policies of Genocide: Jews and Soviet Prisoners of War in Nazi Germany* (London, 1986), 1–14.

18. Hilberg, *Destruction of the European Jews*, I, 291–390.

19. Christopher R. Browning, *Fateful Months: Essays on the Emergence of the Final Solution* (New York, 1985), 57.

20. Gerald Reitlinger, *The Final Solution: The Attempt to Exterminate the Jews of Europe, 1939–1945* (New York, 1961), 243.

21. Hilberg, *Destruction of the European Jews*, II, 543.

22. Jürgen Förster, "Hitlers Entscheidung für den Krieg gegen die Sowjetunion," in Horst Boog et al., *Der Angriff auf die Sowjetunion*, 3–37.

23. See Michael R. Marrus and Robert O. Paxton, "The Nazis and the Jews in Occupied Western Europe, 1940–1944," *Journal of Modern History* 54 (1982), 687–714.

24. Robert Koehl, *The Black Corps: The Structure and Power Struggles of the Nazi SS* (Madison, Wis., 1985), 179; Heinz Höhne, *The Order of the Death's Head: The Story of Hitler's SS*, trans. Richard Barry (London, 1972), 379; Fred E. Katz, "Implementation of the Holocaust: The Behavior of Nazi Officials," *Comparative Studies in Society and History* 24 (1982), 510–29.

25. On France see Eberhard Jäckel, *Frankreich in Hitlers Europa* (Stuttgart, 1966).

26. Browning, *Fateful Months*, 49.

27. Browning, *Final Solution and the German Foreign Office*.

28. Study prepared by Werner Best, August–September 1941, microfilm series, U.S. National Archives, Washington, D.C., Microcopy T-501/101/1367.

29. Michael R. Marrus and Robert O. Paxton, *Vichy France and the Jews* (New York, 1981), 242; Robert O. Paxton, *Vichy France: Old Guard and New Order, 1940–1944* (New York, 1972), 227–28, 295.

30. Marrus and Paxton, "Nazis and the Jews in Occupied Western Europe," 706.

31. Marrus and Paxton, *Vichy France and the Jews;* Georges Wellers, André Kaspi, and Serge Klarsfeld, eds., *La France et la question juive, 1940–1944: Actes du Colloque du Centre de documentation juive contemporaine (10 au 12 mars 1979)* (Paris, 1981).

32. Willy Bok, "Considérations sur les estimations quantitatives de la population juive en Belgique," in *La Vie juive dans l'Europe contemporaine* (Brussels, 1965), 94–95; Hilberg, *Destruction of the European Jews,* II, 607; *Les Crimes de guerre, commis sous l'occupation de Belgique: Persécution antisémite* (Liège, 1947), 28; Reitlinger, *Final Solution,* 343.

33. Marrus and Paxton, *Vichy France and the Jews,* 323–29; Geoffrey Warner, *Pierre Laval and the Eclipse of France, 1931–1945: A Political Biography* (New York, 1968); Fred Kupferman, *Pierre Laval* (Paris, 1976).

34. See Patrice Higonnet, "How Guilty Were the French?" *New York Review of Books,* 3 December 1981, 17; René de Chambrun, *Pierre Laval: Traitor or Patriot,* trans. Elly Stein (New York, 1984).

35. On the Danish rescue see Leni Yahil, *The Rescue of Danish Jewry: Test of a Democracy,* trans. Morris Gradel (Philadelphia, 1969); idem, "Methods of Persecution: A Comparison of the 'Final Solution' in Holland and Denmark," *Scripta Hierosolymita* 23 (1972), 279–300; and idem, "The Uniqueness of the Rescue of Danish Jewry," in Gutman and Zuroff, *Rescue Attempts during the Holocaust,* 617–25; Harold Flender, *Rescue in Denmark* (New York, 1963); Hugo Valentin, "Rescue and Relief Activities on Behalf of Jewish Victims of Nazism in Scandinavia," *YIVO Annual of Jewish Social Science* 8 (1953), 224–51.

36. Meir Michaelis, *Mussolini and the Jews: German-Italian Relations and the Jewish Question in Italy, 1922–1945* (Oxford, 1978). See also Susan Zuccotti, *The Italians and the Holocaust: Persecution, Rescue, and Survival* (New York, 1987); Daniel Carpi, "Il problema ebraicao nella politica italiana fra le due guerre mondiale," *Rivista di Studi Politici Internazionali* 23 (1961), 46–50; idem, "The Rescue of Jews in the Italian Zone of Occupied Croatia," in Yisrael Gutman and Efraim Zuroff, eds., *Rescue Attempts during the Holocaust: Proceedings of the Second Yad Vashem International Historical Conference, April 1974* (Jerusalem, 1977), 465–525; idem, "Notes on the History of the Jews in Greece during the Holo-

caust Period: The Attitude of the Italians," *Festschrift in Honor of Dr. George S. Wise* (Tel Aviv, 1981), 25–62; idem, "Nuovi documenti per la storia dell'Olocausto in Grecia: L'atteggiamento degli Italiani (1941–1943)," in *Michael VII* (Tel Aviv, 1981), 119–200; Renzo De Felice, *Storia degli ebrei italiani sotto il fascismo* (Turnin, 1972); Gene Bernardini, "The Origins and Development of Racial Anti-Semitism in Fascist Italy," *Journal of Modern History* 49 (1977), 431–53; Marrus and Paxton, *Vichy France and the Jews*, 315–21; Michael Ledeen, "The Evolution of Italian Fascist Antisemitism," *Jewish Social Studies* 37 (1975), 3–17. See also the fascinating memoir by Dan Segre, "My Jewish-Fascist Childhood," *Jerusalem Quarterly* 26 (Winter 1983), 3–21.

37. See Frederick B. Chary, *The Bulgarian Jews and the Final Solution, 1940–1944* (Pittsburgh, Pa., 1972), ch. 2.

38. See Yeshayahu Jelinek, "The Holocaust and the Internal Policies of the Nazi Satellites in Eastern Europe: A Comparative Study," *Proceedings of the Eighth World Congress of Jewish Studies* (Jerusalem, 1982), 173–78.

39. Walter Laqueur, *The Terrible Secret: An Investigation into the Suppression of Information about Hitler's "Final Solution"* (London, 1980).

40. *Actes et documents de la Saint-Siège rélatifs à la Seconde Guerre Mondiale* (Vatican City, 1974), VII, 453; Saul Friedlander, *Pius XII and the Third Reich: A Documentation*, trans. Charles Fullman (New York, 1966), 158; Laqueur, *Terrible Secret*, 141.

41. Hilberg, *Destruction of the European Jews*, II, 713–14.

42. Livia Rothkirchen, "Hungary: An Asylum for the Refugees of Europe," *Yad Vashem Studies* 7 (1968), 127–42.

43. Randolph L. Braham, *The Politics of Genocide: The Holocaust in Hungary* (New York, 1981), II, 716–18.

44. Some of the evidence is discussed in S. Fauck, "Das deutsch-slovakische Verhältnis 1941–43 und seine Rückwirking auf die slowakische Judenpolitik," in *Gutachten des Instituts für Zeitgeschichte* (Stuttgart, 1966), II, 61–73; Livia Rothkirchen, "Vatican Policy and the 'Jewish Question' in 'Independent' Slovakia, 1939–1945," *Yad Vashem Studies* 6 (1967), 27–53; Yeshayahu Jelinek, "Slovakia's Internal Policy and the Third Reich, August 1940–February 1941," *Central European History* 4 (1971), 242–70.

45. Yeshayahu Jelinek, "The 'Final Solution': The Slovak Version," *East European Quarterly* 4 (1970), 431–41; idem, "Storm Troopers in Slovakia: the Rodrobrana and the Hlinka Guard," *Journal of Contemporary History* 6 (1971), 111.

46. Hilberg, *Destruction of the European Jews*, II, 735.

47. Dora Litani, "The Destruction of the Jews of Odessa in the Light of Rumanian Documents," *Yad Vashem Studies* 6 (1967), 135–54; Reitlinger, *Final Solution*, 240.

48. Hilberg, *Destruction of the European Jews*, II, 759. In addition to the deportees to Transnistria, Hilberg estimates that the Rumanians "killed around 150,000 indigenous Jews in the Odessa area and Golta."

49. Martin Broszat, "Das dritte Reich und die Rumänische Judenpolitik," in *Gutachten des Instituts für Zeitgeschichte* (Munich, 1958), I, 102–83; Nicholas Nagy-Talavera, *The Green Shirts and the Others* (Stanford, 1970); Stephen Fischer-Galati, "Fascism, Communism and the Jewish Question in Rumania," in Bela Vago and George L. Mosse, eds., *Jews and Non-Jews in Eastern Europe* (New York, 1974); Jean Ancel, "Plans for Deportation of the Rumanian Jews and Their Discontinuance in the Light of Documentary Evidence (July–October 1942)," *Yad Vashem Studies* 16 (1984), 381–420; Joseph B. Schechtman, "The Transnistria Reservation," *YIVO Annual of Jewish Social Science* 8 (1953), 178–96.

50. Chary, *Bulgarian Jews*, xiii.

51. Chary, *Bulgarian Jews*; Nisan Oren, "The Bulgarian Exception: A Reassessment of the Salvation of the Jewish Community," *Yad Vashem Studies* 7 (1968), 83–106; Vicki Tamir, *Bulgaria and Her Jews: The History of a Dubious Symbiosis* (New York, 1979).

52. Braham, *Politics of Genocide*, I, 77; II, 1143–47; Mario D. Fenyo, *Hitler, Horthy, and Hungary* (New Haven, 1972), ch. 10.

53. Randolph L. Braham, *The Hungarian Labor Service System, 1939–1945* (New York, 1977).

54. Braham, *Politics of Genocide*, I, 225–26, 229; and idem, "The Jewish Question in German-Hungarian Relations during the Kallay Era," *Jewish Social Studies* 39 (1977), 183–208. See the excellent review of Braham's work by Istvan Déak, "Could the Hungarian Jews Have Survived?" *New York Review of Books*, 4 February 1982, 24–27; and the polemic "Genocide in Hungary: An Exchange," ibid., 27 May 1982, 54–55.

55. Braham, *Politics of Genocide*, I, 374.

5. PUBLIC OPINION IN NAZI EUROPE

1. For an extremely useful survey of the literature on this subject see O. D. Kulka and Aron Rodrigue, "The German Population and the Jews in the Third Reich: Recent Publications and Trends in Research on German Society and the 'Jewish Question,'" *Yad Vashem Studies* 16 (1984), 421–35.

2. Justin Godart, preface to Léon Poliakov, *L'Etoile jaune* (Paris, 1949), 11.

3. Friedrich Meinecke, *The German Catastrophe: Reflections and Recollections*, trans. Sidney B. Fay (Boston, 1963), 86.

4. Peter Viereck, *Meta-Politics: The Roots of the Nazi Mind* (New York, 1965), 317.

5. Karl Dietrich Bracher, *The German Dictatorship: The Origins, Structure, and Effects of National Socialism*, trans. Jean Steinberg (New York, 1970), 370.

6. Martin Broszat, "Soziale Motivation und Führer-Bindung des Nationalsozialismus," *Vierteljahrshefte für Zeitgeschichte* 18 (1970), 401.

7. Karl Jaspers, *The Question of German Guilt,* trans. E. B. Ashton (New York, 1961), 82.

8. Eva Reichmann, *Hostages of Civilization: The Social Sources of National Socialist Anti-Semitism* (London, 1953), 190.

9. Léon Poliakov, *Brévaire de la haine: Le IIIe Reich et les Juifs,* new ed. (Paris, 1974), 419.

10. Hermann Rauschning, *The Revolution of Nihilism: Warning to the West* (New York, 1939), 53.

11. Reichmann, *Hostages of Civilization,* 233–35. "The idea that a considerable number of the anti-Semites of that time [i.e., the early 1930s] would have approved of the expulsion and physical annihilation of their Jewish fellow citizens, with whom they were acquainted, is against the opinion of all contemporary observers" (p. 234).

12. Michael Muller-Claudius, *Der Antisemitismus und das deutsche Verhängnis* (Frankfurt am Main, 1948), 167–76.

13. Franz Neumann, *Behemoth: The Structure and Practice of National Socialism, 1933–1944,* rev. ed. (New York, 1944), 121. For an interesting discussion of the views of the Frankfurt School (of which Neumann was a part) on antisemitism see Martin Jay, *Permanent Exiles: Essays on the Intellectual Migration from Germany to America* (New York, 1985), ch. 6.

14. See Aryeh L. Unger, "The Public Opinion Reports of the Nazi Party," *Public Opinion Quarterly* 29 (1965), 565–82.

15. For an example of conclusions based upon these reports see William Sheridan Allen, "Die deutsche Offentlichkeit und die 'Reichskristallnacht': Konflikte zwischen Werthierarchie und Propaganda im Dritten Reich," in Detlef Peukert and Jürgen Reulecke, eds., *Die Reihen fast geschlossen: Beiträge zur Geschichte des Alltags unterm Nationalsozialismus* (Wuppertal, 1981), 397–411.

16. Lawrence Stokes, "The German People and the Destruction of the European Jews," *Central European History* 6 (1973), 167–91.

17. Marliss Steinert, *Hitler's War and the Germans: Public Mood and Attitude during the Second World War,* ed. and trans. Thomas E. J. de Witt (Athens, Ohio, 1977).

18. Max H. Kele, *Nazis and Workers: National Socialist Appeals to German Labor, 1919–1933* (Chapel Hill, N.C., 1972), 77; Jeremy Noakes, *The Nazi Party of Lower Saxony, 1921–1933* (Oxford, 1971), 209; Richard Hamilton, *Who Voted for Hitler?* Princeton, N.J., 1982), 606–7 and *passim;* Thomas Childers, *The Nazi Voter: The Social Foundations of Fascism in Germany, 1919–1933* (Chapel Hill, N.C., 1983).

19. Werner T. Angress, "Die 'Judenfrage' im Spiegel amtlicher Berichte 1935," in Ursula Buttner, ed., *Das Unrechtsregime: International Forschung über den Nationalsozialismus. Festschrift für Werner Jochmann:* vol. II, *Verfolgung/Exil/Belasteter Neubeginn* (Hamburg, 1986), 19–43.

20. Ian Kershaw, *Popular Opinion and Political Dissent in the Third Reich: Bavaria, 1933–1945* (Oxford, 1983), viii, which draws upon idem, "Antisemitismus und Volksmeinung: Reaktion auf die Judenverfolgung," in Martin Broszat et al., *Bayern in der NS-Zeit* (Munich, 1979), II, 281–300. See also idem, *Der Hitler: Mythos: Volksmeinung und Propaganda im Dritten Reich* (Stuttgart, 1980); and idem, "The Persecution of the Jews and German Popular Opinion in the Third Reich," *Leo Baeck Institute Year Book* 26 (1981), 261–89.

21. Sarah Gordon, *Hitler, Germans and the "Jewish Question"* (Princeton, N.J., 1984), 301. Looking at the social backgrounds of those accused of these crimes, Gordon finds certain groups "overrepresented" among "opponents of persecution." But it turns out that these are the groups into which Jews were disproportionately integrated—older Germans, independents, and white-collar workers. We are not told how intermarriage affects these statistics.

22. Michael H. Kater, "Everyday Anti-Semitism in Prewar Nazi Germany: The Popular Bases," *Yad Vashem Studies* 16 (1984), 138.

23. Christoph Dipper, "The German Resistance and the Jews," *Yad Vashem Studies* 16 (1984), 68, 85. This article also appeared as "Der deutsche Widerstand und die Juden," *Geschichte und Gesellschaft* 9 (1983), 349–80.

24. Otto Dov Kulka, "'Public Opinion' in Nazi Germany and the 'Jewish Question,'" *Jerusalem Quarterly* 25 (1982), 121–44, and 26 (1983), 34–45; and Kulka and Rodrigue, "German Population and the Jews," 434–35; Walter Laqueur observes that "by the end of 1942, millions in Germany knew that the Jewish question had been radically solved, and that this radical solution did not involve resettlement, in short, that most, or all of those who had been deported were no longer alive. Details about their deaths were known to a much smaller number." Laqueur, *Terrible Secret,* 31–32.

25. Otto Dov Kulka, "Die Nürnberger Rassengesetsze und die deutsche Bevölkerung im Lichte geheimer NS-Lage- und Stimmungsberichte," *Vierteljahrshefte für Zeitgeschichte* 32 (1984), 582–624.

26. Kulka and Rodrigue, "German Population and the Jews," 434.

27. Shulamit Volkov, "Kontinuität und Diskontinuität im deutschen Antisemitismus," *Vierteljahrshefte für Zeitgeschichte* 33 (1985), 221–43. Gordon, *Hitler, Germans and the "Jewish Question,"* 48, also makes this point.

28. See Angress, "Judenfrage," 37–38; Erich Goldhagen, "Weltanschauung und Endlösung: Zum Antisemitismus der nationalsozialistischen Fuhrungsschicht," *Vierteljahrshefte für Zeitgeschichte* 24 (1976), 392.

29. Michael R. Marrus, "The Theory and Practice of Anti-Semitism," *Commentary,* August 1982, 38–42.

30. Christian Streit, *Keine Kameraden: Die Wehrmacht und die sowjetischen Kriegsgefangenen, 1941–1945* (Stuttgart, 1978), 300; idem, "The German Army and the Policies of Genocide," in Gerhard Hirschfeld, ed., *The Policies of Genocide: Jews and Soviet Prisoners of War in Nazi*

Germany (London, 1986), 1–19; Omer Bartov, *The Eastern Front, 1941–45: German Troops and the Barbarisation of Warfare* (Oxford, 1985), chs. 3–4.

31. See Bela Vago and George Mosse, eds., *Jews and Non-Jews in Eastern Europe* (New York, 1974); Bela Vago, *The Shadow of the Swastika: The Rise of Fascism and Anti-Semitism in the Danubian Basin* (London, 1975); Hugh Seton-Watson, "Government Policies towards the Jews in Pre-Communist Eastern Europe," *Soviet Jewish Affairs* 4 (December 1969), 20–25. See also the comprehensive review article by Ezra Mendelsohn, "Recent Work on the Jews in Inter-war East Central Europe: A Survey," *Studies in Contemporary Jewry* 1 (1984), 316–37.

32. Ezra Mendelsohn, *The Jews of East Central Europe between the World Wars* (Bloomington, Ind., 1983).

33. For a sharply dissenting view on Poland see Norman Davies, *God's Playground: A History of Poland:* vol. II, *1795 to the Present* (Oxford, 1981), ch. 9. On prewar Poland see also Celia S. Heller, *On the Edge of Destruction: Jews of Poland between the Two World Wars* (New York, 1977); Ezra Mendelsohn, "Interwar Poland: Good for the Jews or Bad for the Jews?" in Chimen Abramsky, Maciej Jachimczyk, and Antony Polonsky, eds., *The Jews in Poland* (Oxford, 1986), 130–39; and Jerzy Holzer, "Relations between Polish and Jewish Left Wing Groups in Interwar Poland," ibid., 140–46.

34. Hilberg, *Destruction of the European Jews,* III, 1212.

35. There is some sign that the barriers may be wearing down, however. A recent instance is an international conference on Polish Jewish studies held at Oxford in 1984, some of the papers from which have been published in the volume edited by Abramsky, Jachimczyk, and Polonsky noted above.

36. See Joseph Kirmish, introduction to Emmanuel Ringelblum, in Joseph Kirmish and Shmuel Krakowski, eds., *Polish Jewish Relations during the Second World War,* trans. Dafna Allon, Danuta Dabrowska, and Dana Keren, new ed. (New York, 1976); and Yisrael Gutman, "Polish and Jewish Historiography on the Question of Polish-Jewish Relations during World War II," in Abramsky, Jachimczyk, and Polonsky, *Jews in Poland,* 177–89. A recent essay tending to support the present-day Polish and the one-time Bundist perspective is Norman Davies, "The Survivor's Voice," *New York Review of Books,* 20 November 1986, 21–23. See also the provocative observations of Israel Shahak, "'The Life of Death': An Exchange," *New York Review of Books,* 29 January 1987, 45–49.

37. Ringelblum, *Polish-Jewish Relations,* 263.

38. David Engel, "An Early Account of Polish Jewry under Nazi and Soviet Occupation Presented to the Polish Government-in-Exile, February 1940," *Jewish Social Studies* 45 (1983), 12–13.

39. Richard Lukas, *The Forgotten Holocaust: The Poles under German Occupation, 1939–1944* (Lexington, Ky., 1986).

40. See also Wladyslaw Bartoszewski, "Polish-Jewish Relations in Oc-

cupied Poland, 1939–1945," in Abramsky, Jachimczyk, and Polonsky, *Jews in Poland*, 150–51.

41. Norman Davies points out that the Polish resistance "failed to oppose not only the actions against the Jews but equally, until 1943, all the executions and mass deportations of Polish civilians." Davies, *God's Playground*, II, 265.

42. Yisrael Gutman, *The Jews of Warsaw, 1939–1943: Ghetto, Underground, Revolt*, trans. Ina Freidman (Bloomington, Ind., 1982), 254–55; and idem, "Polish Responses to the Liquidation of Polish Jewry," *Jerusalem Quarterly* 17 (Fall 1980), 40–55. See also the account of the Polish-Jewish Communist historian Ber Mark, *Uprising in the Warsaw Ghetto*, trans. Gershon Friedlin (New York, 1975), which refers to support for the Jews "from Polish democratic circles."

43. Gutman, *Jews of Warsaw*, 414.

44. On conditions in the Ukraine see Philip Friedman, "Ukrainian-Jewish Relations during the Nazi Occupation," *YIVO Annual of Jewish Social Science* 13 (1958/59), 259–96; Howard Aster and Peter J. Potichnyj, *Jewish Ukrainian Relations: Two Solitudes* (Oakville, Ontario, 1983); and Taras Hunczak, "Ukrainian-Jewish Relations during the Soviet and Nazi Occupations," in Yuri Boshyk, ed., *Ukraine during World War II: History and Aftermath* (Edmonton, Alberta, 1986), 39–57.

45. See Alexander Dallin, *German Rule in Russia, 1941–1945: A Study of Occupation Policies* (London, 1957); John A. Armstrong, "Collaborationism in World War II: The Integral Nationalist Variant in Eastern Europe," *Journal of Modern History* 40 (September 1968), 396–410.

46. See *The Stroop Report: The Jewish Quarter of Warsaw Is No More!* trans. Sybil Milton (New York, 1979). In reality, of course, the so-called ready-to-help volunteers were not really volunteers at all, having chosen auxilliary training in places like the Trawniki camp in Poland as a way of escaping almost certain death as Soviet prisoners of war. Helge Grabitz, "Die strafrechtliche Verantwortlichkeit der 'Trawnikis' für ihren Einsatz bei der 'Endlösung der Judenfrage' in den Distrikten Lublin und Warsaw," paper delivered at the German Studies Association Conference, Albuquerque, N.M., September 1986. See idem, *NS-Prozesse: Psychogramme der Beteiligten* (Heidelberg, 1986), 59–64.

47. Yehuda Bauer, *A History of the Holocaust* (New York, 1982), 286.

48. Livia Rothkirchen, "Czech Attitudes towards the Jews during the Nazi Regime," *Yad Vashem Studies* 13 (1979), 287–320.

49. For examples see Friedman, "Ukrainian-Jewish Relations," 284; Hunczak, "Ukrainian-Jewish Relations," 46; Dov Levin, *Fighting Back: Lithuania's Armed Resistance to the Nazis, 1941–1945*, trans. Moshe Kohn and Dina Cohen (New York, 1985), 183–84.

50. Michael R. Marrus and Robert O. Paxton, *Vichy France and the Jews* (New York, 1981), ch. 5.

51. John Sweets, *Choices in Vichy France: The French under Nazi Occupation* (New York, 1986), 118–36.

52. There is even evidence for this shift in Slovakia, where considerable popular antisemitism existed. See Lilvia Rothkirchen, "Vatican Policy and the 'Jewish Question' in 'Independent' Slovakia (1939–1945)," *Yad Vashem Studies* 6 (1967), 42.

53. Leonard Gross, *The Last Jews of Berlin* (New York, 1982).

54. B. A. Sijes, "The Position of the Jews during the German Occupation of the Netherlands: Some Observations," *Acta Historae Neerlandicae* 9 (1976), 170.

55. Philip Hallie, *Lest Innocent Blood Be Shed: The Story of Le Chambon and How Goodness Happened There* (New York, 1979); Pierre Sauvage, "A Most Persistent Haven: Le Chambon-sur-Lignon," *Moment*, October 1983, 30–35.

56. See Martin Gilbert, *The Holocaust: A History of the Jews of Europe during the Second World War* (New York, 1985), 499; Gideon Hausner, *Justice in Jerusalem* (New York, 1968), 251; Michael R. Marrus, "Die französischen Kirchen und die Verfolgung der Juden in Frankreich, 1940–1944," *Vierteljahrshefte für Zeitgeschichte* 31 (1983), 483–505; Helen Fein, *Accounting for Genocide: National Responses and Jewish Victimization during the Holocaust* (New York, 1979), ch. 4.

57. Bernard Wasserstein, *Britain and the Jews of Europe, 1939–1945* (London, 1979), 295–301.

58. See B. A. Sijes, "Several Observations concerning the Position of the Jews in Occupied Holland during World War II," in Yisrael Gutman and Efraim Zuroff, eds., *Rescue Attempts during the Holocaust: Proceedings of the Second Yad Vashem International Historical Conference, Jerusalem, April 8–11, 1974* (Jerusalem, 1977), 547.

59. Leni Yahil, *The Rescue of Danish Jewry: Test of a Democracy*, trans. Morris Gradel (Philadelphia, 1969), xviii. See also Harold Flender, *Rescue in Denmark* (New York, 1963); Hugo Valentin, "Rescue and Relief Activities on Behalf of Jewish Victims of Nazism in Scandinavia," *YIVO Annual of Jewish Social Science* 8 (1953), 224–51; Leni Yahil, "Methods of Persecution: A Comparison of the 'Final Solution' in Holland and Denmark," *Scripta Hierosolymita* 23 (1972), 279–300.

60. Meir Michaelis, *Mussolini and the Jews: German-Italian Relations and the Jewish Question in Italy, 1922–1945* (Oxford, 1978); and Susan Zuccotti, *The Italians and the Holocaust: Persecution, Rescue, and Survival* (New York, 1987). See also Daniel Carpi, "Il problema ebraico nella politica italiana fra le due guerre mondiali," *Revista di Studi Politici Internazionale* 23 (1961), 46–50; idem, "The Rescue of Jews in the Italian Zone of Occupied Croatia," in Gutman and Zuroff, *Rescue Attempts during the Holocaust*, 465–525; idem, "Notes on the History of the Jews in Greece during the Holocaust Period: The Attitude of the Italians," in *Festrschrift in Honor of Dr. George S. Wise* (Tel Aviv, 1981), 25–62; idem, "Nuovi documenti per la storia dell'Olocausto in Grecia: L'atteggiamento degli Italiani (1941–1943)," in *Michael VII* (Tel Aviv, 1981), 119–200;

Renzo De Felice, *Storia degli ebrei italiani sotto il fascismo* (Turin, 1972); Marrus and Paxton, *Vichy France and the Jews*, 315–21.

61. Samuel P. Olner, "The Need to Recognize the Heroes of the Nazi Era," *Reconstructionist* 48 (June 1982), 7–14; Moshe Bejski, "The Righteous among the Nations and Their Part in the Rescue of Jews," in Yisrael Gutman and Livia Rothkirchen, eds., *The Catastrophe of the European Jews* (Jerusalem, 1976), 582–607; Kazimierz Iranek-Osmecki, *He Who Saves One Life* (New York, 1971); Peter Hellman, *The Avenue of the Righteous* (New York, 1980).

62. Lawrence Baron, "The Dynamics of Decency: Dutch Rescuers of Jews during the Holocaust," Frank P. Piskor Faculty Lecture, St. Lawrence University, 2 May 1985. Cf. Louis de Jong, "Help to People in Hiding," *Delta: A Review of Arts, Life, and Thought in the Netherlands* 8 (1965), 37–79; Henry L. Mason, "Testing Human Bonds within Nations: Jews in the Occupied Netherlands," *Political Science Quarterly* 99 (1984), 315–45.

63. Louis de Jong, "Jews and Non-Jews in Nazi-Occupied Holland," in Max Beloff, ed., *On the Track of Tyranny* (London, 1960), 145–46; Fein, *Accounting for Genocide*, 269–70.

64. Nechama Tec, *When Light Pierced the Darkness: Christian Rescue of Jews in Nazi-Occupied Poland* (New York, 1986), 59 and *passim*.

65. Ibid., 188.

66. Teresa Prekerowa, "The Relief Committee of the Jews of Poland," in Abramsky, Jachimczyk, and Polonsky, *Jews in Poland*, 161–76; Joseph Kermish, "The Activities of the Council for Aid to the Jews ("Zegota") in Occupied Poland," in Gutman and Zuroff, *Rescue Attempts during the Holocaust*, 367–98; and the comments by Shmuel Krakowski, Abraham (Adolf) Berman, Miriam Peleg, and Yisrael Gutman; and Lukas, *Forgotten Holocaust*, 147–49.

67. Laqueur, *Terrible Secret*, 112; Anita Revel, *Faithful unto Death: The Story of Arthur Zygielbaum* (Montreal, 1980), 178.

68. Laqueur, *Terrible Secret*, 106.

6. THE VICTIMS

1. Yitzhak Arad, *Ghetto in Flames: The Struggle and Destruction of the Jews in Vilna in the Holocaust* (Jerusalem, 1980), 231; Yisrael Gutman, *The Jews of Warsaw, 1939–1943: Ghetto, Underground, Revolt* (Bloomington, Ind., 1983), 305; Emmanuel Ringelblum, *Notes from the Warsaw Ghetto*, trans. and ed. Jacob Sloan (New York, 1974), 310.

2. Raul Hilberg, *The Destruction of the European Jews*, rev. ed. (New York, 1985), III, 1030–31, 1038–39. At the beginning of his book Hilberg makes a curious observation that appears to qualify his assessment: "it should be emphasized again that the term 'Jewish reactions' refers only to ghetto Jews. This reaction pattern was born in the ghetto and it will die there. It is part and parcel of ghetto life. It applies to *all* ghetto Jews—as-

similationists and Zionists, the capitalists and the socialists, the unortho-
dox and the religious" (emphasis in original; I, 27). It is not clear what Hilberg means by "ghetto Jews" in this context, but the term seems to apply to
all Jews whose reactions he examines.

3. For some sense of the intensity of this criticism see Nathan Eck, "Historical Research or Slander?" *Yad Vashem Studies* 6 (1967), 385–430.

4. Raul Hilberg, "The Judenrat: Conscious or Unconscious 'Tool,'" in
Yisrael Gutman and Cynthia J. Haft, eds., *Patterns of Jewish Leadership in
Nazi Europe, 1933–1945: Proceedings of the Third Yad Vashem International Historical Conference, Jerusalem, April 4–7, 1977* (Jerusalem,
1979), 61–63; idem, *Destruction of the European Jews*, III, 1037; idem,
"The Ghetto as a Form of Government: An Analysis of Isaiah Trunk's *Judenrat*," in Yehuda Bauer and Nathan Rotenstreich, eds., *The Holocaust
as a Historical Experience* (New York, 1981), 155–71.

5. Hilberg, "Judenrat," 33.

6. Hannah Arendt, *Eichmann in Jerusalem: A Report on the Banality of
Evil* (New York, 1963), 117–18, 125. For a useful perspective on this
work see Walter Laqueur, "Re-reading Hannah Arendt," *Encounter,*
March 1979, 73–79.

7. Arendt, *Eichman in Jerusalem,* 125–26.

8. For an important critique of Arendt, see Jacob Robinson, *And the
Crooked Shall be Made Straight: The Eichmann Trial, the Jewish Catastrophe, and Hannah Arendt's Narrative* (Philadelphia, 1965).

9. Isaiah Trunk, *Jewish Responses to Nazi Persecution: Collective and
Individual Behavior in Extremis* (New York, 1982), ix.

10. Isaiah Trunk, *Judenrat: The Jewish Councils in Eastern Europe
under Nazi Occupation* (New York, 1972), 1.

11. Ibid., Appendix 1.

12. Raul Hilberg, Stanislaw Staron, and Josef Kermisz, ed., *The Warsaw Diary of Adam Czerniakow: Prelude to Doom,* trans. Stanislaw
Staron et al. (New York, 1979).

13. Ibid., introduction by Raul Hilberg and Stanislaw Staron, 65.

14. Hilberg, "Judenrat," 36. See also idem, "Ghetto as a Form of Government," 155–71.

15. See Aryeh Tartakower, "Adam Czerniakow: The Man and His Supreme Sacrifice," *Yad Vashem Studies* 6 (1967), 55–67; Yosef Kermisz,
"The Judenrat in Warsaw," in Gutman and Haft, *Patterns of Jewish Leadership in Nazi Europe,* 75–90; Gutman, *The Jews of Warsaw, 1939–1943,*
207; Maurice Friedberg, "The Question of the Judenräte," *Commentary,*
July 1973, 61–63; Mendel Kohansky, "The Last Days of Adam Czerniakow," *Midstream* 15 (1969), 61–67.

16. Leonard Tushnet, *The Pavement of Hell* (New York, 1972), 169–
70; Shmuel Huppert, "King of the Ghetto: Mordechai Haim Rumkowski,
the Elder of the Lodz Ghetto," *Yad Vashem Studies* 15 (1983), 150; Philip
Friedman, "Two 'Saviors' Who Failed: Moses Merin of Sosnowiec and
Jacob Gens of Vilna," *Commentary* 26 (1958), 479–91; Bendet Hershko-

vitch, "The Ghetto in Litzmannstadt (Lodz)," *YIVO Annual of Jewish Social Science* 5 (1950), 85–122.

17. For a survey of much of this research see Yehuda Bauer, "Jewish Leadership Reactions to Nazi Policies," in Bauer and Rotenstreich, *Holocaust as a Historical Experience*, 173–92.

18. A fascinating exception is the octogenerian Jewish Germanophile Alfred Nossig, who was tried and shot by the Jewish underground in Warsaw in early 1943. See Michael Zylberg, "The Trial of Alfred Nossig: Traitor or Victim," *Wiener Library Bulletin* 23, nos. 2, 3 (1969), 41–45; Gutman, *Jews of Warsaw*, 341–42.

19. Trunk, *Judenrat*, 17–21, 467–69.

20. Aharon Weiss, "Jewish Leadership in Occupied Poland: Postures and Attitudes," *Yad Vashem Studies* 12 (1977), 335–65. Cf. idem, "The Relations between the Judenrat and the Jewish Polish," in Gutman and Haft, *Patterns of Jewish Leadership*, 201–17.

21. Hilberg, *Destruction of European Jewry*, III, 1212; Christopher Browning, "Nazi Resettlement Policy and the Search for a Solution to the Jewish Question," *German Studies Review* 9 (1986), 497–519.

22. Shalom Cholawsky, "The Judenrat in Minsk," in Gutman and Haft, *Patterns of Jewish Leadership*, 113–32.

23. Yisrael Gutman, "The Concept of Labor," in Gutman and Haft, *Patterns of Jewish Leadership*, 162; Arad, *Ghetto in Flames*, 337. In 1943 Gens still believed in salvation through economic productivity. "Time is on our side," he said at the end of August. "I am convinced that the Soviet Army will reach Vilna by December of this year, and if at that time the ghetto still survives, even though a few will be left in it, I shall know that I completed my task" (p. 427).

24. See the articles by Yosef Kermisz, Yitzhak Arad, Dov Levin, Yisrael Gutman, and Aharon Weiss in Gutman and Haft, *Patterns of Jewish Leadership*; Lucjan Dobroszycki, "Jewish Elites under German Rule," in Henry Friedlander and Sybil Milton, eds., *The Holocaust: Ideology, Bureaucracy, and Genocide: The San José Papers* (Millwood, N.Y., 1980), 221–30; idem, *Chronicle of the Lodz Ghetto, 1941–1944*, trans. Richard Lourie et al. (New Haven, Conn., 1984); Shmuel Huppert, "King of the Ghetto: Mordechai Haim Rumkowski, the Elder of the Lodz Ghetto," *Yad Vashem Studies* 15 (1983), 125–57; Tushnet, *Pavement of Hell*; Yehuda Bauer, "Jewish Leadership Reactions to Nazi Policies," in Bauer and Rotenstreich, *Holocaust as a Historical Experience*, 180. On Rumkowski, see the fictionalized account by Leslie Epstein, *King of the Jews: A Novel of the Holocaust* (New York, 1979). But cf. the reactions in Huppert, "King of the Ghetto," 125–27.

25. See Erich Goldhagen, "The Mind and Spirit of East European Jewry during the Holocaust," *Midstream*, March 1980, 11–14.

26. See Avraham Barkai, "Between East and West: Jews from Germany in the Lodz Ghetto," *Yad Vashem Studies* 16 (1984), 271–332.

27. Clifford Geertz, *The Interpretation of Cultures: Selected Essays* (New York, 1973), 16.

28. *Notes from the Warsaw Ghetto: The Journal of Emmanuel Ringelblum*, ed. and trans. Jacob Sloan (New York, 1974), 178. The optimism quickly collapsed. "That afternoon and the next day came the bitter, sober aftermath. The press did not confirm the news. This mass psychosis, during which a few people actually heard the Others' soldiers talking about Göring's death at the post office, reminds us of the Sabbatian psychosis of the seventeenth century, when Jews who believed that Sabbatai Zevi was really the Messiah sold all their possessions and prepared to journey to Palestine" (p. 179). On rumors see also Christopher Browning and Yisrael Gutman, "The Reports of a Jewish 'Informer' in the Warsaw Ghetto: Selected Documents," *Yad Vashem Studies* 17 (1985), 247–94.

29. Gutman, "Concept of Labor," 162; Goldhagen, "Mind and Spirit of East European Jewry during the Holocaust," 10–14.

30. Jan Karski, *Story of a Secret State* (Boston, 1944), 330.

31. Emil Apfelbaum, ed., *Maladie de famine* (Warsaw, 1946); Leonard Tushnet, *The Uses of Adversity* (New York, 1966).

32. Yehuda Bauer, *A History of the Holocaust* (New York, 1983), 172; Lucy S. Dawidowicz, *The War against the Jews, 1933–1945* (New York, 1975), 242.

33. *The Warsaw Diary of Chaim A. Kaplan*, rev. ed., trans. and ed. Abraham I. Katsh (New York, 1973), 244–45.

34. Arad, *Ghetto in Flames*, 320.

35. Trunk, *Judenrat*, 226.

36. Lucjan Dobroszycki, ed., *The Chronicle of the Lodz Ghetto, 1941–1944*, trans. Richard Lourie et al. (New Haven, 1984), 412.

37. On Jewish emigration see Herbert A. Strauss, "Jewish Emigration from Germany: Nazi Policies and Jewish Response," *Leo Baeck Institute Year Book* 25 (1980), 313–61; and ibid., 26 (1981), 343–409; Werner Rosenstock, "Exodus, 1933–1939: A Survey of Jewish Emigration from Germany," *Leo Baeck Institute Year Book* 1 (1956), 373–90; Helmut Genschel, *Die Verdrängung der Juden aus der Wirtschaft im Dritten Reich* (Göttingen, 1966); Arieh Tartakower and Kurt B. Grossmann, *The Jewish Refugee* (New York, 1944).

38. Abraham Margaliot, "The Problem of the Rescue of German Jewry during the Years 1933–1939: The Reasons for the Delay in their Emigration from the Reich," in Yisrael Gutman and Efraim Zuroff, eds., *Rescue Attempts during the Holocaust: Proceedings of the Second Yad Vashem International Historical Conference, Jerusalem, April 8–11, 1974* (Jerusalem, 1977), 263; idem, "The Dispute over the Leadership of German Jewry, 1933–1938," *Yad Vashem Studies* 10 (1974), 129–48. See also Arnold Paucker, ed., *Die Juden in Nationalsozialistischen Deutschland, 1933–1943* (Tübingen, 1986).

39. George L. Mosse, *German Jews beyond Judaism* (Bloomington, Ind., 1985).

40. Sidney M. Bolkosky, *The Distorted Image: German Jewish Perceptions of Germans and Germany, 1918–1935* (New York, 1975), 184.

41. See Jacob Katz, "Was the Holocaust Predictable?" *Commentary*, May 1975, 41–48.

42. Leonard Baker, *Days of Sorrow and Pain: Leo Baeck and the Berlin Jews* (New York, 1978), 247.

43. O. D. Kulka, "The 'Reichsvereinigung of the Jews in Germany' (1938/9–1943)," in Gutman and Haft, *Patterns of Jewish Leadership*, 45–58.

44. Dawidowicz, *War against the Jews*, 196.

45. Henry Huttenbach, *The Destruction of the Jewish Community of Worms, 1933–1945: A Study of the Holocaust Experience in Germany* (New York, 1981), 36. Cf. H. G. Adler, *Der verwaltete Mensch: Studien zur Deportation der Juden aus Deutschland* (Tübingen, 1974).

46. Livia Rothkirchen, "The Dual Role of the 'Jewish Center' in Slovakia," in Gutman and Haft, *Patterns of Jewish Leadership*, 219–27.

47. Bela Vago, "The Ambiguity of Collaborationism: The Center of the Jews in Romania (1942–1944)," in Gutman and Haft, *Patterns of Jewish Leadership*, 287–309.

48. Yerachmiel [Richard] Cohen, "French Jewry's Dilemma on the Orientation of Its Leadership: From Polemics to Conciliation, 1942–1944," *Yad Vashem Studies* 14 (1981), 167–204; idem, "The Jewish Community of France in the Face of Vichy-German Persecution, 1940–1944," in Frances Malino and Bernard Wasserstein, eds., *The Jews in Modern France* (Hanover, N.H., 1985), 180–203. Cf., Leni Yahil, "The Jewish Leadership of France," in Gutman and Haft, *Patterns of Jewish Leadership*, 317–33.

49. Maurice Rajfus, *Des Juifs dans la collaboration: l'UGIF (1941–1944)* (Paris, 1980). Cf. Cynthia J. Haft, *The Bargain and the Bridle: The General Union of the Israelites of France* (Chicago, 1983).

50. Raymond Raoul Lambert, *Carnet d'un témoin, 1940–1943,* ed. Richard Cohen (Paris, 1985); and Richard Cohen, "A Jewish Leader in Vichy France, 1940–1943: The Diary of Raymond Raoul Lambert," *Jewish Social Studies* 43 (1981), 291–310.

51. Joseph Michman, "The Controversy Surrounding the Jewish Council of Amsterdam," in Gutman and Haft, *Patterns of Jewish Leadership*, 235–57; idem, "The Controversial Stand of the Joodse Raad in the Netherlands: Lodewijk E. Visser's Struggle," *Yad Vashem Studies* 10 (1974), 9–68. See the assessment of H. W. von der Dunk, *Kleio heeft duizend ogen* (Assen, 1974), 50, cited in Michman, "Jewish Council of Amsterdam," 256. See also Jacob Presser, *The Destruction of the Dutch Jews*, trans. Arnold Pomerans (New York, 1969).

52. Michman, "Jewish Council of Amsterdam," 255.

53. Lucjan Dobroszycki, "Jewish Elites under German Rule," in Friedlander and Milton, *Holocaust*, 222.

54. See, however, Eugen Kogen, Hermann Langbein, and Adalbert Rückerl, eds., *Nationalsozialistische Massentötung durch Giftgas* (Frankfurt, 1983); Adalbert Rückerl, *NS-Vernichtungslager im Spiegel deutscher Strafprozesse, Belzec, Sobibor, Treblinka, Chelmno* (Munich, 1977).

55. Olga Wormser-Migot, *Le Système concentrationnaire nazi (1933– 1945)* (Paris, 1968), 559; Eugen Kogon, *Der SS-Staat: Das System der deutschen Konzentrationslager* (Frankfurt am Main, 1946); Yisrael Gutman, "Social Stratification in the Concentration Camps," in Yisrael Gutman and Avital Saf, eds., *The Nazi Concentration Camps: Structure and Aims. The Image of the Prisoner. The Jews in the Camps. Proceedings of the Fourth Yad Vashem International Historical Conference, Jerusalem, January 1980* (Jerusalem, 1984), 151, n. 18.

56. Falk Pingel, *Häftlinge unter SS-Herschaft: Widerstand, Selbstbehauptung und Vernichtung im Konzentrationslager* (Hamburg, 1978), 129–30; Hans Buchheim, "The SS-Instrument of Domination," in Helmut Krausnick et al., *Anatomy of the SS State* (London, 1968), 127–291; Martin Broszat, "The Concentration Camps, 1933–45," ibid., 397–497; Joseph Billig, *L'Hitlérisme et le système concentrationnaire* (Paris, 1967); Benjamin B. Ferencz, *Less Than Slaves: Jewish Forced Labor and the Quest for Compensation* (Cambridge, Mass., 1979); Joseph Borkin, *The Crime and Punishment of I. G. Farben* (London, 1979), 111–27.

57. Hilberg, *Destruction of the European Jews*, III, 1219.

58. See also Tom Segev, "The Commanders of Nazi Concentration Camps," Ph.D. dissertation, Boston University, 1977.

59. Rudolf Höss, *Commandant of Auschwitz*, trans. Constantine Fitz-Gibbon (London, 1959), 148. On Höss see Joachim C. Fest, *The Fact of the Third Reich*, trans. Michael Bullock (New York, 1970), 276–87.

60. Gita Sereny, *Into That Darkness: An Examination of Conscience* (London, 1974), 166, 200. For a critique of Sereny's interview see Lucy S. Dawidowicz, *The Jewish Presence: Essays on Identity and History* (New York, 1978), ch. 16.

61. Höss, *Commandant of Auschwitz*, 196. Cf. W. Glicksman, "Social Differentiation in the German Concentration Camps," in Joshua A. Fishman, ed., *Studies in Modern Jewish History* (New York, 1972), 129–30.

62. Glicksman, "Social Differentiation in the German Concentration Camps," 123–50; Gutman, "Social Stratification in the Concentration Camps," 143–76; Kogon, *Der SS-Staat*.

63. David Rousset, *L'Univers concentrationnaire* (Paris, 1946).

64. Bruno Bettelheim, "Individual and Mass Behavior in Extreme Situations," *Journal of Abnormal Psychology* 38 (1943), 417–52, with a somewhat different version in *Surviving and Other Essays* (New York, 1980), 48–83. See also the related discussion in *The Informed Heart: Autonomy in a Mass Age*, 2d ed. (New York, 1971), chs. 4 and 5.

65. For extensive critiques of Bettelheim see Terrence Des Pres, *The Survivor: An Anatomy of Life in the Death Camps* (New York, 1976), 56–57, 79–80, 103, 116–17, 155–56, 157–63; Eli Pfefferkorn, "The Case of

Bruno Bettelheim and Lina Wertmüller's *Seven Beauties,*" in Gutman and Saf, *Nazi Concentration Camps,* 663–81. See also George M. Kren and Leon Rappoport, *The Holocaust and the Crisis of Human Behavior* (New York, 1980), ch. 4.

66. Quoted in Albert H. Friedlander, *Out of the Whirlwind: A Reader of Holocaust Literature* (New York, 1976), 211.

67. Bettelheim, *Informed Heart,* 134, 151; idem, *Surviving,* 83.

68. Bettelheim, *Surviving,* 108, 287–88, 268.

69. Kren and Rappoport, *Holocaust and the Crisis of Human Behavior,* 74.

70. Elie A. Cohen, *Human Behavior in the Concentration Camp,* trans. M. H. Braaksma (New York, 1954), 144.

71. Anna Pawełczyńska, *Values and Violence in Auschwitz: A Sociological Analysis,* trans. Catherine S. Leach (Berkeley, Calif., 1979), 58.

72. Bettelheim, *Surviving,* 246–57.

73. Des Pres, *Survivor,* 156–58.

7. JEWISH RESISTANCE

1. Isaiah Trunk, *Judenrat: The Jewish Councils in Eastern Europe under Nazi Occupation* (New York, 1972), 456, 469–70.

2. Ibid., 425; Dov Levin, *Fighting Back: Lithuanian Jewry's Armed Resistance to the Nazis, 1941–1944,* trans. Moshe Kohn and Dina Cohen (New York, 1985), 99, 116–25, 158–59.

3. Abraham Fuchs, *The Unheeded Cry* (New York, 1984), 105–6.

4. Yisrael Gutman, "The War against the Jews, 1939–1945," *Yad Vashem Studies* 11 (1976), 333.

5. Lucjan Dobroszycki, ed., *The Chronicle of the Lodz Ghetto, 1941–1944,* trans. Richard Lourie et al. (New Haven, 1984), 113.

6. See the remarks of Yosef Burg, in Moshe M. Kohn, ed., *Jewish Resistance during the Holocaust: Proceedings of the Conference on Manifestations of Jewish Resistance, Jerusalem, April 7–11, 1968* (Jerusalem, 1971), 15–16.

7. Raul Hilberg, *The Destruction of the European Jews,* rev. ed. (New York, 1985), III, 1030–31. For an extended critical evaluation of the issue of Jewish political responses see David Biale, *Power and Powerlessness in Jewish History* (New York, 1986), 141–44 and *passim.*

8. Yehuda Bauer, *The Jewish Emergence from Powerlessness* (Toronto, 1979), 34.

9. Yehuda Bauer, *They Chose Life: Jewish Resistance in the Holocaust* (New York, 1973), 33; idem, *Jewish Emergence from Powerlessness,* 27. Cf. Lionel Kochan, "Resistance: A Constant in Jewish Life," *Midstream,* August/September 1976, 63–68; Emil Fackenheim, "The Spectrum of Resistance during the Holocaust: An Essay in Description and Definition," *Modern Judaism* 2 (1982), 113–30.

10. *Notes from the Warsaw Ghetto: The Journal of Emmanuel Ringelblum*, ed. and trans. Jacob Sloan (New York, 1974), 295. According to Ringelblum, the broadcast had a considerable effect in the Jewish population: "The last few days the Jewish populace has been agitated by the broadcast from London. The news that the world has finally been deeply stirred by the account of the massacres taking place in Poland has shaken us all to the very depths. For long, long months we tormented ourselves in the midst of our suffering with the questions: Does the world know about our suffering? And if it knows, why is it silent?" (p. 296).

11. Levin, *Fight Back*, chs. 4–10. For other examples see Jack Nusan Porter, ed., *Jewish Partisans: A Documentary of Jewish Resistance in the Soviet Union during World War II* (Washington, D.C., 1982), vol. II.

12. See Shimon Redlich, *Propaganda and Nationalism in Wartime Russia: The Jewish Anti-Fascist Committee in the USSR, 1941–1948* (n.p., 1982), 39–50 and *passim*. *Eynikayt* was strongly supportive of Jewish nationalism and printed such columns as "Our Sons and Daughters," "Our Heroes," and "Our Scientists," to emphasize the Jewish contribution to the war effort. Thousands of letters poured into its offices from Soviet Jewish soldiers and officers serving in the Red Army, taking pride in Jewish achievements. According to Redlich, the newspaper was widely distributed abroad. As well, the committee had regular, weekly radio broadcasts by various Jewish personalities in the Soviet Union (pp. 46–49).

13. This was not, however, the tone of the Soviet press itself, as Redlich points out. See ibid., 93 and *passim*.

14. Annie Latour, *The Jewish Resistance in France (1940–1944)*, trans. Irene R. Ilton (New York, 1981), 177.

15. Otto Komoly, "What May Jews Learn from the Present Crisis?" in Andrew Handler, ed., *The Holocaust in Hungary: An Anthology of Jewish Response* (University, Ala., 1982), 51. Komoly was head of a secret rescue committee operating from Budapest in 1943 and 1944 that saved about a thousand Jews. He was killed by the Arrow Cross in January 1945.

16. Levin, *Fighting Back*, 54–56.

17. Christian Streit, *Keine Kameraden: Die Wehrmacht und die sowjetischen Kriegsgefangenen, 1941–1945* (Stuttgart, 1978), 10. Alfred Streim's estimate is 2.5 million fatalities out of 5.3 million captured. *Sowjetische Kriegsgefangene in Hitlers Vernichtungskrieg: Berichte und Dokumente, 1941–1945* (Heidelberg, 1982), 174.

18. Henri Michel, "Jewish Resistance and the European Resistance Movement," *Yad Vashem Studies* 7 (1968), 7–16.

19. Milovan Djilas, *Wartime*, trans. Michael B. Petrovich (New York, 1977), 129.

20. Bauer, *Jewish Emergence from Powerlessness*, 29.

21. Yisrael Gutman, *The Jews of Warsaw, 1939–1943: Ghetto, Underground, Revolt*, trans. Ina Friedman (Bloomington, Ind., 1982), 344, 348, 360, 366, 395; Shmuel Krakowski, *The War of the Doomed: Jewish*

Armed Resistance in Poland, 1942–1944, trans. Ora Blaustein (New York, 1984), 176–89.

22. See the detailed report on the German operations in *The Stroop Report: The Jewish Quarter of Warsaw Is No More!* trans. Sybil Milton (New York, 1979).

23. Ibid., 394.

24. Gutman, *Jews of Warsaw*, 426–30.

25. See the incidents described in Shmuel Spector, "The Jews of Volhynia and Their Reaction to Extermination," *Yad Vashem Studies* 15 (1983), 168–75.

26. Yitzhak Arad, "Jewish Family Camps in the Forests: An Original Means of Rescue," in Yisrael Gutman and Efraim Zuroff, eds., *Rescue Attempts during the Holocaust: Proceedings of the Second Yad Vashem International Historical Conference, Jerusalem, April 8–11, 1974* (Jerusalem, 1977), 333–53.

27. Yehuda Bauer, *A History of the Holocaust* (New York, 1982), 270.

28. Krakowski, *War of the Doomed*, 3, 11.

29. Levin, *Fighting Back*, 227.

30. For an excellent survey see Ezra Mendelsohn, *The Jews of East Central Europe between the World Wars* (Bloomington, Ind., 1983).

31. Gutman, "Youth Movements in the Underground and Ghetto Revolts," in Kohn, *Jewish Resistance during the Holocaust*, 260–81; George M. Kren and Leon Rappoport, *The Holocaust and the Crisis of Human Behavior* (New York, 1980), ch. 5. On prewar German-Jewish youth see Werner T. Angress, "Jüdische Jugend zwischen nationalsozialistischer Verfolgung und jüdischer Wiedergeburt," in Arnold Paucker, ed., *Die Juden im nationalsozialistichen Deutschland* (Tübingen, 1986), 211–21.

32. Trunk, *Judenrat*, 455.

33. Yitzhak Arad, *Ghetto in Flames: The Struggle and Destruction of the Jews of Vilna during the Holocaust* (Jerusalem, 1980), 393–94.

34. Gutman, "Youth Movements in the Underground and Ghetto Revolts," 275–76.

35. Jan Karski, *Story of a Secret State* (Boston, 1944), 322.

36. Levin, *Fighting Back*.

37. Dov Levin, "July 1944: The Crucial Month for the Remnants of Lithuanian Jewry," *Yad Vashem Studies* 16 (1984), 333–35.

38. Yuri Suhl, "The Resistance Movement in the Ghetto of Minsk," in Yuri Suhl, ed., *They Fought Back: The Story of the Jewish Resistance in Nazi Europe* (New York, 1975), 231–38; Shalom Cholawsky, "The Judenrat in Minsk," in Yisrael Gutman and Cynthia J. Haft, eds., *Patterns of Jewish Leadership in Nazi Europe, 1933–1945: Proceedings of the Third Yad Vashem International Historical Conference, Jerusalem, April 4–7, 1977* (Jerusalem, 1979), 113–32.

39. Philip Friedman, "Ukrainian-Jewish Relations during the Nazi Occupation," *YIVO Annual of Jewish Social Science* 12 (1958/59), 259–96. For a different view see Taras Hunczak, "Ukrainian-Jewish Relations dur-

ing the Soviet and Nazi Occupations," in Yuri Boshyk, ed., *Ukraine during World War II: History and Aftermath* (Edmonton, Alberta, 1986), 39–57.

40. See Yisrael Gutman and Avital Saf, eds., *The Nazi Concentration Camps: Structure and Aims. The Image of the Prisoner. The Jews in the Camps. Proceedings of the Fourth Yad Vashem International Conference, Jerusalem, January 1980* (Jerusalem, 1984); Falk Pingel, "Resistance and Resignation in Nazi Concentration and Extermination Camps," in Gerhard Hirschfeld, ed., *The Policies of Genocide: Jews and Soviet Prisoners of War in Germany* (London, 1986), 30–72.

41. Bruno Baum, *Widerstand in Auschwitz* (Berlin, 1957); Hermann Langbein, *Menschen in Auschwitz* (Vienna, 1972), pt. 2, ch. 12; Tzipora Hager Halivni, "The Birkenau Revolt: Poles Prevent a Timely Insurrection," *Jewish Social Studies* 41 (1979), 123–54; Rudolf Vrba and Alan Bestic, *I Cannot Forgive* (New York, 1964); Erich Kulka, "Five Escapes from Auschwitz," in Suhl, *They Fought Back*, 196–218; idem, "Escapes of Prisoners from Auschwitz-Birkenau and Their Attempts to Stop Mass Extermination," in Gutman and Saf, *Nazi Concentration Camps*, 401–16. Non-Jews probably constituted a majority of the inmates in Auschwitz until 1944, most Jews being killed immediately upon their arrival in the camp. There was an underground movement in non-Jewish portions of the camp which was in touch, occasionally, with the Polish Home Army. It helped to organize several escapes and planned a final uprising, but only "if there were a chance of a general uprising against the Germans with the help of local partisans and very strong assistance from the western Allies." Such conditions did not present themselves. Josef Garliniski, "The Underground Movement in Auschwitz Concentration Camp," in Stephen Hawes and Ralph White, eds., *Resistance in Europe, 1939–45* (Harmondsworth, England, 1976), 55–76.

42. Jean François Steiner, *Treblinka* (New York, 1967); Alexander Pechersky, "Revolt in Sobibor," in Suhl, *They Fought Back*, 7–50; Alexander Donat [pseud.], ed., *The Death Camp Treblinka: A Documentary* (New York, 1979); Yitzhak Arad, "Jewish Prisoner Uprisings in the Treblinka and Sobibor Extermination Camps," in Gutman and Saf, *Nazi Concentration Camps*, 357–99; Richard Raschke, *Escape from Sobibor* (Boston, 1982); Miriam Novitch, ed., *Sobibor: Marytrdom and Revolt* (New York, 1980); Krakowski, *War of the Doomed*, ch. 12.

43. Bauer, *Jewish Emergence from Powerlessness*, 31.

44. Quoted in Livia Rothkirchen, "Escape Routes and Contacts during the War," in Kohn, *Jewish Resistance during the Holocaust*, 411.

45. See Walter Laqueur, *The Terrible Secret: An Investigation into the Suppression of Information about Hitler's "Final Solution"* (London, 1980), 144–45, 146n.

46. Livia Rothkirchen, "The Dual Role of the 'Jewish Center' in Slovakia," in Gutman and Haft, *Patterns of Jewish Leadership*, 219–27. See also idem, "The Czech and Slovak Jewish Leadership," in Gutman and Zuroff, *Rescue Attempts during the Holocaust*, 423–34.

47. Fuchs, *Unheeded Cry,* is a strong defense of Weissmandel; Monty Noam Penkower, *The Jews Were Expendable: Free World Diplomacy and the Holocaust* (Urbana, Ill., 1983) presents a sympathetic picture, drawing on a very wide range of documentation. A much more critical perspective is that of Yehuda Bauer, *American Jewry and the Holocaust: The American Joint Distribution Committee, 1939–1945* (Detroit, 1981).

48. Randolf Braham, *The Politics of Genocide: The Holocaust in Hungary* (New York, 1981), II, 704–5; Frederick E. Werbell and Thurston Clarke, *Lost Hero: The Mystery of Raoul Wallenberg* (New York, 1982), 51–54.

49. See Livia Rothkirchen, "Hungary: An Asylum for the Refugees of Europe," *Yad Vashem Studies* 7 (1968), 127–42.

50. Braham, *Politics of Genocide,* II, 932–33.

51. Ibid., 997–1011; Asher Cohen, "He-Halutz Underground in Hungary: March–August 1944," *Yad Vashem Studies* 14 (1981), 247–67.

52. Lucien Steinberg, "Quelques problèmes relatifs à l'étude de la participation des Juifs dans les forces armées alliées," in Kohn, *Jewish Resistance during the Holocaust,* 537. Cf. Lucien Steinberg, *La Révolte des justes: Les Juifs contre Hitler* (Paris, 1970).

53. See Michael R. Marrus and Robert O. Paxton, *Vichy France and the Jews* (New York, 1981), 190–91, 207–8; Simon Pétrement, *La Vie de Simone Weil* (Paris, 1973), II, 476–77; John Hellman, *Simone Weil: An Introduction to Her Thought* (Waterloo, Ontario, 1982), 72–73.

54. See the debates on this subject in the special issue of *Le Monde juif,* no. 118, April–June 1985.

55. Renée Poznanski, "La résistance juive en France," *Revue d'histoire de la deuxième guerre mondiale,* no. 137 (1985), 9.

56. Bauer, *American Jewry and the Holocaust,* 269–70.

57. Lucien Steinberg, *Le Comité de défense des Juifs en Belgique, 1942–1944* (Brussels, 1973), 83–109; Jacob Gutfreind, "The Jewish Resistance Movement in Belgium," in Suhl, *They Fought Back,* 304–11.

58. Jacques Adler, *Face à la persécution: Les organisations juives à Paris de 1940 à 1944,* trans. André Charpentier (Paris, 1985).

59. Haim Avni, "The Zionist Underground in Holland and France and the Escape to Spain," in Gutman and Zuroff, *Rescue Attempts during the Holocaust,* 555–90.

60. See Steinberg, *Comité de défense des Juifs en Beligique,* 70.

61. See Ralph White, "The Unity and Diversity of European Resistance," in Hawes and White, *Resistance in Europe,* 8–9; and M. R. D. Foot, "What Good Did Resistance Do?" ibid., 204–20.

8. BYSTANDERS

1. David S. Wyman, *The Abandonment of the Jews: America and the Holocaust, 1941–1945* (New York, 1984); Monty Noam Penkower, *The*

Jews Were Expendable: Free World Diplomacy and the Holocaust (Urbana, Ill., 1983).

2. Jacob Katz, "Was the Holocaust Predictable?" *Commentary,* May 1975, 41.

3. Yehuda Bauer, *The Holocaust in Historical Perspective* (Seattle, 1978), 18. "As far as the actual information was concerned, there can be no doubt at all that whoever read the papers, listened to the radio, or read the Jewish Telegraphic Agency's daily reports could have had all the information about Europe's Jews that was needed to establish the facts about the mass murder" (p. 19).

4. Robert H. Abzug, *Inside the Vicious Heart: Americans and the Liberation of Nazi Concentration Camps* (New York, 1985), 127.

5. *Trials of War Criminals before the Nuremberg Military Tribunals* (Nuremberg, 1947–49), IV, 450, quoted in Nathan Eck, "Historical Research or Slander?" *Yad Vashem Studies* 6 (1967), 419.

6. "If the Poles showed less sympathy and solidarity with Jews than many Danes and Dutch, they behaved far more humanely than Romanians and Ukrainians, than Lithuanians and Latvians. A comparison with France would be by no means unfavourable for Poland. In view of the Polish prewar attitudes towards Jews, it is not surprising that there was so little help, but that there was so much." Walter Laqueur, *The Terrible Secret: An Investigation into the Suppression of Information about Hitler's "Final Solution"* (London, 1980), 107.

7. Ibid., 56; John F. Morley, *Vatican Diplomacy and the Holocaust, 1939–1943* (New York, 1980).

8. Yehuda Bauer, "When Did They Know?" *Midstream,* April 1968, 51–58.

9. Reigner's source, we now know, was Eduard Schulte, a prominent German businessman in touch with Allied intelligence agents. On Schulte see Walter Laqueur and Richard Breitman, *Breaking the Silence* (New York, 1986).

10. For additional discussion see Walter Laqueur, "Hitler's Holocaust: Who Knew What, When, and How?" *Encounter,* July 1980, 12–14; Yehuda Bauer, *American Jewry and the Holocaust: The American Jewish Joint Distribution Committee, 1939–1945* (Detroit, 1981), 190–91; Pentkower, *Jews Were Expendable,* ch. 3; Wyman, *Abandonment of the Jews,* ch. 3. Wyman misleadingly, in my view, entitles his chapter on the Reigner telegram "The Worst Is Confirmed."

11. Laqueur, *Terrible Secret,* 145–46. Laqueur cites the Slovak Jewish leader Oscar Neumann on this point: "There was total resistance in our hearts to believe the news. . . . Of course, there had been certain rumours about the horrible events in Auschwitz. But they were flying about like bats at night, they were not tangible" (p. 146).

12. Martin Gilbert, *Auschwitz and the Allies* (New York, 1981). Drawing on American documentation Richard Breitman cites several Polish reports on Auschwitz before that of the 1944 escapees. See Richard Breit-

man, "Auschwitz and the Archives," *Central European History* 18 (1985), 369–72.

13. "German Record in Poland," *Times* (London), 10 July 1942.

14. Deborah E. Lipstadt, *Beyond Belief: The American Press and the Coming of the Holocaust, 1933–1945* (New York, 1986). See also Robert W. Ross, *So It Was True: The American Protestant Press and the Nazi Persecution of the Jews* (Minneapolis, Minn., 1980).

15. Bauer, *American Jewry and the Holocaust*, 39–40; Lipstadt, *Beyond Belief*, 127.

16. John W. Dower, *War without Mercy: Race and Power in the Pacific War* (New York, 1986).

17. Bradley Smith, *The Road to Nuremberg* (New York, 1981), 115.

18. Lipstadt, *Beyond Belief*, 163–64.

19. Bernard Wasserstein, *Britain and the Jews of Europe, 1939–1945* (London, 1979), ch. 4; Laqueur, *Terrible Secret*, 223–28; John P. Fox, "The Jewish Factor in British War Crimes Policy in 1942," *English Historical Review* 92 (1977), 82–107.

20. Laqueur, *Terrible Secret*, 6.

21. Ibid., 3. Cf. idem, "Jewish Denial and the Holocaust," *Commentary*, December 1979, 44–55.

22. See Penkower, *Jews Were Expendable;* Michael R. Marrus, *The Unwanted: European Refugees in the Twentieth Century* (New York, 1985); Kurt R. Grossmann, *Emigration: Geschichte der Hitler-Flüchtlinge, 1933–1945* (Frankfurt am Main, 1969); Ruth Fabian and Corinna Coulmas, *Die deutsche Emigration in Frankreich nach 1933* (Munich, 1978); JeanCharles Bonnet, *Les Pouvoirs publics français et l'immigration dans l'entre-deux-guerres* (Lyon, 1976); Alfred A. Häsler, *The Lifeboat Is Full: Switzerland and the Refugees, 1933–1945*, trans. Charles Lam Markmann (New York, 1969); Irving Abella and Harold Troper, *None Is Too Many: Canada and the Jews of Europe, 1933–1948* (Toronto, 1982); Yehuda Bauer, *My Brother's Keeper: A History of the American Jewish Joint Distribution Committee, 1929–1939* (Philadelphia, 1974); A. J. Sherman, *Island Refuge: Britain and Refugees from the Third Reich, 1933–1939* (London, 1973); Saul S. Friedman, *No Haven for the Oppressed: United States Policy towards Refugees* (Detroit, 1973); Henry Feingold, *The Politics of Rescue: The Roosevelt Administration and the Holocaust, 1938–1945* (New Brunswick, N.J., 1970); David S. Wyman, *Paper Walls: America and the Refugee Crisis, 1938–1941* (Boston, 1968); idem, *Abandonment of the Jews*.

23. Sherman, *Island Rescue;* Michael J. Cohen, *Palestine: Retreat from Mandate: The Making of British Policy, 1936–1945* (London, 1978), ch. 5; Noah Lucas, *The Modern History of Israel* (London, 1974); Nicholas Bethell, *The Palestine Triangle: The Struggle between the British, the Jews, and the Arabs, 1935–1948* (London, 1980), ch. 3; Martin Gilbert, *Exile and Return: The Emergence of Jewish Statehood* (London, 1978); Grossmann, *Emigration*, 162–76; Werner Rosenstock, "Exodus, 1933–1939:

A Survey of Emigration from Germany," *Leo Baeck Institute Year Book* 1 (1956), 373–90.

24. Wasserstein, *Britain and the Jews of Europe,* 17. Cf. the very different view of Cohen, *Retreat from Mandate,* 187.

25. Bauer, *American Jewry and the Holocaust,* 48, 66.

26. Haim Avni, *Spain, Franco and the Jews,* trans. Emanuel Shimoni (Philadephia, 1982), 186.

27. Wyman, *Abandonment of the Jews,* 335–36.

28. Abella and Troper, *None Is Too Many,* 41–42.

29. Assistant Secretary of State Breckinridge Long in Washington and Deputy Minister of Mines and Resources Frederick Charles Blair in Ottawa.

30. Ronald Zweig, "The Political Uses of Military Intelligence: Evaluating the Threat of a Jewish Revolt against Britain during the Second World War," in Richard Langhorne, ed., *Diplomacy and Intelligence during the Second World War* (Cambridge, 1985), 109–25.

31. Wyman, *Abandonment of the Jews,* xi, 190. Cf. the similar assessment of Peter Grose: "Roosevelt failed to act on the information available to him; so did many others, Jews and Gentiles alike, who might have been able to goad the President into action had they tried. The options for action open to the United States government were pitifully few. But even the possibilities scarcely came up for discussion. There was none of the competitive give and take, none of the brainstorming, through which Roosevelt exercised his leadership. Roosevelt's guilt, the guilt of American Jewish leadership and of the dozens and hundreds of others in positions of responsibility, was that most of the time they failed to try." *Israel in the Mind of America* (New York, 1983), 133.

32. Wasserstein, *Britain and the Jews of Europe,* 259. For a much more critical view of Churchill see Michael J. Cohen, "Churchill and the Jews: The Holocaust," *Modern Judaism,* February 1986, 27–48; and idem, *Churchill and the Jews* (London, 1985), ch. 8.

33. Wasserstein, *Britain and the Jews of Europe,* 351–53.

34. Henry Feingold, "Who Shall Bear Guilt for the Holocaust: The Human Dilemma," *American Jewish History* 68 (1979), 261.

35. Monty N. Penkower, "The Bermuda Conference and Its Aftermath: An Allied Quest for 'Refuge' during the Holocaust," *Prologue,* Fall 1982, 145–73.

36. Wyman, *Abandonment of the Jews,* 287.

37. Letter to the Hechalutz office in Geneva, 23 December 1942, quoted in Abraham Fuchs, *The Unheeded Cry* (New York, 1984), 105. Cf. Weissmandel's letter of 31 May 1943: "We beg you with tear-filled eyes. . . . Please do all you can and more. How good and pleasant it would be if we were able to breathe a soul into these letters; then we could command them saying, 'Go before our brethren, the Jews abroad in the lands of freedom, and talk to them and cry out before them about the souls of the old men and women who are stabbed in the streets, who are shot to death on their beds, about the souls of the thousands of beautiful children, pure children

who are murdered in the camps, who are buried alive in communal graves; about the souls of the millions who were strangled by smoke of murder in the gas chambers'" (p. 115).

38. Walter Laqueur, "Jewish Denial and the Holocaust," *Commentary*, December 1979, 44–55.

39. Feingold, "Guilt for the Holocaust," 279.

40. Dina Porat, "The Role Played by the Jewish Agency in Jerusalem in the Efforts to Rescue the Jews in Europe, 1942–1945," Ph.D. dissertation[Hebrew], Tel Aviv University, 1983; and idem, *An Entangled Leadership: The Yishuv and the Holocaust, 1942–1945* [Hebrew] (Tel Aviv, 1986); idem, "Palestinian Jewry and the Jewish Agency: Public Response to the Holocaust," in Richard Cohen, ed., *Vision and Conflict in the Holy Land* (New York, 1985), 246–73; Laqueur, *Terrible Secret*, 183; Yehuda Slutzki, "The Palestine Jewish Community and Its Assistance to European Jewry in the Holocaust Years," in Kohn, *Jewish Resistance during the Holocaust*, 414–26.

41. Y. Gothelf, *Davar*, 10 December 1942, quoted in Laqueur, *Terrible Secret*, 182–87.

42. Slutzki, "Palestine Jewish Community," 416.

43. See Yoav Gelber, "Zionist Policy and European Jewry (1939–1942)," *Yad Vashem Studies* 13 (1979), 169–210; Yehuda Bauer, *From Diplomacy to Resistance: A History of Jewish Palestine, 1939–1945*, trans. Alton M. Winters (New York, 1973); Dina Porat, "Al-domi: Palestinian Intellectuals and the Holocaust," *Studies in Zionism* 5 (1984), 97–124; Laqueur, *Terrible Secret*, 179–95.

44. Gelber, "Zionist Policy and European Jewry," 209. Bela Vago's judgment is even harsher: "the Yishuv leadership was rather late in grasping the dimensions of the Holocaust; it was immersed in its own problems at the expense of the attention that the fate of European Jews should have commanded. Its participation in the help and rescue activities was below its capacities and competence, and it failed to fully exploit the given circumstances." "Some Aspects of the Yishuv Leadership's Activities during the Holocaust," in Randolph L. Braham, ed., *Jewish Leadership in the Nazi Era: Patterns of Behavior in the Free World* (New York, 1985), 65.

45. *American Jewry during the Holocaust* (New York, 1984). For a sharp critique see Yehuda Bauer, "The Goldberg Report," *Midstream*, February 1985, 25–28.

46. See Leonard Dinnerstein, "Jews and the New Deal," *American Jewish History* 72 (1982/83), 461–76; Henry L. Feingold, "Stephen Wise and the Holocaust," *Midstream*, January 1983, 45–49; Melvin Urofsky, *A Voice That Spoke for Justice: The Life and Times of Stephen S. Wise* (Albany, N.Y., 1982).

47. Wyman, *Abandonment of the Jews*, ch. 8. See also Monty N. Penkower, "In Dramatic Dissent: The Bergson Boys," *American Jewish History* 70 (1981), 281–309; idem, "Jewish Organizations and the Creation of the U.S. War Refugee Board," *Annals of the American Academy of*

Political and Social Science 450 (July 1980), 122–39; Edward Pinsky, "American Jewish Unity during the Holocaust: The Joint Emergency Committee, 1943," *American Jewish History*, 17 (1981/82), 477–94; Sarah Peck, "The Campaign for an American Response to the Holocaust, 1943–1945," *Journal of Contemporary History* 15 (1980), 367–400; Eliahu Matz, "Policial Actions vs. Personal Relations," *Midstream*, April 1981, 41–48; Zvi Ganin, "Activism versus Moderation: The Conflict between Abba Hillel Silver and Stephen Wise during the 1940s," *Studies in Zionism* 5 (1984), 71–95.

48. See Yehuda Bauer, "Jewish Foreign Policy during the Holocaust," *Midstream*, December 1984, 22–25; Henry L. Feingold, "'Courage First and Intelligence Second': The American Jewish Secular Elite, Roosevelt, and the Failure of Rescue," *American Jewish History* 72 (1982/83), 424–60; Lucy Dawidowicz, "Indicting American Jews," *Commentary*, June 1983, 36–44; Marie Syrkin, "What American Jews Did during the Holocaust," *Midstream*, October 1982, 6–12; Bernard Wasserstein, "The Myth of 'Jewish Silence,'" *Midstream*, August/September 1980, 10–16. See also the exchange of letters in ibid., March 1981, 59–64.

49. Wyman, *Abandonment of the Jews*, 71.

50. Abella and Troper, *None Is Too Many*, 145–47 and *passim*.

51. Bernard Wasserstein, "Patterns of Jewish Leadership in Great Britain during the Nazi Era," in Braham, *Jewish Leadership in the Nazi Era*, 29–43; Chaim Bermant, *The Cousinhood: The Anglo-Jewish Gentry* (London, 1971).

52. Gerhart Riegner, "Switzerland and the Leadership of Its Jewish Community during the Second World War," in Braham, *Jewish Leadership in the Nazi Era*, 67–86.

53. Marrus, *Unwanted*, 138–41. On the grim fate of the few refugees who did manage to reach the Soviet Union see David Pike, *German Writers in Soviet Exile, 1933–1945* (Chapel Hill, N.C., 1982); Wolfgang Leonhard, *Child of the Revolution*, trans. C. M. Woodhouse (London, 1957); Margarete Buber, *Under Two Dictators*, trans. Edward Fitzgerald (London, 1949).

54. Marrus, *Unwanted*, 195–99; Grossmann, *Emigration*, 177–90; Ben-Cion Pinchuk, "Jewish Refugees in Soviet Poland, 1939–1941," *Jewish Social Studies* 40 (1978), 142–45; Shimon Redlich, "The Jews in the Soviet-Annexed Territories, 1939–1941," *Soviet Jewish Affairs* 1 (1971), 81–90; Tartakower and Grossmann, *Jewish Refugee*, 271.

55. Mark Harrison, *Soviet Planning in Peace and War, 1938–1945* (Cambridge, Mass., 1985), 63–79; Yisrael Gutman, "Jews in General Anders' Army in the Soviet Union," *Yad Vashem Studies* 12 (1977), 233–34. See also Dov Levin, "The Attitude of the Soviet Union toward the Rescue of Jews," in Yisrael Gutman and Efraim Zuroff, eds., *Rescue Attempts during the Holocaust: Proceedings of the Second Yad Vashem International Historical Conference, Jerusalem, April 8–11, 1974* (Jerusalem, 1977), 230, 235.

56. Solomon Schwarz, *The Jews in the Soviet Union* (Syracuse, 1951), 197–98; Marrus, *Unwanted*, 245.

57. Tartakower and Grossmann, *Jewish Refugee*, 268.

58. Gutman, "Jews in General Anders' Army," 231–96.

59. Lady Cheetam at the British Foreign Office nevertheless suggested this, in September 1944. See Wasserstein, *Britain and the Jews of Europe*, 318; Gilbert, *Auschwitz and the Allies*, 319.

60. Gilbert, *Auschwitz and the Allies*, 337–38. The text of the Soviet report as broadcast by the Soviet news agency Tass on 7 May 1945 is in the Public Record Office: FO 371/51185/WR1417.

61. Levin, "Soviet Policy toward Rescue," 236.

62. Avni, *Spain, Franco and the Jews*, 182; John P. Willson, "Carlton J. H. Hayes, Spain, and the Refugee Crisis, 1942–1945," *American Jewish Historical Quarterly* 62 (1972), 99–110.

63. Marrus, *Unwanted*, 258–65; Malcolm Proudfoot, *European Refugees, 1939–52: A Study in Forced Population Movement* (London, [1956]), chs. 2, 3; Bauer, *American Jewry*, ch. 8; Hugh Kay, *Salazar and Modern Portugal* (London, 1970), ch. 7.

64. Carl Ludwig, *La Politique pratiquée par la Suisse à légard des réfugiés au cours des années 1933 à 1955* [Annexe au rapport du Conseil fédéral à l'Assemblée fédérale sur la politique pratiquée par la Suisse à l'égard des réfugiés au cours des années 1933 à nos jours] (Bern, 1957).

65. The remark was made by Federal Councillor Edouard von Steiger, federal minister of justice and police. Häsler, *Lifeboat Is Full*, 175.

66. Bauer, *My Brothers' Keeper*, 173; Eliahu Ben Elissar, *La Diplomatie du IIIe Reich et les Juifs* (Paris, 1981), 267–68; Tartakower and Grossmann, *Jewish Refugee*, 286–91; Häsler, *Lifeboat Is Full*; Ludwig, *Politique pratiquée par la Suisse*; Riegner, "Swiss Jewish Leadership"; Ladislas Mysyrowicz and Jean-Claude Favez, "Refuge et représentation d'intérêts, étrangers," *Revue d'histoire de la deuxième guerre mondiale* 31 (1981), 109–20; Urs Schwarz, *The Eye of the Hurricane: Switzerland in World War Two* (Boulder, Colo., 1980), 122–28.

67. Avni, *Spain, the Jews and Franco*, ch. 5; Christopher R. Browning, *The Final Solution and the German Foreign Office: A Study of Referat D III of Abteilung Deutschland, 1940–43* (New York, 1978), 154–58 and *passim*. The Turks, admittedly, took some time before they were prepared to extend protection to the Jewish nationals. See ibid., 156.

68. Hugo Valentin, "Rescue and Relief Activities in Behalf of Jewish Victims of Nazism in Scandinavia," *YIVO Annual of Jewish Social Science* 8 (1953), 224–51; Barry Rubin, "Ambassador Laurence A. Steinhardt: The Perils of a Jewish Diplomat, 1940–1945," *American Jewish History* 70 (1981), 331–46.

69. On Wallenberg see Leni Yahil, "Raoul Wallenberg: His Mission and His Activities in Hungary," *Yad Vashem Studies* 15 (1984), 7–53; Randolph L. Braham, *The Politics of Genocide: The Holocaust in Hun-*

gary (New York, 1981), II, 1077–95; Franklin D. Scott, *Sweden: The Nation's History* (Minneapolis, Minn., 1977), 503–9; Jacques Derogy, *Le Cas Wallenberg* (Paris, 1980); Frederick E. Werbell and Thurston Clarke, *Lost Hero: The Mystery of Raoul Wallenberg* (New York, 1982); Harvey Rosenfeld, *Raoul Wallenberg: Angel of Rescue* (Buffalo, 1982); Elenore Lester, *Wallenberg: The Man in the Iron Web* (Englewood Cliffs, N.J., 1982); Kati Marton, *Wallenberg* (New York, 1982).

70. See Eric Bentley, ed., *The Storm over "The Deputy"* (New York, 1964); Leonidas E. Hill, "History and Rolf Hochhuth's *The Deputy*," in R. G. Collins, ed., *From an Ancient to a Modern Theatre* (Winnipeg, 1972), 145–57; *Actes et documents de la Saint-Siège relatifs à la seconde guerre mondiale* (Vatican City, 1965–81); Carlo Falconi, *The Silence of Pope Pius XII*, trans. B. Wall (New York, 1970); Saul Friedlander, *Pius XII and the Third Reich: A Documentation*, trans. Charles Fullman (New York, 1966); John S. Conway, "The Silence of Pius XII," in Charles Delzell, ed., *The Papacy and Totalitarianism between the Two World Wars* (New York, 1974), 79–108; idem, "Catholicism and the Jewish People during the Nazi Period and Afterwards," in *Papers Presented to the International Symposium on Judaism and Christianity under the Impact of National Socialism (1919–1945)* (Jerusalem, 1982), 347–75; idem, "Records and Documents of the Holy See Relating to the Second World War," *Yad Vashem Studies* 15 (1983), 327–45; John Morley, *Vatican Diplomacy and the Jews during the Holocaust, 1939–1943* (New York, 1980); Léon Papeleux, *Les Silences de Pie XII* (Brussels, 1980).

71. Stewart A. Stehlin, *Weimar and the Vatican, 1919–1939: German-Vatican Diplomatic Relations in the Interwar Years* (Princeton, N.J., 1984); François Delpech, "La Papauté et la persécution nazie," in Georges Wellers, André Kaspi, and Serge Klarsfeld, eds., *La France et la question juive, 1940–1944: Actes du colloque du Centre de documentation juive contemporaine (10 au 12 mars 1979)* (Paris, 1981), 197–209.

72. Heinz-Albert Raem, *Pius XI und der Nationalsozialismus: Die Enyklika "Mit brennender Sorge" vom 14, März 1937* (Paderborn, 1979).

73. Michael R. Marrus and Robert O. Paxton, *Vichy France and the Jews* (New York, 1981), 200–202; Morley, *Vatican Diplomacy and the Jews*, 51–54.

74. Laqueur, *Terrible Secret*, 54–57.

75. Summing up the activity of Vatican diplomats Morley concludes: "their involvement in the Jewish problem was tangential at best, and minimal at worst. By a lack of total response to the Jews in their hour of greatest need, the nuncios failed to live up to the high calling that they proclaimed for themselves." *Vatican Diplomacy and the Jews*, 200.

76. See Leonidas E. Hill, "The Vatican Embassy of Ernst von Weizsäcker, 1943–1945," *Journal of Modern History* 39 (1967), 138–59; Robert Katz, *Death in Rome* (New York, 1967); Meir Michaelis, *Mussolini and the Jews: German-Italian Relations and the Jewish Question in*

Italy, 1922–1945 (London, 1978), 364–66; Owen Chadwick, "Weizsäcker, the Vatican, and the Jews of Rome," *Journal of Ecclesiastical History* 28 (1977), 179–99; Papeleux, *Silences de Pie XII,* 242–29.
77. Hansjacob Stehle, *Eastern Politics of the Vatican, 1917–1979,* trans. Sandra Smith (Athens, Ohio, 1981), 213.
78. Papeleux, *Silences de Pie XII,* 238–41.
79. Morley, *Vatican Diplomacy and the Jews, passim;* Michael R. Marrus, "Die französischen Kirchen und die Verfolgung der Juden in Frankreich, 1940–1944," *Vierteljahrshefte für Zeitgeschichte* 31 (1983), 483–505; Livia Rothkirchen, "Vatican Policy and the'Jewish Problem' in Independent Slovakia," *Yad Vashem Studies* 6 (1967), 27–53.
80. Guenter Lewy, *The Catholic Church and Nazi Germany* (New York, 1965), 304–5. For a similar judgment see Ernst Christian Helmreich, *The German Churches under Hitler: Background, Struggle, and Epilogue* (Detroit, 1979), 365.
81. Morley, *Vatican Diplomacy and the Jews,* 209.
82. Hill, "History and Rolf Hochhuth's *The Deputy,*" 149.

9. THE END OF THE HOLOCAUST

1. Quoted in Monty Noam Penkower, *The Jews Were Expendable: Free World Diplomacy and the Holocaust* (Urbana, Ill., 1983), 281.
2. See Livia Rothkirchen, "The 'Final Solution' in its Last Stages," *Yad Vashem Studies* 8 (1970), 7–28.
3. Raul Hilberg, *The Destruction of the European Jews,* rev. ed. (New York, 1985), II, 823–24, 842–46; III, 1132–40.
4. Martin Gilbert, *Auschwitz and the Allies* (New York, 1981), 205. See also John S. Conway, "Der Holocaust in Ungarn: Neue Kontroversen und Überlegungen," *Vierteljahrshefte für Zeitgeschichte* 32 (1984), 179–212.
5. Yehuda Bauer, "Genocide: Was It the Nazis' Original Plan?" *Annals of the American Academy of Political and Social Science* 450 (July 1980), 43–44; idem, *The Holocaust in Historical Perspective* (Seattle, 1978), ch. 4; idem, *The Jewish Emergence from Powerlessness* (Toronto, 1979), 7–25; idem, "The Negotiations between Saly Mayer and the Representatives of the SS in 1944–1945," in Yisrael Gutman and Efraim Zuroff, eds., *Rescue Attempts during the Holocaust: Proceedings of the Second Yad Vashem International Historical Conference, Jerusalem, April 8–11, 1974* (Jerusalem, 1977), 5–45.
6. Peter Black, *Ernst Kaltenbrunner: Ideological Soldier of the Third Reich* (Princeton, N.J., 1984), 233.
7. See the relevant passage in Hitler's testament, in Yitzhak Arad, Yisrael Gutman, and Abraham Margaliot, eds., *Documents on the Holocaust: Selected Sources on the Destruction of the Jews of Germany and Austria, Poland, and the Soviet Union* (Jerusalem, 1981), 162.
8. Bernard Wasserstein, *Britain and the Jews of Europe, 1939–1945*

(London, 1979), 259. For a very different interpretation, highly critical of Churchill, see Michael J. Cohen, *Churchill and the Jews* (London, 1985), 290–93.

9. Michael R. Marrus, *The Unwanted: European Refugees in the Twentieth Century* (New York, 1985), 282–95; Henry Feingold, *The Politics of Rescue: The Roosevelt Administration and the Holocaust, 1938–1945* (New Brunswick, N.J., 1970); Saul S. Freidman, *No Haven for the Oppressed: United States Policy toward Jewish Refugees, 1938–1945* (Detroit, 1973); Yehuda Bauer, *American Jewry and the Holocaust: The American Jewish Joint Distribution Committee, 1939–1945* (Detroit, 1981); David S. Wyman, *The Abandoment of the Jews: America and the Holocaust, 1941–1945* (New York, 1985); John S. Conway, "Between Apprehension and Indifference: Allied Attitudes to the Destruction of Hungarian Jewry," *Wiener Library Bulletin* 27 (1973/74), 37–48; Penkower, *Jews Were Expendable,* ch. 7.

10. See W. Z. Laqueur, "The Kastner Case: Aftermath of the Catastrophe," *Commentary* 20 (1955), 500–511.

11. Rudolf Vrba, quoted in Gilbert, *Auschwitz and the Allies,* 205. See also Conway, "Holocaust in Ungarn," 192–212.

12. Andre Biss, *Der Stopp der Endlösung* (Stuttgart, 1966); Randolph L. Braham, "The Official Jewish Leadership of Wartime Hungary," in Yisrael Gutman and Cynthia J. Haft, eds., *Patterns of Jewish Leadership in Nazi Europe, 1933–1945: Proceedings of the Third Yad Vashem International Historical Conference, Jerusalem, April 4–7, 1977* (Jerusalem, 1979), 267–85.

13. Randolph L. Braham, *The Politics of Genocide: The Holocaust in Hungary* (New York, 1981), II, 973; Bauer, *Holocaust in Historical Perspective,* 106–7.

14. See Penkower, *Jews Were Expendable,* 253; Abraham Fuchs, *The Unheeded Cry* (New York, 1984), 75–77; Moshe Shonfeld, *The Holocaust Victims Accuse* (New York, 1977), 73–82.

15. Yehuda Bauer, "'Onkel Saly': Die Verhandlungen des Saly Mayer zur Rettung der Juden, 1944/45," *Vierteljahrshefte für Zeitgeschichte* 25 (1977), 188–219; idem, "Negotiations between Saly Mayer and the SS"; idem, *American Jewry and the Holocaust,* ch. 9 and *passim.*

16. See also Feingold, *Politics of Rescue,* 276–80; Wyman, *Abandonment of the Jews,* 247; Braham, *Politics of Genocide,* II, 967–68.

17. See especially Martin Gilbert, "The Question of Bombing Auschwitz," in Yisrael Gutman and Avital Saf, eds., *The Nazi Concentration Camps: Structure and Aims. The Image of the Prisoner. The Jews in the Camps. Proceedings of the Fourth Yad Vashem International Historical Conference, Jerusalem, January 1980* (Jerusalem, 1984), 417–73; idem, *Auschwitz and the Allies;* Wasserstein, *Britain and the Jews of Europe,* 307–20; David S. Wyman, "Why Auschwitz Was Never Bombed," *Commentary,* May 1978, 37–46; idem, *Abandonment of the Jews,* ch. 15; Penkower, *Jews Were Expendable,* ch. 7.

18. The photographs of this and subsequent American intelligence flights have been published in Dino A. Brugioni and Robert G. Poirer, "The Holocaust Revisited: A Retrospective Analysis of the Auschwitz-Birkenau Extermination Complex," United States Central Intelligence Agency publication ST-79-10001 (Washington, 1979).

19. Wasserstein, *Britain and the Jews of Europe,* 311, 316.

20. Wyman, *Abandonment of the Jews,* 291.

21. Present-day discussions about the likely practical efficacy of the bombing of Auschwitz is, in strict historical terms, beside the point, since what matters for the evaluation of this episode is what contemporaries thought about it and why. Nevertheless, there has been some discussion of what the likely effects of various proposed raids would have been. While most would agree that the Germans could repair interdicted rail lines quickly, there is a strong feeling that, as Wyman says, "destruction of the gas chambers and crematoria would have saved many lives." Wyman, *Abandonment of the Jews,* 301. Albert Speer had a different view, however, suggesting to the Israeli political scientist Shlomo Aronson that Hitler's likely response would have been to accelerate the Final Solution. Shlomo Aronson, "Die dreifache Falle: Hitlers Judenpolitik, die Allierten, und die Juden," *Vierteljahrshefte für Zeitgeschichte* 32 (1984), 60. On this point see also Conway, "Holocaust in Ungarn," 189–90.

22. See Wasserstein, *Britain and the Jews of Europe,* 305–7.

23. Martin Gilbert, *Finest Hour: Winston S. Churchill, 1939–1941* (London, 1983), 851–52. On the other hand, Churchill seems to have changed his mind momentarily on the last day of 1942, proposing retaliatory attacks on Berlin as "reprisals for the persecution of Jews and Poles." See Martin Gilbert, *Road to Victory: Winston S. Churchill, 1941–1945* (London, 1986), 287. His suggestion was not adopted.

24. Wasserstein, *Britain and the Jews of Europe,* 309–10; Gilbert, *Auschwitz and the Allies,* 255–56. When Weizmann lunched with Churchill at Chequers on 4 November 1944 the Zionist leader did not even mention the Jewish Agency's earlier request to bomb Auschwitz and the rail lines leading to it, concentrating instead on pressing Britain for a Jewish state. See Gilbert, *Road to Victory,* 1050.

25. See Hilberg, *Destruction of the European Jews,* III, 979–89.

26. Ibid., 980; Rothkirchen, "'Final Solution' in Its Last Stages," 22–23.

27. Biss, *Stopp der Endlösung;* Hilberg, *Destruction of the European Jews,* III, 980.

28. Bernadotte became U.N. mediator for Palestine in May 1948, and was assassinated in September, presumably by extreme right-wing Jewish nationalists. The fullest account of these intricate negotiations is Leni Yahil, "Scandinavian Countries to the Rescue of Concentration Camp Prisoners," *Yad Vashem Studies* 6 (1967), 181–20. See also Hugo Valentin, "Rescue and Relief Activities in Behalf of Jewish Victims of Nazism in Scandinavia," *YIVO Annual of Jewish Social Science* 8 (1953), 224–51;

Penkower, *Jews Were Expendable*, 265–68. The most recent summary of the German perspective is in Black, *Kaltenbrunner*, 231–33.

29. Martin Broszat and Helmut Krausnick, *Anatomy of the SS State*, trans. Dorothy Lang and Marion Jackson (London, 1970), 249.

30. Yehuda Bauer, "The Death-Marches, January–May 1945," *Modern Judaism* 3 (1983), 1–21.

31. Ibid., 9.

32. Gerald Reitlinger, *The Final Solution: The Attempt to Exterminate the Jews of Europe, 1939–1945* (New York, 1961), 465–70; Rothkirchen, "'Final Solution' in Its Last Stages," 26–27.

33. Robert H. Abzug, *Inside the Vicious Heart: Americans and the Liberation of Nazi Concentration Camps* (New York, 1985), 26.

34. H. R. Trevor-Roper, *The Last Days of Hitler*, 3d ed. (New York, 1962), 119 and *passim;* Reitlinger, *Final Solution*, 455, 465–66. Drawing on documents from the International Red Cross, Reitlinger cites Eichmann's discussion with Paul Dunand of the Swiss Red Cross in April 1945: "Eichmann added that he did not approve of all the more humane measures which Himmler intended to introduce towards the Jews, but, *en tant que bon soldat,* he obeyed Himmler's orders blindly" (p. 472).

35. Abzug, *Inside the Vicious Heart*, 171. See also Leonard Dinnerstein, *America and the Survivors of the Holocaust* (New York, 1982); Marrus, *Unwanted*, 331–39.

36. Benedikt Kautsky, *Teufel und Verdammte: Erfahrungen und Erkenntnisse aus sieben Jahren in Deutschen Konzentrationslager* (Vienna, 1948), 77; Report of Brigadier H. L. Glyn Hughes, in Sir Henry Letherby Tidy, ed., *Interallied Conferences on War Medicine, 1942–1945* (London, 1947). See also Eberhard Kolb, *Bergen-Belsen: Geschichte des "Aufenhaltslagers," 1943–1945* (Hannover, 1962).

37. Yehuda Bauer, *A History of the Holocaust* (New York, 1982), 295–96; Wolfgang Jacobmeyer, "Jüdische Uberlebene als 'Displaced Persons': Untersuchungen zur Bezatzungspolitik in den deutschen Westzonen und zur Zuwanderung osteuropaïscher Juden, 1945–1947," *Geschichte und Gesellschaft* 9 (1983), 421–52; Dinnerstein, *America and the Survivors of the Holocaust*, 24; Malcolm Proudfoot, *European Refugees, 1939–1945* (London, [1956]), 321; Bauer, "Death-Marches," 1–4.

38. See Salo Baron, "European Jewry before and after Hitler," *American Jewish Yearbook* 63 (1962), 3–49; Léon Poliakov, *Brévaire de haine* (Paris, 1951), 498–505; Georges Wellers, "Le Nombre des victimes de la «solution finale» et le rapport Korherr," *Le Monde juif*, no. 86 (April–June 1977), 63–84; idem, *Les Chambres à gaz ont existé: Des documents, des témoignages, des chiffres* (Paris, 1981), pt. 2.

39. Serge Klarsfeld, *Le Mémorial de la déportation des Juifs de France* (Paris, 1978).

40. Hilberg, *Destruction of the European Jews*, III, 1203–6.

41. J[acob] R[obinson], "Holocaust," in *Encyclopaedia Judaica* (Jerusalem, 1971), VIII, 889–90.

42. Hilberg, *Destruction of the European Jews,* III, 1207–20. In his *The Final Solution,* published in 1953 and reprinted in 1961, Gerald Reitlinger concluded that the losses stood between 4,194,200 and 4,581,200. Reitlinger, *Final Solution,* 489–501.

43. Philip Friedman, "Research on the Recent Jewish Tragedy," *Jewish Social Studies* 12 (1950), 25. See the similar observations of Abraham G. Duker, "Comments," ibid., 79.

44. "Recording the Holocaust," *Jerusalem Post International Edition,* 28 June 1986, 8.

45. Quoted in Geoff Eley, "Holocaust History," *London Review of Books,* 3–17 March 1986, 7–8.

46. Bauer, *Holocaust in Historical Perspective,* 5.

47 Lucy S. Dawidowicz, *The Holocaust and the Historians* (Cambridge, Mass., 1981), 142–46.

SUGGESTIONS FOR

FURTHER READING

Readers will find in the notes many of the books and articles consulted in the writing of this book. In the following section I have selected a few of what I believe to be the most important works in English, with an emphasis, where appropriate, upon the most recent publications.

I. GENERAL: SURVEYS AND PERSPECTIVE

Salo Baron, "European Jewry before and after Hitler," *American Jewish Yearbook* 63 (1962), 3–49.

Yehuda Bauer, *A History of the Holocaust* (New York, 1982).

——, *The Holocaust in Historical Perspective* (Seattle, 1973).

——, "The Place of the Holocaust in Contemporary History," *Studies in Contemporary Jewry* 1 (1984), 201–24.

Lucy S. Dawidowicz, *The Holocaust and the Historians* (Cambridge, Mass., 1981).

——, ed., *A Holocaust Reader* (New York, 1976).

——, *The War against the Jews* (New York, 1975).

Raul Hilberg, *The Destruction of the European Jews*, 3 vols., rev. ed. (New York, 1985).

——, ed., *Documents of Destruction: Germany and Jewry, 1933–1945* (Chicago, 1971).

Jacob Katz, *From Prejudice to Destruction: Anti-Semitism, 1700–1933* (Cambridge, Mass., 1980).

Ian Kershaw, *The Nazi Dictatorship: Problems and Perspectives of Interpretation* (London, 1985).

Gerd Korman, "The Holocaust in American Historical Writing," *Societas* 2 (1972), 251–70.

George M. Kren and Leon Rappoport, *The Holocaust and the Crisis of Human Behavior* (New York, 1980).

Nora Levin, *The Holocaust: The Destruction of European Jewry, 1939–1945* (New York, 1973).

Michael R. Marrus, "The Theory and Practice of Antisemitism," *Commentary*, August 1982, 38–42.

John Mendelsohn, ed., *The Holocaust: Selected Documents in Eighteen Volumes* (New York, 1982).

George L. Mosse, *The Crisis of German Ideology* (New York, 1981).

———, *Toward the Final Solution: A History of European Racism* (London, 1978).

Léon Poliakov, *Harvest of Hate* (Syracuse, 1954).

Gerald Reitlinger, *The Final Solution: The Attempt to Exterminate the Jews of Europe, 1939–1945* (New York, 1961).

J. L. Talmon, "European History: Seedbed of the Holocaust," *Midstream*, May 1973, 3–25.

Eugen Weber, "Jews, Antisemitism, and the Origins of the Holocaust," *Historical Reflections* 5 (1978), 1–17.

2. THE FINAL SOLUTION

Martin Broszat, "Hitler and the Genesis of the 'Final Solution': An Assessment of David Irving's Thesis," *Yad Vashem Studies* 13 (1979), 73–125.

Christopher R. Browning, *Fateful Months: Essays on the Emergence of the Final Solution* (New York, 1961).

———, *The Final Solution and the German Foreign Office: A Study of Referat DIII of Abteilung Deutschland* (New York, 1978).

———, "Nazi Resettlement Policy and the Search for a Solution to the Jewish Question, 1939–1941," *German Studies Review* 9 (1986), 497–519.

Gerald Fleming, *Hitler and the Final Solution* (Berkeley, Calif., 1984).

Saul Friedlander, "From Anti-Semitism to Extermination: A Historiographical Study of Nazi Policies toward the Jews," *Yad Vashem Studies* 16 (1984), 1–50.

Philip Friedman, "The Lublin Reservation and the Madagascar Plan: Two Aspects of Nazi Jewish Policy during the Second World War," in Joshua A. Fishman, ed., *Studies on Modern Jewish Social History* (New York, 1972), 354–80.

Gerhard Hirschfeld, ed., *The Policies of Genocide: Jews and Soviet Prisoners of War in Nazi Germany* (London, 1986).

Heinz Höhne, *The Order of the Death's Head: The Story of Hitler's SS*, trans. Richard Barry (London, 1972).

Eberhard Jäckel, *Hitler in History* (Hanover, N.H., 1984).

———, *Hitler's Weltanschauung: A Blueprint for Power*, trans. Herbert Arnold (Middletown, Conn., 1972).

Ihor Kamenetsky, *Secret Nazi Plans for Eastern Europe: A Study of Lebensraum Policies* (New York, 1961).

Robert L. Koehl, *RKFVD: German Resettlement and Population Policy,*

1939–1945: A History of the Reich Commission for the Strengthening of Germandom (Cambridge, Mass., 1957).

Helmut Krausnick and Martin Broszat, *Anatomy of the SS State*, trans. Dorothy Lang and Marian Jackson (London, 1968).

Robert Jay Lifton, *The Nazi Doctors: Medical Killing and the Psychology of Genocide* (New York, 1986).

Jonny Moser, "Nisko: The First Experiment in Deportation," *Simon Wiesenthal Annual* 2 (1985), 1–30.

Karl Schleunes, *The Twisted Road to Auschwitz: Nazi Policies toward the Jews, 1933–1939* (Urbana, Ill., 1970).

Gitta Sereny, *Into That Darkness* (London, 1974).

3. GERMANY'S ALLIES, VANQUISHED STATES, AND COLLABORATIONIST GOVERNMENTS

Randolph L. Braham, *The Politics of Genocide: The Holocaust in Hungary*, 2 vols. (New York, 1981).

Frederick Chary, *The Bulgarian Jews and the Final Solution, 1940–1944* (Pittsburgh, 1972).

Helen Fein, *Accounting for Genocide: National Responses and Jewish Victimization during the Holocaust* (New York, 1979).

Harold Flender, *Rescue in Denmark* (New York, 1963).

Yeshayahu Jellinek, "The 'Final Solution': The Slovak Version," *East European Quarterly* 4 (1970), 431–44.

———, "The Holocaust and the Internal Policies of the Nazi Satellites in Eastern Europe: A Comparative Study," in *Proceedings of the Eighth World Congress of Jewish Studies* (Jerusalem, 1982), 173–78.

Michael R. Marrus and Robert O. Paxton, "The Nazis and the Jews in Occupied Western Europe," *Journal of Modern History* 54 (1982), 687–714.

———, *Vichy France and the Jews* (New York, 1981).

Meir Michaelis, *Mussolini and the Jews: German-Italian Relations and the Jewish Question in Italy, 1922–1945* (Oxford, 1978).

Nicholas Nagy-Talavera, *The Green Shirts and the Others* (Stanford, 1970).

Nisan Oren, "The Bulgarian Exception: A Reassessment of the Salvation of the Jewish Community," *Yad Vashem Studies* 7 (1968), 83–106.

Jacob Presser, *The Destruction of the Dutch Jews*, trans. Arnold Pomerans (New York, 1969).

Joseph B. Schechtman, "The Transnistria Reservation," *YIVO Annual of Jewish Social Science* 8 (1953), 178–96.

B. A. Sijes, "The Position of the Jews during the German Occupation of the Netherlands: Some Observations," *Acta Historiae Neerlandicae* 9 (1976), 170–92.

Vicki Tamir, *Bulgaria and Her Jews: The History of a Dubious Symbiosis* (New Haven, Conn., 1979).

Leni Yahil, "Methods of Persecution: A Comparison of the 'Final Solution' in Holland and Denmark," *Scripta Hierosolymita* 23 (1972), 279–300.

———, *The Rescue of Danish Jewry: Test of a Democracy*, trans. Maurice Gradel (Philadelphia, 1969).

Susan Zuccotti, *The Italians and the Holocaust: Persecution, Rescue, and Survival* (New York, 1987).

4. PUBLIC OPINION IN NAZI EUROPE

Chimen Abramsky, Maciej Jachimczyk, and Antony Polonsky, eds., *The Jews in Poland* (Oxford, 1986).

Christoph Dipper, "The German Resistance and the Jews," *Yad Vashem Studies* 16 (1984), 51–93.

Philip Friedman, "Ukrainian-Jewish Relations during the Nazi Occupation," *YIVO Annual of Jewish Social Science* 13 (1958/59), 259–96.

Sarah Gordon, *Hitler, Germans and the "Jewish Question"* (Princeton, N.J., 1984).

Yisrael Gutman, *The Jews of Warsaw, 1939–1943: Ghetto, Underground, Revolt*, trans. Ina Friedman (Bloomington, Ind., 1982).

———, "Polish Responses to the Liquidation of Polish Jewry," *Jerusalem Quarterly* 17 (Fall 1980), 40–55.

Philip Hallie, *Lest Innocent Blood Be Shed: The Story of Le Chambon and How Goodness Happened There* (New York, 1979).

Taras Hunczak, "Ukrainian-Jewish Relations during the Soviet and Nazi Occupations," in Yuri Boshyk, ed., *Ukraine during World War II: History and Aftermath* (Edmonton, Alberta, 1986), 39–57.

Louis de Jong, "Jews and Non-Jews in Nazi Occupied Holland," in Max Beloff, ed., *On the Track of Tyranny* (London, 1960), 139–55.

Michael Kater, "Everyday Antisemitism in Prewar Nazi Germany: The Popular Bases," *Yad Vashem Studies* 16 (1984), 129–59.

Ian Kershaw, "The Persecution of the Jews and German Popular Opinion in the Third Reich," *Leo Baeck Institute Year Book* 26 (1981), 261–89.

———, *Popular Opinion and Political Dissent in the Third Reich: Bavaria, 1933–1945* (Oxford, 1983).

Otto Dov Kulka, "'Public Opinion' in Nazi Germany and the 'Jewish Question,'" *Jerusalem Quarterly* 25 (1982), 121–44; and 26 (1983), 34–45.

O. D. Kulka and Aron Rodrigue, "The German Population and the Jews in the Third Reich: Recent Publication and Trends in Research on German Society and the 'Jewish Question,'" *Yad Vashem Studies* 16 (1984), 421–35.

Walter Laqueur, *The Terrible Secret: An Investigation into the Suppression of Information about Hitler's "Final Solution"* (London, 1980).

Richard Lukas, *The Forgotten Holocaust: The Poles under German Occupation, 1939–1944* (Lexington, Ky., 1986).

Ezra Mendelsohn, *The Jews of East Central Europe between the World Wars* (Bloomington, Ind., 1983).

Emmanuel Ringelblum, *Polish Jewish Relations during the Second World War*, ed. Joseph Kirmisch and Shmuel Krakowski, trans. Dafna Allon, Danuta Dabrowska, and Dana Keren (New York, 1976).

Livia Rothkirchen, "Czech Attitudes towards the Jews during the Nazi Regime," *Yad Vashem Studies* 13 (1979), 287–320.

Lawrence Stokes, "The German People and the Destruction of the European Jews," *Central European History* 6 (1973), 167–91.

Nechama Tec, *When Light Pierced the Darkness: Christian Rescue of Jews in Nazi Occupied Poland* (New York, 1986).

Hans-Heinrich Wilhelm, "The Holocaust in National Socialist Rhetoric and Writings: Some Evidence against the Thesis That Before 1945 Nothing Was Known about the 'Final Solution,'" *Yad Vashem Studies* 16 (1984), 95–127.

5. THE VICTIMS

Yitzhak Arad, *Ghetto in Flames: The Struggle and Destruction of the Jews in Vilna in the Holocaust* (Jerusalem, 1980).

Hannah Arendt, *Eichmann in Jerusalem: A Report on the Banality of Evil* (New York, 1963).

Bruno Bettelheim, *The Informed Heart: Autonomy in a Mass Age* (New York, 1971).

———, *Surviving and Other Essays* (New York, 1980).

Yerachmiel [Richard] Cohen, "French Jewry's Dilemma on the Orientation of Its Leadership: From Polemics to Conciliation," *Yad Vashem Studies* 14 (1981), 167–204.

———, "The Jewish Community of France in the Face of Vichy-German Persecution, 1940–1944," in Frances Malino and Bernard Wasserstein, eds., *The Jews in Modern France* (Hanover, N.H., 1985), 180–203.

Terrence Des Pres, *The Survivor: An Anatomy of Life in the Death Camps* (New York, 1976).

Lucjan Dobroszycki, ed., *The Chronicle of the Lodz Ghetto, 1941–1944*, trans. Richard Lourie et al. (New Haven, 1984).

Alexander Donat, *The Holocaust Kingdom* (New York, 1965).

Martin Gilbert, *The Holocaust: A History of the Jews of Europe during the Second World War* (London, 1986).

W. Glicksman, "Social Differentiation in the German Concentration Camps," in Joshua A. Fishman, ed., *Studies in Modern Jewish Social History* (New York, 1972), 381–408.

Yisrael Gutman, *The Jews of Warsaw, 1939–1943: Ghetto, Underground, Revolt*, trans. Ina Friedman (Bloomington, Ind., 1983).

Yisrael Gutman and Cynthia J. Haft, eds., *Patterns of Jewish Leadership in Nazi Europe, 1933–1945: Proceedings of the Third Yad Vashem Inter-*

national Historical Conference, Jerusalem, April 4–7, 1977 (Jerusalem, 1979).

Yisrael Gutman and Avital Saf, eds., *The Nazi Concentration Camps: Structure and Aims. The Image of the Prisoner. The Jews in the Camps. Proceedings of the Fourth Yad Vashem International Historical Conference, Jerusalem, January 1980* (Jerusalem, 1984).

Raul Hilberg, Stanislaw Staron, and Josef Kermisz, eds., *The Warsaw Diary of Adam Czerniakow: Prelude to Doom,* trans. Stanislaw Staron et al. (New York, 1979).

Jacob Katz, "Was the Holocaust Predictable?" *Commentary,* May 1975, 41–48.

Eugen Kogon, *The Theory and Practice of Hell,* trans. Heinz Norden (New York, 1953).

Primo Levi, *Survival in Auschwitz,* trans. Stuart Woolf (New York, 1969).

Anna Pawełczynksa, *Values and Violence in Auschwitz: A Sociological Analysis,* trans. Catherine S. Leach (Berkeley, Calif., 1979).

Jehuda Reinharz, ed., *Living with Antisemitism: Modern Jewish Responses* (Hanover, N.H., 1987).

Emmanuel Ringelblum, *Notes from the Warsaw Ghetto,* trans. and ed. Jacob Sloan (New York, 1974).

Jacob Robinson, *And the Crooked Shall Be Made Straight: The Eichmann Trial, the Jewish Catastrophe, and Hannah Arendt's Narrative* (Philadelphia, 1965).

Isaiah Trunk, *Jewish Responses to Nazi Persecution: Collective and Individual Behavior in Extremis* (New York, 1982).

———, *Judenrat: The Jewish Councils in Eastern Europe under Nazi Occupation* (New York, 1972).

Leonard Tushnet, *The Pavement of Hell* (New York, 1972).

Rudolf Vrba and Alan Bestic, *I Cannot Forgive* (New York, 1964).

Aharon Weiss, "Jewish Leadership in Occupied Poland: Postures and Attitudes," *Yad Vashem Studies* 12 (1977), 335–65.

6. JEWISH RESISTANCE

Reuben Ainsztein, *Jewish Resistance in Nazi-Occupied Eastern Europe* (New York, 1974).

Yehuda Bauer, *The Jewish Emergence from Powerlessness* (Toronto, 1979).

———, *They Chose Life: Jewish Resistance in the Holocaust* (New York, 1973).

Yisrael Gutman, *The Jews of Warsaw, 1939–1943: Ghetto, Underground, Revolt,* trans. Ina Friedman (Bloomington, Ind., 1983).

Moshe Kohn, ed., *Jewish Resistance during the Holocaust: Proceedings of the Conference on Manifestations of Jewish Resistance, Jerusalem, April 7–11, 1968* (Jerusalem, 1971).

Shmuel Krakowski, *The War of the Doomed: Jewish Armed Resistance in Poland, 1942–1944*, trans. Ora Blaustein (New York, 1984).

Annie Latour, *The Jewish Resistance in France*, trans. Irene R. Ilton (New York, 1981).

Dov Levin, *Fighting Back: Lithuanian Jewry's Armed Resistance to the Nazis, 1941–1944*, trans. Moshe Kohn and Dina Cohen (New York, 1985).

Henri Michel, "Jewish Resistance and the European Resistance Movement," *Yad Vashem Studies* 7 (1968), 7–16.

Yuri Suhl, ed., *They Fought Back: The Story of the Jewish Resistance in Nazi Europe* (New York, 1975).

Isaiah Trunk, *Judenrat: The Jewish Councils in Eastern Europe under Nazi Occupation* (New York, 1972).

———, "Note: Why Was There No Armed Resistance against the Nazis in the Lodz Ghetto?" *Jewish Social Studies* 43 (1981), 329–34.

7. BYSTANDERS

Irving Abella and Harold Troper, *None Is Too Many: Canada and the Jews of Europe, 1933–1948* (Toronto, 1982).

Chaim Avni, *Spain, Franco and the Jews*, trans. Emanuel Shimoni (Philadelphia, 1982).

Yehuda Bauer, *American Jewry and the Holocaust: The American Jewish Joint Distribution Committee, 1939–1945* (Detroit, 1981).

Randolph L. Braham, ed., *Jewish Leadership in the Nazi Era: Patterns of Behavior in the Free World* (New York, 1985).

Owen Chadwick, "Weizsäcker, the Vatican, and the Jews of Rome," *Journal of Ecclesiastical History* 28 (1977), 179–99.

Michael J. Cohen, *Churchill and the Jews* (London, 1985).

John S. Conway, "Records and Documents of the Holy See Relating to the Second World War," *Yad Vashem Studies* 15 (1983), 327–45.

———, "The Silence of Pius XII," in Charles Delzell, ed., *The Papacy and Totalitarianism between the Two World Wars* (New York, 1974), 79–108.

Henry Feingold, "Courage First and Intelligence Second: The American Jewish Secular Elite, Roosevelt, and the Failure of Rescue," *American Jewish History* 72 (1982/83), 424–60.

———, *The Politics of Rescue: The Roosevelt Administration and the Holocaust, 1938–1945* (New Brunswick, N.J., 1970).

Saul Friedlander, *Pius XIII and the Third Reich: A Documentation*, trans. Charles Fullman (New York, 1966).

Saul S. Friedman, *No Haven for the Oppressed: United States Policy toward Refugees* (Detroit, 1973).

Abraham Fuchs, *The Unheeded Cry* (New York, 1984).

Martin Gilbert, *Auschwitz and the Allies* (New York, 1981).

Alfred A. Häsler, *The Lifeboat Is Full: Switzerland and the Refugees, 1933–1945,* trans. Charles Lam Markhmann (New York, 1969).

Leonidas B. Hill, "History and Rolf Hochhuth's *The Deputy,*" in R. G. Collins, ed., *From an Ancient to a Modern Theatre* (Winnipeg, 1972), 145–57.

Walter Laqueur, *The Terrible Secret: An Investigation into the Suppression of Information about Hitler's "Final Solution"* (London, 1980).

Deborah E. Lipstadt, *Beyond Belief: The American Press and the Coming of the Holocaust, 1933–1945* (New York, 1986).

Michael R. Marrus, *The Unwanted: European Refugees in the Twentieth Century* (New York, 1985).

John F. Morley, *Vatican Diplomacy and the Holocaust, 1939–1943* (New York, 1980).

Monty Noam Penkower, *The Jews Were Expendable: Free World Diplomacy and the Holocaust* (Urbana, Ill., 1983).

Dina Porat, "Palestinian Jewry and the Jewish Agency: Public Response to the Holocaust," in Richard Cohen, ed., *Vision and Conflict in the Holy Land* (New York, 1985), 246–73.

Bernard Wasserstein, *Britain and the Jews of Europe, 1939–1945* (London, 1979).

David S. Wyman, *The Abandonment of the Jews: America and the Holocaust, 1941–1945* (New York, 1984).

Leni Yahil, "Raoul Wallenberg: His Mission and His Activities in Hungary," *Yad Vashem Studies* 15 (1984), 7–53.

8. THE END OF THE HOLOCAUST: RESCUE OPTIONS AND LIBERATION

Robert H. Abzug, *Inside the Vicious Heart: Americans and the Liberation of Nazi Concentration Camps* (New York, 1985).

Yehuda Bauer, "The Death Marches, January–May 1945," *Modern Judaism* 3 (1983), 1–21.

———, *The Holocaust in Historical Perspective* (Seattle, 1973).

———, *The Jewish Emergence from Powerlessness* (Toronto, 1979).

Randolph L. Braham, *The Politics of Genocide: The Holocaust in Hungary,* 2 vols. (New York, 1981).

John Conway, "Between Apprehension and Indifference: Allied Attitudes to the Destruction of Hungarian Jewry," *Wiener Library Bulletin* 27 (1973/74), 37–48.

Leonard Dinnerstein, *America and the Survivors of the Holocaust* (New York, 1982).

Martin Gilbert, *Auschwitz and the Allies* (New York, 1981).

Michael R. Marrus, *The Unwanted: European Refugees in the Twentieth Century* (New York, 1985).

Monty Noam Penkower, *The Jews Were Expendable: Free World Diplomacy and the Holocaust* (Urbana, Ill., 1983).

Livia Rothkirchen, "The 'Final Solution' in its Last Stages," *Yad Vashem Studies* 8 (1970), 7–28.

Bernard Wasserstein, *Britain and the Jews of Europe, 1939–1945* (London, 1979).

Alex Weissberg, *Desperate Mission: Joel Brand's Story* (New York, 1958).

David S. Wyman, *The Abandonment of the Jews: America and the Holocaust, 1941–1945* (New York, 1984).

Leni Yahil, "Scandinavian Countries to the Rescue of Concentration Camp Prisoners," *Yad Vashem Studies* 6 (1967), 181–20.

INDEX

The Tauber Institute for the Study of European Jewry, established by a gift to Brandeis University from Dr. Laszlo N. Tauber, is dedicated to the memory of the victims of Nazi persecutions between 1933 and 1945. The Institute seeks to study the history and culture of European Jewry in the modern period. The Institute has a special interest in studying the causes, nature, and consequences of the European Jewish catastrophe and seeks to explore them within the context of modern European diplomatic, intellectual, political, and social history. The Tauber Institute for the Study of European Jewry is organized on a multidisciplinary basis, with the participation of scholars in history, Judaic studies, political science, sociology, comparative literature, and other disciplines.

THE TAUBER INSTITUTE FOR THE STUDY OF EUROPEAN JEWRY SERIES

Jehuda Reinharz, General Editor

The MERIDIAN Quality Paperback Collection
(0452)

☐ **VOICES FROM THE HOLOCAUST edited by Sylvia Rothchild. Introduction by Eli Wiesel.** A vivid, moving, and totally honest re-creation of the lives of 30 ordinary people caught in the tragic cataclysm of the war against the Jew; this unique oral history tells what it was like to grow up Jewish in Europe, to survive Hitler's "final solution," and to rebuild a new life in America. The stories are taken from tapes held in the William E. Weiner Oral History Library. (008603—$10.95)

☐ **THE GERMANS by Gordon A. Craig.** Written by one of the most distinguished historians of modern Germany, this provocative study traces the evolution of the postwar German character by carefully looking at the past and offering a fascinating perspective on German today. (008972—$9.95)

☐ **THE TERRORISM READER: A Historical Anthology edited by Walter Laqueur.** This unique anthology brings together the most notable proponents, critics, and analysts of terrorism from ancient times to today. (008433—$12.95)

☐ **F.D.R.: An Intimate History by Nathan Miller.** Here is a portrait that captures all sides of Franklin Delano Roosevelt, the nation's only four-term president, and the man whose New Deal changed government in the United States forever. The brilliance, charm, and remarkable talents of both the political and private personality are seen in this fascinating and comprehensive biography. (006767—$10.95)

☐ **SIN, SICKNESS AND SANITY: A History of Sexual Attitudes by Vern Bullough and Bonnie Bullough.** This book examines, in historical context, the myths, misinformation and taboos that have distorted our view of sexual behavior; the attempts of early Christian Sects to promote total chastity; homosexual practices among the Arabs; the havoc wrought by the onset of syphilis in Europe; Victorian theories about masturbation and madness; sexist dogmas that have long limited feminine potential; social attitudes toward abortion over the centuries; and much more. (007841—$9.95)

All prices higher in Canada.

Titles of Related Interest from MERIDIAN

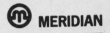